ROBERT ROGERS OF THE RANGERS

ROBERT ROGERS

OF THE

RANGERS

John R. Cuneo

NEW YORK
Oxford University Press
1959

Dedicated to the Memory of
DR. RANDOLPH G. ADAMS

ILLUSTRATIONS

Major Robert Rogers

Elizabeth Browne Rogers

A Plan of the City of Albany

Plan of Fort St. Frédéric

Plan of Fort Edward

A View of Fort Ticonderoga

A North East View of Crown Point

Sketch of the Fort at Michilimackinac

Between pages 84 and 85

LIST OF MAPS

CONTENTS

CONTENTS

ACKNOWLEDGMENTS

MY chief regret is that Dr. Randolph G. Adams, who induced me to write this book, is not alive. He introduced me to the treasures of Clements Library, Ann Arbor; those who followed him, Colton Storm and Howard W. Peckham, aided by William S. Ewing and the entire staff, made every facility of that fabulous storehouse open to me.

Second only to Clements Library has been the Fort Ticonderoga Museum Library. The friendly co-operation of John H. G. Pell, Eleanor Murray, and Edward P. Hamilton made available the tremendous collection housed in the restored fort, itself an inspiration to research in the period covered by this study. Work past closing hours once gave me a chance to walk the fort's walls by moonlight: I could almost make out what the ghosts were trying to tell me. Here I met John W. Shy, whose military background aided by sound scholarship has opened up new views of campaigns whose retelling had grown hackneyed. Opportunity to participate in a small way in archaeological work at the fort, particularly with J. Duncan Campbell, aided my research. Closely allied with the fort is Harrison K. Bird, Jr., who was brought up on Lake George and whose particular interest is Robert Rogers. His knowledge of the terrain was particularly helpful.

My law practice restricted the time I could give to research. G. R. Mellor pursued the faint traces of Rogers not only through the various public and private archives of England but even to burial registers rescued from bombed-out cellars. I am sorry that death also claimed him before he could see how greatly he assisted me. Alice J. Thompson did a great deal of work in New Hampshire records, while A. N. Morton scurried over northeastern Massachusetts on my behalf. Both ran down a great many blind leads for which I could not have spared the time.

Scores of others gave me valuable assistance. Curators and librarians examined materials in their libraries; manuscript owners gave me copies or gave me access to the documents; experts criticized portions of my book or shared their specialist knowledge. Among them are Captain W.

B. Armit of the Canadian Army Museum (Halifax), Alan S. Brown, Albert Campbell of Belfast, Charlotte D. Conover of the New Hampshire Historical Society Library, Norma Cuthbert of the Huntington Library, Jane M. Lape of the New York State Historical Association Library (Ticonderoga), the Earl of Dartmouth, Alice M. Hadley of Dunbarton, N. H., Major Reginald Hargreaves, Ernest Harvey of Londonderry (N. Ireland), Ross Henderson of Newtonstewart (N. Ireland), Margaret L. Johnson of the Public Record Office of Northern Ireland, Lucile Kane of the Minnesota Historical Society Library, Bernhardt Knollenberg, William Kaye Lamb of the Public Archives of Canada, Mildred P. McKay of the New Hampshire State Library, Harold E. Peterson, Mrs. Kenneth Roberts, the late Kenneth Roberts, James S. Schoff, and S. R. Sellwood.

Institutions aiding me include the American Philosophical Society, the British Museum, the John Carter Brown Library, the Public Archives of Canada, Colonial Williamsburg, the Library of Congress, the Connecticut State Library, the Detroit Public Library, the Frick Art Reference Library, Guildhall Library (London), Harvard University Library, Henry E. Huntington Library, Hufeland Memorial Library, Public Record Office of Northern Ireland, Public Record Office (London), Massachusetts Historical Society, Minnesota Historical Society, National Archives, the Newberry Library, the New Hampshire State Library, the New Hampshire Historical Society, the New-York Historical Society, the New York Public Library, the New York State Historical Association, the Historical Society of Pennsylvania, the Redpath Library of McGill University, the Vermont Historical Society, the Wisconsin Historical Society, and Yale University Library.

My Contoura camera and microfilm enabled me to subject my materials to a careful study at home, which would have been impossible during brief trips to the various libraries. Robert Seidman helped me immeasurably with suggestions from a lay reader's point of view. I also thank Harry Edgar Bryan for his aid in the preparation of the maps.

JOHN R. CUNEO

Westport, Connecticut
March 1959

ROBERT ROGERS OF THE RANGERS

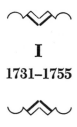

I
1731–1755

'For Whie Should Such Anoest Man Be Killed?'

UNTIL the drums of war called, Robert Rogers was a farmer on the New Hampshire frontier. Like most of his class—the yeomen of the eighteenth century—he left few traces of this phase of his life. But his beginnings must be projected against this background: it marked him for life.

The yeomen were a rough and rude class. Their daily life-or-death struggle amid the fresh stumps of fallen forest giants hardened them both to the rigors of nature and the culture of men. It sharpened their individualism and put a premium on initiative, but their fight was as likely to be with the bonds imposed by men as with the limitations imposed by nature. Poverty rampant on the frontier produced a society cynical of tidewater wealth, ready to dare anything for financial return, and hungry for land as a means not of sustaining life but of producing the ever-elusive fortune. Law and order commanded little respect when standing between a yeoman and his objective.

Perhaps this picture requires modification, but it is far truer than the picture painted by the agrarian tradition, vestiges of which are still with us. The lithograph of the sober,

industrious, and pious pioneer in clean homespun, the pleas-
ant-faced wife in plain but neat dress, the chubby children
gamboling among the trees is an over-cheerful representation
of the bleak reality. Against the rosy-hued print of tradition
Robert Rogers is an anomaly, as would be the vast majority
of his yeoman associates.

Robert Rogers was born to James and Mary Rogers on 18
November 1731* in Methuen, a small frontier town in northeastern Massachusetts Bay Colony. The brief entry by the
town clerk is the earliest known record of his parents; there
is not even a wisp of tradition about any forebears.

Tenuous evidence indicates that James and Mary were of
Scotch stock from Northern Ireland. Heavy emigration of the
Ulster Scotch had begun in 1717, but Robert's parents seem
to have come over much later. Burdened with three small
sons, Samuel, Daniel, and James, they may have arrived only
a short time before Robert's birth.

Their predecessors had found no warm welcome in New
England. The Puritans eyed them coldly as a 'parcel of Irish'
and damned them—Presbyterians to the man—as 'black Pa-
pists.' Some communities barred them. At least Methuen was
hospitable enough to leave undisturbed those of the Ulster
Scotch who in 1728 dared to settle on outlying common-land.
Perhaps this opportunity attracted James. No deed attests to
any purchase, but town records after Robert's birth tacitly
recognize the Rogers' squatter's claim to a farm on the western out-lands toward Dracut.

Nothing details the struggles of Robert's parents to provide
food and shelter for him but there is proof of their concern
about the fate of his soul. Hell was the certain destiny of any
unbaptized babe: James and Mary swallowed their Presby-

---

* In the text all dates prior to 2 September 1752 have been advanced eleven
days to correspond to the modern calendar.

terian pride and carried the infant Robert seven days after his birth to the local Puritan minister. There was no other church in the community. Their names appear only twice again in the ecclesiastical annals: to mark the baptism of a son Richard, two and half years later, and to note the same event in the life of their first daughter, Mary, in the midsummer of 1736.

The unchronicled eight years spent by Robert in Methuen were undoubtedly happy. Outside the door, nature seemed created solely for a small boy's pleasure. He was too young to comprehend the daily fight carried on by his parents with the same nature against nakedness and starvation, but children only slightly older knew and hated the grim existence.

The Rogers youngsters, in the way of boys from the beginnings of time, soon became friendly with those on a neighboring farm. Perhaps through them James Rogers became acquainted with the other father, Joseph Pudney. Ulster Scotch were inclined to be clannish; Pudney was American-born and of English extraction. But prejudices were forgotten and the two became close friends.

Something called these men away from Methuen. Neither held legal title to his land although Pudney was an old inhabitant; perhaps they wanted to find a tract whose paper title could be purchased as security against conflicting claims. Or perhaps they merely felt the magic tug of the wilderness.

Their hearts' desire was the 'Great Meadow,' some thirty-five miles northwest of Methuen and west of the line of settlements along the Merrimack River. There tall grass waved in the sun on naturally cleared meadow lying on a series of high ridges. The tract was part of a grant from the Massachusetts Bay legislature to veterans of an Indian campaign. Rogers and Pudney purchased rights in the land: on 12 November 1738 Rogers received a deed to an undivided one-sixth interest in 'twenty-one Hundred & ninty Acres be it more or less . . . being ye Grant . . . known by ye name of Lovewells Grant.' Twelve days later Pudney acquired a similar interest in the same tract.

Early in the next spring the two families packed their personal belongings in ox-carts and with their few precious cattle trailed northerly along the eastern bank of the Merrimack. Possibly they crossed on John Goffe's ferry near Cohas Brook. Soon all signs of habitation were behind them; the blue sky and colored tapestry of spring along the open road were replaced by a dark-green canopy and a floor of shadow-flaked brown. Finally, after following a brook from its junction with the Merrimack, the small caravan emerged from the forest's shadow into the bright clearing. Great Meadow soon had another name spelled in a wondrous variety: Mountalona. Did this corner of the New World remind James and Mary of their distant home in the Sperrin Mountains of Northern Ireland?

A farm had to be carved in soil never touched by a plow. Here there were no helping neighbors. Years passed before any came. Even then there were only isolated homes interconnected by rough trails. Rumford, some ten miles to the northeast, was the nearest community. Tradition tells how young Robert cut poles from the yellow birches lining Great Meadow. Ends were slivered into thin, flat splints and the opposite end of each was carved into the handle of an 'Indian broom.' These he carried to Rumford to earn a few precious pennies.

Like his associates Robert received little formal education. He was a poor speller, although we should not be too critical: his was a society where the primary means of communication was oral and all spelling was treated phonetically. He may have started school in Methuen, but there was none in Mountalona and Rumford's schoolhouse was too distant. Probably the Bible was Robert's hornbook and encyclopedia. In the introduction to his printed *Journals* he spoke as if his 'early education' was simply lore gained from Indians. There were few of this race left in eighteenth-century New Hampshire. Before 1700 the ragged, defeated remnants of the Pennacook confederacy had fled from the lands of their fathers. Some trailed the setting sun into New York; others chose Canada. Many of the latter joined other New England exiles, the Abnaki, in the village of St. Francis near the St. Lawrence River, and helped to keep alive the bitter feud with the invading English. Only scattered, individual families clung in poverty to ancestral sites in the Merrimack valley. Perhaps here young Robert gained his basic training in woodcraft.

Robert's formative years were spent amid the alarms and excursions of war. When in 1744 news arrived in New England that France had declared war against Great Britain, mounted couriers thudded out of tidewater cities to spread the news inland. For a time there was only the threat but, beginning in the second half of 1745, a series of hit-and-run attacks by French-led Indians struck the frontier. The raiders fanned out from St. Francis, Montreal, or St. Frédéric, France's stone fortress at Crown Point on Lake Champlain, and drifted through the woods in small bands, impossible to anticipate or to pursue. Sudden, brief, and barbaric, the unpredictable assaults forced reluctant farmers to withdraw to more populated centers for mutual protection. Deserted farms were worked by co-operative effort. Some toiled while others, with cocked flintlocks, scanned the inscrutable forest wall. The Rogers family and the Pudneys went to Rumford; in 1746 they are listed among those assigned to certain fortified houses (garrisons) in the town.

During the spring of that year the raids seemed to stop. Inevitably vigilance relaxed—as the patient foe expected. In mid-August a war party ambushed eight militiamen within earshot of their commander, Captain Daniel Ladd, and the remainder of his company. Five were killed and the corpses were stripped, scalped, hearts and entrails jerked out, limbs and genitals hacked off. Two were made captive, to be hurried off to face unspeakable torture. One escaped and his excited tale merely supplemented the horror of the mangled bodies. Alarm reverberated throughout New Hampshire.

Ladd asked for replacements. Among the volunteers was Robert, now fourteen and, by frontier standards, old enough to take his place among men. He was probably happy to exchange the cramped garrisons with their squalling babies and clacking female tongues for the roistering, free life of a militiaman. The company warily beat the woods but the Indians had become one with the forest's shadows. October saw disbandment: the harvest required the help of all. The garrisoned settlers dared to separate to their homes under winter's cover, but spring forced them together again. Robert was held to aid the communal tilling of fields until midsummer; then he was among the first to enlist in Captain Ebenezer Eastman's company. As usual, the men searched but found no foe.

In the spring of 1748 the two families decided to risk staying on their Mountalona farms. It was foolhardy: French and Indian raiders had only been waiting until the worse of winter was passed. In April evidence of their presence was discovered near Rumford; bells tolled and couriers galloped along forest trails to alert outlying farms. Aroused at night, the families from Mountalona stumbled in the darkness in headlong flight to Rumford.

In the morning the men returned for the cattle. Aghast they stared at the clearing. A thin pall of smoke hung in the still April air over charred timbers; butchered cattle sprawled on the cool spring grass. Fruit trees lay among scattered blossoms; whimsically, only one was left standing. The dearly bought results of almost ten years of labor had been destroyed.

After a brief desultory search among the ashes, the men turned their backs on Mountalona. Rebuilding must await the war's end.

By late summer peace was in the air but brought no comfort. The Rogerses and Pudneys seemed about to lose their land to another enemy more civilized but hardly less rapacious than the raiders from Canada. The frontier well knew the new foe: the tidewater proprietors who always seemed to have the law's assistance in ousting pioneer settlers from hard earned homes. James Rogers and Joseph Pudney were caught in the toils of a long-standing dispute over the territorial limits of Massachusetts Bay, which colony had set up a claim to lands west of the Merrimack River. It was to one of its grants in this region that Rogers and Pudney traced their title. However, in 1740, simultaneously with the establishment of a separate governorship for New Hampshire, the northern boundary of Massachusetts Bay was determined as running west from Pawtucket Falls. This seemed to validate the title of Captain John Mason, the original grantee of the area, and a syndicate of twelve New Hampshire citizens purchased the claim from his heirs. After reassuring their native province by confirming all its grants, the new proprietors began to distribute townships west of the Merrimack, disregarding prior grants by Massachusetts Bay.

A group of Ulster Scotch from Londonderry headed by Archibald Stark now petitioned for land including Mountalona. In October 1748 the Masonian proprietors gave the group permission to survey and to lay out a town in the area. Panic-stricken, Rogers and Pudney hired a Londonderry attorney to present their story. Claiming that they and their respective six sons had purchased the entire twenty-one hundred acres, they asked for the same acreage in the new town.

The syndicate, flooded by other petitions from claimants under Massachusetts Bay, made a decision in December. James and Joseph were each awarded a share equal to each Londonderry petitioner while their eldest sons received one share in common. Eventually each shareholder in the new town—first Starkstown but later Dunbarton—received two hundred acres.

It is interesting to note the exaggeration of the original Rogers and Pudney purchase. Actually the two heads had only purchased two-sixths of the total interest in Lovewell's Grant. But the frontier cared little about the niceties of such matters; besides the 'honest labor' of the two families had in the eyes of yeomen created a perfect title to the entire tract.

Undoubtedly the result was a bitter blow to the younger sons of James and Joseph. Land was one of the principal contemporary badges of wealth and the loss was a serious setback to the expectations of all.

In 1752 Robert left Starkstown for a small farm further south which had apparently been purchased for him when he was a boy. His heart was not in husbandry: there soon was a tenant and we next find him in the woods with another expedition.

In March 1753 he was one of twenty men starting out 'to survey and mark a road' to the fertile Coös Meadows on the Connecticut River under authorization of the New Hampshire Assembly. First the Merrimack and then the Pemigewasset were followed to the latter's junction with the Baker; then the trail went northwesterly along the Baker's bank. The men on snowshoes trudged deeper into the hills, past the spot where the preceding year, their guide, John Stark, had been captured by Indians, past the source of the Baker until finally they

emerged from the forest on a height overlooking the Connecticut. At their feet the river valley stretched to the north and
south, the wide, level meadows in its famous bends attractive
to the eyes of the farmers. To the west stretched pine and fir
trees dark against the snow to distant mountains. The party
halted there only one night and then turned for home: the
St. Francis Indians had threatened bloody retaliation for any
penetration into the region. The ax-marks on the trees were
almost effaced before any settlers dared to follow the trail.
It was to be Robert Rogers who wiped out the danger from
the north.

A deed of May 1753 places Robert back in Starkstown.
Perhaps the death of his father drew him home. Tradition
says James was mistaken for a bear and shot by an old
hunter friend whom he was going to visit. Robert did not stay
long; in September he purchased land in Merrimack and
from that time he was usually identified in deeds as a resident
of this community.

The call to arms still claimed him above everything. In midsummer 1754 a series of Indian forays forced the governor to
call out the militia. Robert served under Lieutenant John
Goffe, patrolling between the Merrimack and Contoocook
rivers. Signs of the enemy were everywhere; enemy guns
were discharged so often in the surrounding hills that the
men believed that the redskins were taunting them. Still
there was no actual encounter; Robert was discharged late in
September.

Robert Rogers felt the urge to know what was beyond the
distant hills. He seems to have covered most of New Hampshire's frontier: there are his recorded services and his
description of his experiences in the White Mountains. But
his curiosity outran the limitations imposed on him by the
demands of farming to which he was compelled to give a

minimum of attention. He constantly talked with hunters and
Indians about 'the uncultivated desert,' listening and questioning about the mountains, valleys, rivers, lakes, and passes.
Thus he was not only inured to the hardships faced in the
wilderness but also singularly prepared for service in the
wilderness adjacent to his native province.

He was physically equal to such tasks. The Stark family tradition pictures him 'six feet in stature, well proportioned, and
one of the most athletic men of his time—well known in all
trials of strength or activity among the young men of his vicin-
ity, and for many miles around.' It attributed to him 'great
presence of mind, intrepidity, perseverance and . . . a plausible
address.' The first three traits were not uncommon but the
last was to enable him to gain the assistance of some of the
greatest men of his time.

It was soon evident that success was not to be his in farming on the frontier. To purchase the land in Merrimack he had
given the seller a note. A year later the payee sued and the
only possession the sheriff could find for attachment was a
hat. This circumstance, common as it was in debt-ridden but
litigious frontier society, made Robert an easy mark for a
clever scoundrel, Owen Sullivan, a specialist in engraving and
passing counterfeit money. Sullivan's sensational success was
undoubtedly due to his recognition of the inordinate desire
of debtors for currency. Acts curtailing legal tender caused
people to claim counterfeiting 'was No Sin, for it would
make Money plentier among poor People.' The outraged
splutterings of the 'honest' wealthy about the enormous crimes
of villainous counterfeiters fell on cynical ears. Sullivan and
his accomplices never lacked a sympathetic public among
the masses.

Sullivan apparently made his own plates and passed the
worthless notes by himself or through local gangs organized

by him, as payment for commodities or cattle. He usually disappeared, like Old Nick himself, just before the authorities swooped down, but he did not always escape: in 1749 he stood in the pillory for two hours and received twenty lashes on his bare back for plying his trade in Boston; two years later in Providence both of his ears were cropped and the letter 'C' was branded on both cheeks. In late summer 1754 a narrow escape from the authorities in Newport, Rhode Island, induced him to seek the cooler clime of New Hampshire's green hills. Here his success was so great that the legislature provided each of its members with an unsigned sheet of bills made from authentic plates to enable them to detect counterfeit money.

Late that fall Robert Rogers, hunting in Goffstown, encountered a stranger who introduced himself as 'John McDaniel' and said he wanted to purchase cattle. He made the situation obvious by pulling out a large roll of 'money' before the bulging eyes of the young man, from which he peeled off a twenty pound note to pay in advance for pasturing his horse for two days. Robert was in no position to collect the cattle in a hurry: when he finally had them, Sullivan, the fictitious 'McDaniel,' had disappeared. He left behind a local ring and when Robert saw the ease with which he disposed of a few bills he managed to obtain, he contemplated joining it. Rumor claimed that prominent Joseph Blanchard, Jr. was involved. Robert approached Blanchard who—to quote testimony given by Robert—answered 'that he was not concerned nor never should be in such a devilish act and . . . strongly cautioned me against being concerned in any such thing.' Robert took the advice. The local gang (whose waverings along the path of crime had once caused exasperated Sullivan to cry, 'I never was Concerned with Such a pack of Damned fools') had expected Robert with the cattle. When he failed to appear, his name was dismissed with a curse.

Late in January 1755 provincial authorities in Portsmouth issued warrants for the arrests of nineteen suspects including Robert and his younger brother Richard. On 7 February fifteen—including Robert—stood with witnesses before a panel of four examining justices of peace, one of whom was Joseph Blanchard, Jr. A scribe hurriedly took down the testimony and the scraps used by him attest to the scarcity of paper. Pleading 'Not Guilty,' Robert told his story, denying that he knew the money was counterfeit. His friend, John Stark, was compelled to contradict him. Stark told how Robert claimed to have been 'cheated' when Sullivan disappeared because he had hoped to get a large quantity of counterfeit bills. However, Stark loyally testified that Robert had assured him 'he would not be concerned anymore in any such things.'

At the conclusion of the hearings Robert and nine others were held for trial in Portsmouth, assigned for 12 February. (His brother Richard was clearly not involved in the incident.) Robert and five others were released on bond while the four principals went to jail. None was ever tried. The real culprit had escaped and there was no popular demand for prosecution of the local participants.

When the arresting officers had first appeared in Mountalona, Robert had become frightened and sent a hurried note to a friend, Carty Gilman, to whom he had passed some bogus bills. Instead of tearing it up, Gilman kept it until a deputy-sheriff appeared. Then he tried to swallow it but the officer managed to get it out of his mouth and produced the scrap in court—the earliest known manuscript in Robert Rogers' handwriting.

It was an excited and badly spelled appeal that Gilman 'do the work you promised Me' as Robert's 'life Lays att your providence . . .' 'Ons more I adjur you by your Maker to Do it for whie should such anonest man be Killed?' At least by frontier standards this plea of innocence was probably true.

Then at this moment when his tortured imagination was picturing him a martyr about to be led to the branding iron or the scaffold, Robert suddenly heard of a new opportunity. War with France was breaking out; Massachusetts Bay was seeking recruits for a campaign in Nova Scotia.

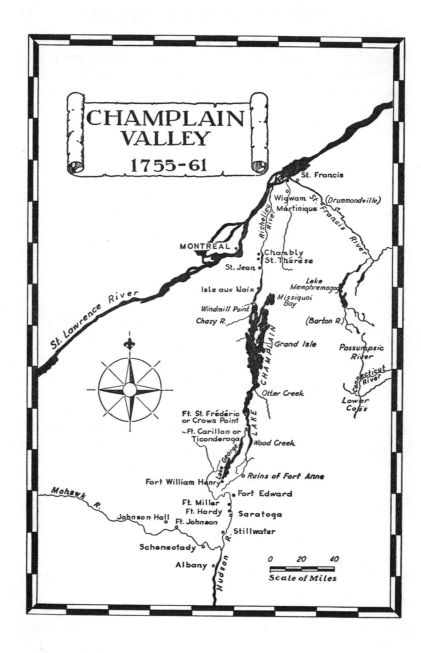

CHAMPLAIN VALLEY
1755-61

St. Francis

Wigwam St. (Drummondville)
Martinique

MONTREAL

Chambly
St. Thérèse
St. Jean

Isle aux Noix

Lake Memphremagog
Missisquoi Bay

Windmill Point
Chazy R.

(Barton R.)

Grand Isle

Passumpsic River

LAKE CHAMPLAIN

Otter Creek

Lower Coös

Ft. St. Frédéric or Crown Point
Ft. Carillon or Ticonderoga

Wood Creek

Ruins of Fort Anne

Fort William Henry

Fort Edward

Mohawk R.
Johnson Hall

Ft. Miller
Ft. Hardy
Ft. Johnson

Saratoga

Stillwater

Schenectady

Albany

Hudson R.

St. Lawrence River

Richelieu River

St. Francis River

Connecticut River

Lake George

0   20   40
Scale of Miles

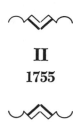

II
1755

'He Is the Most Active Man in Our Army'

IN 1755 French Canada encircled the narrow fringe of English colonies huddled along the Atlantic seaboard. The Monongahela and Ohio watersheds in the west had already witnessed the first clashes between French and British colonial troops. In the northeast the French had invaded Nova Scotia, erecting forts at the head of the Bay of Fundy and inciting the Acadians to revolt. The winds of war for control of an American empire were already whistling through the land.

On 12 February 1755 Governor William Shirley of Massachusetts issued a call for volunteers for a regiment under John Winslow to help drive the French from the Bay of Fundy. Recruiting drums now began to thump throughout New England.

For Robert Rogers the heady excitement of war could not have been more opportune. What better defense to the counterfeiting charge than the firm shield of patriotism? He contacted a recruiting officer, Major Joseph Frye, and offered to enlist twenty or more men. Frye advanced a small sum to be paid the recruits and Robert soon beguiled twenty-four New Hampshire men to volunteer.

Meanwhile the theater of the war had enlarged. There was to be an expedition to force the French from Crown Point.

New Hampshire voted on 20 March to raise five hundred men for this purpose and could not afford to permit Rogers to recruit within its borders for Massachusetts Bay. He was ordered to come 'directly' to Portsmouth for orders from Governor Benning Wentworth. Obviously he now had an even greater opportunity to ingratiate himself with the authorities. His recruits were soon sworn in 'as Private Soldiers in a Company of foot in a Regiment . . . to be under the Command of the Hon. Jos. Blanchard Esq.'

Robert notified Frye and frankly explained the circumstances compelling him to turn his men over to New Hampshire. Frye cared nothing about Rogers' personal difficulties and wanted the men: he complained to Shirley, who wrote Wentworth. Winslow, regimental commander, joined in, but the New Hampshire governor brushed aside their complaints and refused to interfere.

Robert amply repaid the latter's confidence in him. On 24 April when the New Hampshire regiment was officially activated, he had brought in over fifty men. His unit became 'Company One' of the regiment; he was captain and John Stark was his lieutenant.

Imperial orders widened the British offensive: thrusts against Fort Duquesne by regulars under General Braddock and against Fort Niagara by forces under Shirley as major-general were added to the Nova Scotia and Crown Point expeditions. The last was placed under William Johnson, an ambitious Irishman living on the frontier along the north bank of the Mohawk, whose political control over the neighboring Iroquois was almost as legendary as the tales of his prowess among the confederacy's daughters. Johnson's force was to rendezvous at Albany, about a hundred miles south of Crown Point on a direct line. Wentworth was reluctant to leave the New Hampshire frontier unguarded during the concentration period. Accordingly, Blanchard's regiment was to assemble at the blockhouse in Stevenstown (now in modern Franklin), march along the trail blazed in '53 to the Coös on the Connecticut, patrol the frontier until word came of Johnson's arrival at Crown Point, and then pierce the wilderness to join him.[1] It was a foolhardy plan: two forces without communication between them could hardly hope for a successful junction in wilderness under the very nose of the enemy.

It was mid-July before the regiment was able to move northward. The head of the column—presumably Robert's company—had not advanced far along the Pemigewasset when a mounted courier reached it after an all-night ride. Orders were changed: the column was to return to Stevenstown. Governor Wentworth had given up his plan; the unit was to proceed to Albany. On 21 July it left but without visible haste: the final elements did not march until evening of the following day. The regiment tramped southwesterly to the fort at No. 4 on the Connecticut and then southerly along the river to Fort Dummer. Then they disappeared—presumably to cut across the wilderness to the Hudson River and Albany.

In the meantime Johnson's army had assembled on the 'Flats' along the Hudson a few miles north of Albany. Its ranks were chiefly made up of farmers, tradesmen, mechanics, and laborers, their muskets their sole identification as soldiers. Johnson had hoped for better soldiers from New Hampshire, having been assured that they were 'inured to hardship and bred in the woods.' But where were they? Wentworth had not been frank about his plans; Johnson could not understand the delay. He fumed: the first division of his army marched in mid-July with no sign of the New Hampshire men; the second in early August under similar circumstances and even he left on the 8th with the last, still with no news of the missing regiment.

Three days later Colonel Blanchard arrived in Albany with about half his men; the remainder straggled in during the next two weeks. No provisions had been left and Johnson had to send back orders to cut the red tape for the almost starving men.

To Rogers and his companions Albany undoubtedly seemed a foreign city. They crowded the wide main street that ran from the river to the hilltop fort. They gawked at the one- and two-story brick houses with dates and heart designs of black brick set in stepped gable-ends. They spat with deliberate insolence into the scrubbed street under the gaze of Dutch burghers sitting on their stoops and smoking long-stemmed pipes. To the New Englanders these prosperous men were fat with the profits of Indian trade in loot from the homes of the very provincials now defending them. They eyed the red-cheeked, buxom Dutch girls in clean, rustling skirts and white caps. Few were as frank as the New England boy who later confided to his diary: 'I went to Bed Dreamed about Playing with a Dutch garl.'

In mid-August Johnson ordered Blanchard to convoy provision trains up the Hudson. On 26 August Captain Rogers with a hundred men was given this detail. The slow column toiled northward in the summer's heat, first on the west bank of the Hudson, fording the river at Saratoga (now Schuylerville), and then following the road recently cleared and widened by the army's first division. Finally the camp at the Great Carrying Place came into view. Johnson had already gone on, leaving Major-General Lyman of Connecticut with a New York regiment to construct a three bastioned log fort as laid out by the expedition's military engineer. The men were grumbling; morale was low. The Yorkers decided to work off their feelings on the New Hampshire guards coming in.

Rogers and his men kept their tempers until Colonel Blanchard arrived on 4 September with practically the remainder of the regiment. Then civil war broke out: several men were badly beaten up in the resulting Donnybrook. Fortunately, the French and Indians did not choose the moment for an appearance at the ringside.

Rogers was out on reconnaissance when the French under Baron Dieskau attacked Johnson's camp at Lake George on 8 September. The defense managed to repel the attack but there was no pursuit of the defeated French. The provincials were 'All fatigued in Body and mind'; mortally afraid of the enemy, they cowered behind their log breastwork and imagined new, overwhelming attacks.

Johnson badly needed to know what was going on beyond the blank wall of forested mountains separating him from the French and their Indian allies. Rumor and fear were killing the will of the army to push on. Without intelligence he had no answer to Shirley, now commander in chief, who refused to believe reports of French strength. At this critical point Johnson's trusted scouts, the Mohawks, deserted him. With assurances that they were only following a custom and that it was their intention to return, they departed on 11 September. Their intention soon changed; not only did they fail to return but they turned back other Indians they encountered on the way. Desperate, Johnson inquired of the New Hampshire regiment—now at Lake George—for men of scouting ability. Colonel Blanchard recommended Robert Rogers, who reported to the general.

It was a fateful meeting for both, but unfortunately never recorded by an observer. Rogers, one day to have Johnson for an implacable enemy, now knew only the warm welcome reserved for a needed subordinate. He was ordered to reconnoiter Crown Point at once—to penetrate the enemy-held wilderness, over routes no white had passed without Indian guides since the campaign opened, to the heart of the enemy's territory and to return with intelligence of his position and strength.

Evening darkness covered the Lake George camp from hostile eyes on 14 September when a bateau pulled away down the lake, carrying Rogers and four men. They rowed warily through the dark, damp night and landed at dawn in a bay on the west side of Lake George. The bateau was carried into the underbrush and left in the custody of two Connecticut volunteers. The three other men melted into the foliage and only the ordinary sounds of the forest and lake came to the ears of the two guards crouching behind bush and rock.

Rogers and his two companions threaded their way northerly in the valley between the mountains lining the lake's westerly shore and another chain further west. There were blind mazes of thickets to be solved; steep rocky gorges to be crossed and always the endless succession of dark trunks, anyone of which might conceal a hostile musket. Insects swarmed and bit: 'Our situation was by no means agreeable having nothing to cover us from the Natts and Musketoes (with which that country abounds beyond description) but a Shirt and Breech Clout,' wrote a later scout of the same wilderness. No fires comforted them during the cold, damp September nights. Finally, two and a half days later, they peered out of sheltering foliage at the projection of land on which lay Fort St. Frédéric. At night they slipped by a few farmhouses south of the fort into a small entrenchment running to its very walls. Here, within earshot of the sentries, they crouched, hoping to seize some unwary Frenchman. None came and threatening dawn drove them back to a mountain some two miles to the southwest, 'where there was a clear view of all the Fort and appurtenances.' Below their eyrie lay a small bay beyond which the land almost reached the opposite shore. On its far edge stood the dour gray walls of Fort St. Frédéric, square and small, with three regular bastions capped by projecting round sentry-boxes and a citadel set in an irregularly shaped bastion. A drawbridge over a small ditch led into the parade via a gateway out through a stone barracks. Within the walls crowded a stone chapel and other buildings. In the northwest corner stood the stone citadel, octagonal in shape, four stories high, with a château-like, round, shingled roof rising to a point, surrounded by six tall chimneys. This was the final redoubt with its own small moat and drawbridge.

White tents dotted the open plain south of the fort. To the east was a stone windmill—about a thousand feet estimated Rogers in his report. Further south were scattered farmhouses. From their mountain lookout the three scouts judged they saw about five or six hundred white-coated soldiers intermixed with naked, tawny warriors. A few worked at the entrenchment, some hunted pigeons in near-by fields, while others drilled. There seemed to be no sense of apprehension; the scouts froze in their position when a hunting party chased game close to their hideout.

At nightfall they retired into the forest and began the wearisome journey back. Hunger and fatigue kept them from halting at Ticonderoga where a small stream connected Lake George and Lake Champlain. They heard the noise of bugles and the discharge of muskets. Finally they reached their cache only to find that the guards' nerves had not been equal to their task: they had gone with the boat. The three wearily marched on, and late in the night of 23 September stumbled into camp 'not a little fatigued and distressed from hunger and cold.'

Rogers made his report, clear and concise. Johnson allowed him three days of rest and then, troubled about the French at Ticonderoga, ordered Rogers there on 27 September. This time Rogers and four men slipped out cloaked by friendly night. Silently they skimmed the star-pricked waters of Lake George in a light birchbark canoe, passing the campfires of hostile parties never dreaming of English patrols. Landfall at the first sign of dawn was a mere seven miles south of the portage bypassing the falls in the connecting river between the lakes.[2] Three guards were left with the canoe; Rogers and one companion slipped away. They found an advanced camp of 'about one thousand French and Indians' and further on—an estimated mile and a half—came on a fort being built in a 'Grand Encampment' of about three thousand French and Indians. After withdrawing to the dark security of the forest where they passed the night, Rogers and his companion returned to their canoe.

There the guards excitedly told them that a large Indian canoe with nine Indians and a Frenchman had just gone by. Heedless of being deep in hostile territory Rogers deployed his men on a point of land projecting into the lake, awaiting the canoe's return. Back it came, carelessly near the shore. When it was under the very muzzles of their muskets, the English fired: some of the enemy slumped to the bottom of the canoe. The survivors desperately stabbed their paddles into the water, shrilling defiant war whoops. Rogers and his men jumped into their canoe to give chase, but three other enemy canoes, hurrying to the spot, appeared in the distance. Rogers swung his canoe around and fled up the lake, making the camp by evening.

Rogers became camp hero. His were the first shots fired in heat since the battle of Lake George. He had challenged the French in the heart of their territory. His name was on everyone's lips. One of the surprisingly large number of diary-keepers in the expedition summed up the general opinion: 'a bold adventure it was.'

Johnson was worried about his army and his waning reputation. The army's morale was rapidly deteriorating from what he described as 'the Epidemical Disease . . . Home Sickness.' Rumors that Lyman was held back by Johnson refused to be choked off. Shirley wrote to urge him on, suggesting that if Johnson's wound received in the Lake George battle held him in camp, Lyman should take over. Even letters from New York friends were growing critical. Rogers' intelligence seemed a heaven-sent answer to such criticism: a superior, entrenched foe faced them. Johnson attached Rogers' reports to his letters. They were carried to Albany by Peter Wraxall, Johnson's aid-de-camp, who was sent to confer with New York officials. Wraxall found the latter difficult to convince. They ridiculed any supposed weakness as compared to the French. They branded Rogers' information as untrustworthy. Johnson, they said, should send out other parties again and again. Wraxall hotly insisted that he did not believe 'there was another Man in the Army [who] would go' besides Rogers. The officials scoffed and told him to 'try if there is not.'

Wraxall was proved right. Time and again other scouting parties were sent out, only to return without results. On 4 October Lieutenant Philip Lord started out boldly enough but turned around ten miles out and simply reported no signs of the enemy. Fifty men ordered out on a five-day scout stampeded back to camp on the third day because they 'heard or thought they heard some Party of the Enemy . . . The Cap't says his Men had the *Start* and would not stay out.' Of two parties sent out between the 10th and 13th, John Toulin with fifty men dared to venture five or six miles, then raced back to report no discovery of any enemy, while Henry Babcock got ten or twelve miles before turning. 'Discovered no Enemy, returned to Camp' was his laconic report.

On the 13th Johnson ordered Captain William Symes of

New Hampshire out on scout. He camped three miles distant from the main encampment and dispatched individual scouts who found nothing. 'Towards Evening,' Symes later reported, 'I posted Century out one of w'ch was shot and scalp'd a hatched was left in his head . . .' Panic seized the men and Symes sent posthaste for orders from Johnson. Lieutenant Jelles Fonda was dispatched to rally the force. He ordered the men to march; all refused to proceed. He tried to seize their provisions and blankets; the men refused to surrender them. In desperation Fonda challenged, 'All of you that are cowards come and I'll take your names down.' To his dismay 'They Come so thick that I Could see but 10 or 12 Left of the whole party . . .' He gave up; all returned to camp.

On 6 October the enlistment period of the New Hampshire regiment expired. Rogers, Captain Symes, and five or six men stayed on. On the following day while discharged men were beginning the long walk back from Lake George to their New Hampshire farms, Rogers led out his largest force to date, fifty men. Other men now viewed Ticonderoga and the advanced camp. They reported heavy forces, apparently confirming Rogers' prior intelligence.

In the meantime a deserter had come in reporting that Ticonderoga was weakly held. But he had left before Rogers had visited the locality; reinforcements might have come down from Crown Point during the interval between his departure and Rogers' observation. Although perplexed, Johnson staunchly supported Rogers. '[Rogers'] Bravery & Veracity stands very clear in my Opinion & of all who know him, tho his Reg't is gone, he remains here a Volunteer, & is the most active Man in our Army.' He had heard that insinuations to Rogers' disadvantage had been made and added to Governor Hardy that 'I believe him to be as brave & as honest a Man as any I have equal knowledge of, & both myself & all the Army are convinced that he has distinguished himself since he has been among us, superior to most, inferior to none of his Rank in these troops.' He repeated his words to Governors Fitch of Connecticut and Phips of Massachusetts. Johnson—for reasons of his own—was Rogers' best publicist.

On his next scout to Crown Point, Rogers and a companion tried to capture a Frenchman. 'But he refused to take Quarter so we kill'd him and Took of his Scalp in plain sight of the fort . . .' The grisly trophy created a sensation in the camp. True, scalping was as common by the whites as by Indians, but these men had seen only their own companions mutilated —a diarist in one instance described one man 'we brot in alive with the back part of his scull cut off, and his brains naked'—and they felt a savage joy to see the same barbarism practiced on the foe.

Rogers had returned with an estimate of two thousand men at Ticonderoga but found Johnson wavering. Five more deserters came in telling of weak forces at the foot of the lake. Finally on 30 October Johnson recommended an attack down the lake. But his Council of War hesitated, hoping for further intelligence from Rogers, who was out. On this occasion Rogers tried to waylay a French canoe but, aside from an exciting brush with the enemy, returned empty-handed.

Suddenly all thoughts of an advance were forgotten. On 2 November Johnson had sent out two of the few remaining Mohawks. Nine days later they emerged from the wilderness, reporting an enemy encampment near the foot of Lake George 'so large that they never see the like and the Encamp't at this Lake was nothing in Comparison. . . .' It was taken to mean that the French were advancing; 'Our Hol army was mustered that Night,' wrote a private, and Johnson prepared messages warning Fort Edward and calling for reinforcements from Albany. By midnight the letters were ready when Rogers came to the marquee. He had just returned from Ticonderoga where he found the French 'very busy at work' on the new fort. The Indians must be mistaken; they must have seen the camp at Ticonderoga. Johnson called in the principal Indian. The Mohawk faced the frontiersman over the table of the red-coated general in the murky light of the lanterns. The Indian insisted he knew the country and that the enemy was not at Ticonderoga. Rogers repeated that he was wrong and the other Indian was called in: he warmly supported his fellow-scout. Johnson took no chances: a courier received the letters, sprang to horse, and dissolved into the darkness down the road to Fort Edward. Sorely perplexed Johnson then sat up until three in the morning of 12 November, wearily going over the story with the Indians, who remained adamant. Later in the morning he spoke again with Rogers and was inclined to agree with him.

Reconnaissance parties were, as usual, futile. For example one-third of a unit under Lieutenant Waterbury 'declined to proceed. . . .' The remainder started off, but the firing of an alarm gun dissolved their courage. 'It was the General vote of the popel to Return . . . So We Retorn'd with sped.' The camp rested uneasily behind log ramparts. Johnson fretted but realized that the passage of each day lessened the likelihood of any enemy advance. Gradually tension lessened. Finally a scout under Richard Rogers returned, definitely placing the only enemy at Ticonderoga. The Indians were in error; Robert Rogers' reputation again soared high.

There was a final effort from the rear to force the army to move on, but on 22 November the Council of War voted against it, pointing to the imminence of winter, insufficient clothing, inadequate provisions, lack of bateaux, and the poor morale of the men. The campaign was over.

Johnson lingered at Lake George, which no longer reflected the clear blue of summer skies but was gray under pelting

November rains, only long enough to confer with commissioners from Massachusetts Bay, Connecticut, and New York about the winter defense of the frontier. It was voted to raise seven hundred and fifty men to garrison Fort Edward and Fort William Henry (the latter being the new log fort at Lake George under the command of Colonel Joseph Bagley). Like other contingents, the New Hampshire officers of the new regiment which had arrived in October, were allowed to name a captain. Their choice was Robert Rogers. Of the four hundred and two men assigned to Fort William Henry, the New Hampshire regiment was to leave ninety-five to form Robert's company.

Johnson and the discharged men left hastily on 27 November. Many of those supposedly left behind in the unfinished fort disappeared almost as rapidly. When Colonel Bagley mustered his force in the dawn after Johnson's departure, he found only two hundred and six men. Robert Rogers counted a mere thirty-two. Dispiritedly those remaining faced the coming winter.

Only a few wanted to carry the fight to the enemy. One was Robert Rogers.

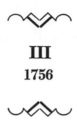

III
1756

'Captain of an Independent Company of Rangers'

DURING the winter of 1755-56 Rogers carried out a series of scouts and raids upon the enemy which laid the basis for his later ranging tactics. Two characteristics were revealed. One was his aggressiveness: he carried the fight to the enemy. The other was his uncanny woodsmanship: he conquered the wilderness under the most adverse circumstances, including the rigorous limitations imposed by warfare. Time and time again Rogers carried out his orders in the heart of the enemy's territory in stormy, freezing weather under combat conditions and returned with his unit intact.

Mid-December found him and three companions watching the French garrison improve new Fort Carillon at Ticonderoga. Heavy snow and piercing cold accompanied them back to their hidden bateau. Before launching it, they 'dugg up our Bottle which we had hid with about one Quart of Rum in it which revived our Spirits greatly then set home with good

Courage and about 2 of the Clock in the Morning Arrived at Fort William Henry in good time to hold Christmas.' In the next month he led seventeen men on skates to the First Narrows of Lake George, then by night through the forested mountains past Carillon to lie in snowy ambush along the narrow thread of Lake Champlain between Ticonderoga and Crown Point. A sleigh with two occupants was intercepted; the horse was slain, its carcass, together with the sleigh and its cargo of fresh beef, was shoved into a hole hastily chopped in the snow. Rogers, his men and the two prisoners faded into the frozen wastes. Ten days after his arrival back at Fort William Henry he was leading fifty men down to peer at Fort St. Frédéric from 'a greate Mounton to the west'rd of Crown Point about one Mile.' One prisoner fell into an ambush laid near the fort, two others were pursued to within gunshot of its walls. Grain-filled barns and farmhouses were set afire, cattle, hogs, and horses were killed before the party turned back. En route one man became ill. Rather than to endanger the whole party by halting, yet unwilling to leave the sick man, Rogers sent all on except himself and seven men. He trailed in twenty-two hours after the main body. Late in February he led sixty men on a fifteen-day scout in the most bitter weather of the winter in the hostile region from Ticonderoga to north of Fort St. Frédéric. Three other provincial captains were members of the party and they could not have helped being impressed by Rogers' ability.

In the eighteenth century winter ended military campaigns; and any activity received undue attention. Rogers' coolly executed expeditions excited unprecedented notices throughout the English colonies. Newspapers were filled with details. Even the military shared the excitement. 'A number of officers at Albany made a collection and presented Captain Rogers with a handsome suit of clothes; and about 161 shillings of

New York Currency, to be laid out in refreshments for him and his men.' In February the New York General Assembly sitting in New York voted Rogers 'as a gratuity for his Extraordinary Courage, Conduct and Dilligence . . . One Hundred and Twenty-five Spanish Milled Pieces of Eight.' Sir Charles Hardy, the governor, wrote the other heads of colonies concerning 'the Behaviour and good Services of Cap't Rogers,' suggesting they duplicate the action of the New York legislature. But tight-fisted New Englanders failed to follow the New York example.

William Shirley in Massachusetts Bay, governor and commander in chief of the British army in North America, had been one of those forwarding Hardy's proposal to the legislature. Its failure to heed the suggestion did not deter him: he had something else in mind and summoned Robert to Boston. Rogers received this order on March 15, the day after his return from the gruelling fifteen-day scout, yet within two days he was on his way, and on 24 March climbed the stairs leading into the Province House in Boston. He must have wondered if Shirley still harbored any ill feeling about the loss of the New Hampshire recruits for the '55 campaign in Nova Scotia. If he did, his mind was soon set at ease. The governor, whose 'every word and every action discovers the gentleman and great politician,' extended a warm welcome to him. Shirley, almost to a fault, loved to discuss warfare on a grand scale; Rogers' activities had opened up a novel aspect of the subject. Both were soon deep in the matter of the role of rangers in an army. Shirley later summarized the thoughts of this conference in a letter to Henry Fox. '. . . It is absolutely necessary for his Majesty's Service, that one Company at least of Rangers should be constantly employ'd in different Parties upon Lake George and Lake Iroquois (alias Lake Champlain), and the Wood Creek and Lands

adjacent. . . .' His outline of their duties summarized Rogers'
activities to date: 'to make Discoveries of the proper Routes
for our own Troops, procure Intelligence of the Enemy's
Strength and Motions, destroy their out Magazines and Settlements, pick up small Parties of their Battoes upon the Lakes,
and keep them under continual Alarm. . . .'

'. . . I Do therefore Hereby Constitute and Appoint you the
Said Robert Rogers to be Captain of an Independent Company of Rangers to be forthwith raised and Employ'd . . .' So
ran Shirley's commission to Rogers dated 23 May 1760. He
was authorized to enlist sixty privates—only courageous men
experienced in hunting, tracking, and long marches—who
were to be paid three shillings (New York currency) per day,
three sergeants at four, an ensign at five, two lieutenants at
seven, while Rogers as captain received ten. Ten Spanish
dollars were allowed each man for clothing, arms and blankets.
By contemporary standards the pay schedule was liberal.
Officers were to receive almost the same salary as regular
officers; the men received twice as much as provincial troops,
who in turn were paid more than privates in the regular army.
    The 'Independent Company of Rangers' was—and yet was
not—a part of the regular army. Formed by the commander
in chief of the regulars and paid from royal funds, it was
subject to regular army discipline and orders. This raised it
from lowly provincial status and undoubtedly contributed to
its esprit de corps. On the other hand it had no permanent
status. The commanding general had created it; he could
end its existence in a moment. This meant that the unit's
leader could never afford to rest on any imagined laurels; he
must constantly prove its value to the army.
    Robert knew of only one source of men measuring up to
Shirley's qualifications: New Hampshire. His brother Richard,

lieutenant in the company, had preceded him to Boston with dispatches; both were soon galloping over frozen roads northward from Boston. Portsmouth came first. Circumstances had radically changed for Robert from the year before, when he, a frightened backwoods farmer, stood in the shadow of the branding iron and scaffold; now he was the shining defender of the northern borders. The gentry, who a year previously damned him as a pest of society, opened their doors to the hero of the day. Symbolic was his acceptance into the local masonic lodge. Its chaplain was the jowled Reverend Arthur Browne, rector of Queen's Chapel, the church of the governor. The lodge's members were the community's principal men.

Elizabeth, the minister's slim fourteen-year-old daughter, undoubtedly had heard of the renowned captain. Perhaps she caught a glimpse of the tall, sturdy young man. He was not the immature frontier farmer of 1755 frightened by his first brush with the law, unaccustomed to men of authority. Now he had behind him months of being a leader, accustomed to meeting important personages and to seeing respect in their eyes and voices. Self-confidence, a deepening sense of responsibility, an eagerness to press on to greater heights in his chosen field—all were attributes of the young ranger captain.

Robert had not returned to bask in the limelight. He was belatedly turning in the muster roll of Company One in Colonel Blanchard's regiment; until this was done, he could not pay the men. The legislature allowed it and all claims were paid. There was an ominous silence when he inquired about pay for his company now at Fort William Henry. Lack of time compelled him to abandon for the moment any further action on the point. He and Richard hurried to recruit among the yeomen he knew in the neighborhood of Rumford. At Starkstown Robert sought out John Stark who could not resist the appeal: he accepted a lieutenant's commission, second in rank to Richard. Both the reputation of Rogers and the rate of pay played a part in the rapid completion of the company. By mid-April thirty-seven new recruits were swinging over the hills to the west under the watchful eyes of experienced officers.

At No. 4 on the Connecticut Rogers divided the party: twenty under Richard went on to Albany, the remainder under Robert turned north to approach Fort St. Frédéric from a new route. He reconnoitered the post, killed cattle on temporarily deserted farms, and on 11 May came in at Fort William Henry. Nine days after his arrival he was off to Ticonderoga with eleven men. At the southern end of the portage he watched a palisaded post being erected; he estimated a thousand men at Fort Carillon. An ambush was prepared along the portage road; muskets roared when a French work detail of twenty-two walked into it. Six dropped. Another was made captive by the rangers, who then hastily turned back to their base. The prisoner revealed that French and Indian raiders were out to intercept English convoys. The morning after his return Robert was out combing the woods for invaders. None were found.

On 6 June Rogers' provincial company formed to protect the front during the winter and early spring was officially disbanded. The men had received no pay because no colony was willing to acknowledge itself liable for the obligation; naturally they were disgruntled. Only fourteen elected to stay on. The others probably shouldered their packs under a barrage of half-envious gibes and trudged out of the fort's gate, happily lifting their faces to the south on the first leg of a long journey home.

Shirley and Rogers had planned to cut the French line of communication between Canada and Crown Point. It could only be done on the water: boats were necessary. Bateaux were too clumsy; canoes, too flimsy. There was another type: long, slim whaleboats, light but sturdy, with a bold sheer, sharp and raking at both ends. But how to get them north of the intervening French forts?

On 13 June darkness covered the departure of Rogers and thirty-seven rangers in five bateaux down the lake. A camp was made on the eastern shore; Rogers left with a few trusted men into the green curtain of the mountains. Secrecy shrouded the project. He probed here and there seeking a portage route from Lake George to Wood Creek. One was discovered; satisfied, he returned to the main body. The passage down the lake was resumed and a routine reconnaissance of the French followed. When about to withdraw a man was reported missing. Rogers was worried: did the ranger desert? Would he tell the French of the search for a portage? After a wait Rogers reluctantly turned back, still refusing to believe the man a deserter, leaving cached provisions. On 17 June the party made the fort. Six days later the missing man staggered in, weak from hunger: he had slipped away from the main body to recover a forgotten knapsack.

The whaleboats arrived at Fort William Henry accompanied by Shirley's orders 'to proceed immediately to Lake Champlain, to cut off, if possible, the provisions and flying parties of the enemy.' On 28 June five boats, each manned by ten rangers, pulled away from the dark shadow of the fort's wooden walls. By the second day out the men had hauled the boats out of the water at the portage. The difficulties of portaging are attested by the fact that it took four days to cover a distance of about four miles on an air line. The graceful whaleboats were clumsy and heavy out of their native element. Portaging them under combat conditions in midsummer was a task which would give pause to anyone acquainted with the roughness of the terrain over which the rangers labored. Finally the whaleboats were lightly bobbing in the muddy waters of Wood Creek.[1]

During the following night the boats crept down to within six miles of Fort Carillon. Threatening dawn forced them ashore until dark. Again under way, they finally saw the campfires twinkling on the peninsula on which Fort Carillon stood. Edging along the irregular eastern shore, the boats inched by the danger point. Rogers coolly tried to guess how many men were camped there, reporting 'about two thousand.' French sentries heard only the slapping of the water on the lake shore, the subdued murmur of a slumbering camp, and the lonely calls of a nocturnal bird. Their calm challenges came clearly over the lake to the ears of the silent rowers.

The first tinges of light in the skies caught the expedition only five miles below the fort; boats were hurriedly dragged ashore into the purple shadows of the forest on the eastern bank. During the day bateau after bateau filed before the eyes of the hidden rangers, discharging passengers or cargo at Fort Carillon then passing back en route to Fort St. Frédéric. River traffic halted at night; the moon was too bright for the rangers to risk the narrows at Crown Point. Daylight saw the French resume their activity; 'near one hundred Boats passed us.' A group of seven almost landed where the men lay hidden; however, the officer in charge 'went further on & Landed about 25 Rods from us where they Dined in our View But did not think it advisable to Attack them in the Situation we were in.' That night the whaleboats slipped by Fort St. Frédéric.

Now Lake Champlain widened; less caution was needed. Ten miles were covered before refuge was taken in the woods. French lake traffic the next day even included a light schooner of 35 or 40 tons. That night the rangers rowed only to one o'clock, when Rogers ordered them into shore. Scouts slipped into the darkness. Almost immediately they returned

to report the schooner at anchor a mile down the lake. Whaleboats were made ready, but before they could be manned
two French bateaux appeared out of the early morning mist,
heading directly for the rangers who could only open fire. The
bateaux lost headway; Rogers shouted to offer quarter if they
would pull into shore. A voice accepted and the English ceased
firing. It was a ruse: the bateaux turned for the opposite shore.
Pursuit was swift and they were soon overtaken. Of the twelve
men in them, three were dead and two, wounded. Boats and
cargo of wheat, flour, rice, wine, and brandy were quickly
sent to the lake bottom, 'excepting Some few Casks of Brandy
& Wine which we hid in very secure Places.' The prisoners
claimed to be the vanguard of a large party; the gunfire must
have carried to hostile ears. Whaleboats were carefully concealed on the western shore. One of the wounded prisoners
was mortally injured and could not be moved. He was quickly
dispatched and his scalp brought the total to four. Then
the rangers and their two prisoners beat a quick retreat into
the woods.

This was on the morning of 8 July. Four days later the party
broke out of the woods on the western edge of Lake George
many miles north of Fort William Henry. The men were too
exhausted to cross the intervening mountains. Richard Rogers was sent ahead for relief. In the evening of the 14th the
latter reappeared with thirty men and ten bateaux. 'Ye 15th
at two of the Clock we arrived safe with all my Party &
Prisners. . . .'

The otherwise idle provincial army at the fort grew excited
about the conjectured alarm of the French at the threat to
their line of communication. '. . . A brave action,' wrote army
surgeon Thomas Williams to his wife (sometimes affectionately addressed as 'My Dear Rib'), 'it will undoubtedly fill them
with consternation, if they can find out what has become of
their party, it will oblige them to leave their habitations,

& draw into their strong-holds.' The blow was a bright moment in a lackluster campaign. The fame of Rogers and his rangers soared high, totally disproportionate to the actual achievement.

IV
1756–1757

'All Ranks . . . Are Pleased with Your Conduct'

THE '56 campaign would bring no glory to British arms: there was to be a stunning defeat at Oswego and a sobering failure of a provincial army to move from its base at the southern end of Lake George. But the year was at least one of change: a shift in the high command, a transfer of the burden of campaigning in the Champlain valley to British regulars. The latter were to find no common ground with the provincials whose ability to wage warfare came to be doubted and who were gradually relieved of front-line duties. Of all the native troops only the rangers were to grow both in size and in the respect of the regulars. The reason: Robert Rogers.

William Shirley's successor had been named in January 1756: John Campbell, Earl of Loudoun, a man more distinguished by the deliberateness of his pace than by the sparkle of his martial glory. He finally embarked for New York on 20 May surrounded by baggage, bustle, and an aid-de-camp, secretary, 'Secretary Extraordinary,' valet, cook, groom, coachman, postillon, footmen, and mistress. New York gaped at this entourage on 23 July. The government had rushed a commission to let his third in command, Daniel Webb, assume temporary leadership in America. Webb practically flew, by contemporary British standards, to arrive in New York on

7 June. He halted to let the second in command, James Abercromby, catch up and then both made Albany by 25 June and relieved Shirley. Loudoun finally came up the Hudson, to assume formal charge on 11 August.

Times were propitious for Rogers and his rangers. Letters and newspapers had carried his fame across the sea. Not only did his forays constitute the sole British successes but they undoubtedly stirred romantic imaginations: rangers silently threading through green forests or slipping in birchbark canoes over autumn-tinted waters; rangers crunching on snowshoes through a silent, frozen maze of rocks and trees under the bluish-silver of a winter moon; dark, menacing shadows, ambushes, sudden gunfire amid terrifying warwhoops, and always the successful penetration by British rangers into the heart of enemy-held territory. The high command was impressed even before putting a foot on American soil. Only a few days after his appointment Loudoun interviewed a newly returned officer about Rogers' unit. Both Webb and Abercromby were instructed 'to get as great a number of Rangers as possible in the Troops to be furnished by the Colonies.'

As the regulars gathered in Albany, Rogers seems to have been a principal topic of conversation. Charlotte Brown, matron of the army's general hospital, recorded the ranger captain's activities in her journal almost from the day of her arrival. Harry Gordon, Royal Engineer, writing back to England, simply referred to Robert as 'the famous cap't.'

General Abercromby was met with cries for more rangers. Shirley, while leaving, repeated warnings from William Johnson that a unit was necessary to secure the line of communication between Albany and Oswego. This was followed by a report from Robert of his Lake Champlain raid together with a brash recommendation that the ranger force be enlarged and that Richard Rogers be appointed captain of the new company. Backed by a decision of his Council of War, Abercromby agreed. Richard hurried home to recruit. Thirty-five men were swept together in New Hampshire and twenty-five more while en route to Albany, where he arrived on 29 August. Although Oswego had fallen he was sent to serve under General Webb west of Albany. He failed to satisfy the nervous general and was soon ordered by Loudoun to Fort Edward.

Anticipating the demand for rangers, Shirley had taken two steps before receiving news of his recall: Winslow was ordered to raise three companies from the New Englanders returning from the '55 Nova Scotia campaign, and the Stockbridge Indians were to form a company of fifty. In the first case the New Englanders had landed and had scattered to their homes before the order was received. Only two partially filled companies under Captains Hobbs and Speakman drifted into Albany in September: a nondescript lot largely from the Boston waterfront, 'the best of their Men, Irish Roman Catholicks, and others mostly Sailors and Spaniards.' They did practically nothing in the fall of '56. Thirty Stockbridge Indians, however, put in an appearance and were promptly incorporated into Rogers' ranging companies.

Loudoun found Winslow claiming his army of provincials was ready to advance down Lake George but upon inquiry discovered that the command did not have the slightest idea of what existed at the other end of the lake. Provincials and regulars began to wrangle. The disgust and revulsion of the regulars are clear in the reports describing provincial camps where sickness and death were rampant: 'The Fort stinks enough to Cause an infection . . . Their Camp nastier than anything I could Conceive, their Necessary houses [latrines], Kitchens, Graves and places for Slaughtering Cattle, all mix through their Encampment . . . .' Regular eyes found insufficient guards and no discipline; during the six days Lieutenant-Colonel Burton inspected Fort William Henry, no scouting party was sent out. Some British felt that the provincials at this fort were the 'Lowest Dregs of the People, both officers and men.' Desertion was common. Loudoun not only abandoned any idea of an offensive but was frankly worried about any effective defense should the French launch an attack.

Rogers had a run of ill luck. In early August while preparing an ambush near Fort St. Frédéric, he and his men were discovered and forced to decamp in a hurry. He wanted to continue the offensive planned by Shirley and asked permission from Loudoun to raid into Canada. Receiving no answer, he foolishly risked his career by setting out without orders. A futile gesture: a thirty-eight-day scout resulted only in the capture of a frightened French family of three near Fort St. Frédéric. Loudoun overlooked Rogers' indescretion; perhaps he was only too happy to see some signs of initiative in local troops. But he did not want the rangers far afield. He drew them in, concentrating them at Fort Edward on a forty-acre island in the Hudson across a narrow, shallow portion of the river from the fort itself. From here—'The Island'—the rangers conducted local patrols for the regular command apprehensive of a French thrust from Ticonderoga.

Occasionally there were flashes of the old spirit. On 22 October Rogers went out to take a prisoner near Fort Carillon at Ticonderoga. His small party lay in ambush without luck until Rogers decided to force matters.

I at length discovered two men, centries to the picquet guard of the French army, one of which was posted in the road that leads from the fort to the woods; I took five of my party, and marched directly down the road in the middle of the day, till we were challenged by the centry. I answered in French, signifying that we were friends; the centinel was thereby deceived, till I came close to him, when perceiving his mistake, in great surprize he called, Qui etes vous? I answered, Rogers, and led him from his post in great haste, cutting his breeches and coat from him, that he might march with the greater ease and expedition.

Beginning with a patrol on 7 September, regular officers or volunteers attached to the regiments began to go out 'on party' under Robert Rogers' leadership. Their experiences generally evoked admiration for the ranger leader. Contrast, for example, the glowing letter of Captain James Abercrombie, nephew and aid-de-camp of General Abercromby, with the usual disgusted descriptions of provincial officers and men written by regulars:

You cannot imagine how all ranks of the people here are pleased with your conduct, and your mens behaviour; for my part, it is no more than I expected; I was so pleased with their appearance when I went out with them, that I took it for granted they would behave well whenever they met the enemy. When I returned I reported them as such, and am glad they have answered my expectation.

Rogers continued to urge Loudoun to use the rangers on offensive missions. When Loudoun came up to Fort Edward, the tall ranger captain, who was meeting the short Scotsman personally for the first time, besieged him with both oral and written proposals to raid into enemy territory. He would attack St. Francis, the heart of the hostile Indians; he would winter at No. 4 with his rangers, both as a cover for New England and as a base for forays into Canada. But Loudoun wanted him at hand. Winter raiders were expected from Ticonderoga. Ignorant of the futility of defensive tactics based on interception of small parties in the limitless wilderness, he confidently expected that the rangers, perhaps joined by regulars, would cut off the enemy. As he told New York's

Governor Hardy: 'One rebuff of this kind will put an entire
end to that sort of War.' He also needed Robert Rogers for
reconnaissance. It enabled him to know when all dangers of
a thrust from Ticonderoga ended and it was safe to go into
winter quarters. His reports home citing Rogers' name made
even the high ministers of state familiar with the name of the
ranger captain.

Hobbs' and Speakman's rangers at Fort William Henry
together with Rogers' two companys at Fort Edward were
now to patrol the northern front. Winter snows soon piled
high against wooden fort walls, limiting the range of missions.
Richard Rogers went to New England to recruit and to seek
payment for Robert's company which served during the winter
of '55-'56.

The gray days passed. Finally Robert was ordered out on
a distant reconnaissance of the French forts: what was the
enemy doing?

15 January 1757. In the gray, bitterly cold darkness of
winter's dusk Robert Rogers, John Stark, and fifty-one rangers
filed into Fort William Henry, having come through the snow
from Fort Edward. While the men dispersed to the welcome
warmth of smoky barracks, Rogers reported to Major Eyre,
post commandant. Additional men were needed. Thirty-three,
including Captain Speakman and Rogers' older brother James
who was an ensign in Speakman's unit, volunteered from the
two ranger companies at the post. Two days were spent in
careful preparation; late in the afternoon of the 17th the force
was mustered. Regulars silently watched from the sidelines
while ranger corporals and sergeants inspected the men and
ranger officers grouped around Rogers for final instructions.
Two weeks' food ration and sixty rounds of powder and ball
were issued. Each man had snowshoes slung over his back;
off his left shoulder hung a food knapsack, below it a canteen

with diluted rum, under the right arm hung a powder horn. Now blankets were passed, Indian-style, over their heads like monks' hoods and fastened in their waist-belts. Mittens, tied to the neck by cords, were drawn on. With guns clubbed over their shoulders, they passed specter-like out of the fort's gateway to the lake shore, donned skates, and disappeared into the cold gloom.

It was rough going in the darkness. When camp was made at the First Narrows, eleven men had suffered incapacitating injuries and were sent back in the morning. The others went on, first in the shadow of the hills on the lake's eastern side, then crossing when the sun swung to the left. By midmorning of the 19th, an estimated nineteen miles beyond the First Narrows, Rogers judged a further advance on the lake too dangerous. Snowshoes were substituted for skates. Then the rangers tramped off northwesterly into the frozen mountains. By evening of the next day they were camping under snow-burdened pines and firs three miles west of Lake Champlain.

Rain was falling the next morning. Concealed fires had to be lit to dry out wet muskets. Then the rangers filed due east under dripping trees and came out on the narrow lake about midway between Crown Point and Ticonderoga. Almost immediately a French sleigh was sighted coming from the direction of Carillon. Stark was dispatched down the lake to halt any attempted breakthrough to the north; Speakman held the center while Rogers hurried along the shore to cut off any retreat. Then the latter saw in the murky grayness about ten other sleighs following far in the rear of two leaders. Two men received hurried orders to warn Stark to let the first sleighs pass. But when they came up to Stark, he and his men were already streaming out onto the ice. Rogers and his men hurried out; the two foremost sleighs slithered to a halt. Rogers was the first to take a prisoner, but three mounted French guards managed to wheel and escape. Rangers desperately tried to reach the rearmost sleighs; they turned and were wildly careening back toward Ticonderoga. Pursuit was futile.

Seven prisoners separately interrogated revealed the desperate plight of the rangers. Two hundred Canadians and forty-five Indians had just arrived at Carillon; fifty more were momentarily expected. All were ready to march. Now a strong and alerted enemy stood poised between the raiders and their base.

Rogers lost no time. The rangers swiftly returned to the camp of the previous night; coals were rekindled to dry sodden firelocks. Then the party started south, forcing the march in slippery, wet snow. Rogers led the forward division. The French and Indians were waiting. Rogers' advanced guard had just topped the western height of a valley between two steep hills when enemy muskets roared, echoing amid the silent mountains. Two rangers fell dead; others were wounded; a ball grazed Robert's head. The advanced party of the rangers fell back before a charge of shouting French and whooping Indians. Rogers ordered a retreat to the opposite ridge, held by the rear guard, where the prisoners were being 'knock'd . . . on the Head' for fear they 'should Escape and give Information to the Enemy. . . .' The French followed closely, cutting off the retreat of some rangers, raking others with murderous fire. Yet Rogers finally managed to form a thin wavering line, beating off all attacks. 'We continued a constant fire on both Sides till Sunset. . . .'

Both sides realized that the rangers were hopelessly pinned down without chance of succor while reinforcements and more ammunition were available to the foe from the near-by fort. The French tried to take advantage of it, reported Rogers, 'calling to us, and desiring us to accept of Quarters, promising that we should be . . . used kindly, and at the same Time called to me by Name and threatened us that if we did not embrace their Offers, as soon as the Party joined them from the Fort, which they expected every Moment, they would cut us to Pieces. . . .' The whooping of the Indians, the dangling of ranger scalps, the screams and moans of the wounded underlined the offers. Rogers laughed at them; he shouted back that his rangers would be the ones to do the cutting to pieces. 'About Sun setting I received a slanting Wound in my hand thro my Wrist which disabled me from loading my Gun, on which I sent a Man to the Rest of my Officers desiring them not to be discouraged but maintain their Ground, which they did very gallantly till Daylight ceased when both Sides left off Firing. . . .' The silence was startling by contrast.

Private Thomas Brown, a volunteer from Speakman's company, later wrote an unusually graphic description of the fight:

I receiv'd a Wound . . . (the first Shot they made on us) thro' the Body, upon which I retir'd into the Rear, to the Prisoner I had taken on the Lake, knock'd him on the Head and killed him . . . ; and as I was going to place myself behind a large Rock, there started up an Indian from the other Side; I threw myself backward into the Snow, it being very deep, sunk so low that I broke my Snowshoes (I had Time to pull 'em off, but was obliged to let my Shoes go with them) one Indian threw his Tomahawk at me, and another was just upon seizing me; but I happily escaped and got to the Centre of our Men, and fix'd myself behind a large Pine, where I loaded and fir'd every Opportunity; after I had discharged 6 or 7 Times, there came a Ball and cut off my Gun just at the Lock. About half an Hour after, I receiv'd a Shot in my Knee; I crawled again into the Rear, and as I was turning about receiv'd a Shot in my Shoulder. The Engagement held, as near as I could guess, 5½ Hours, and as I learnt after I was taken, we Killed more of the Enemy than we were in Number. By this Time it grew dark and the Firing Ceased on both Sides. . . .

The ranger officers crawled to the rear; a council of war decided to disperse quietly, and to carry off the wounded.

Morning came and the first French shots were unanswered: the rangers had gone.

The same darkness that covered the successful withdrawal also led to overlooking some of the wounded. Brown was one. Crawling out of battle range, he had fallen in with two wounded men, Captain Speakman and Mr. Baker, a volunteer from the regulars. Misery and pain made them careless: they kindled a fire. Then they noted the silence around them; guarded calls revealed that they were alone. Brown saw an Indian approaching and hastily crawled away from the fire. He escaped notice but saw the Indian strip and scalp Captain Speakman alive and take off Baker, who was prevented from committing suicide.

Seeing this dreadful Tragedy, I concluded, if possible, to crawl into the Woods and there die of my Wounds: But not being far from Capt. Spikeman, he saw me and beg'd me *for God's sake! to give him a Tomahawk, that he might put an end to his Life!* I refus'd him, and Exhorted him as well as I could to pray for Mercy, as he could not live many Minutes in that deplorable Condition, being on the frozen Ground, cover'd with Snow. He desir'd me to let his Wife Know *if I lived to get home* the dreadful Death he died.

Brown was finally captured and saw Speakman's head on a pole. Later he watched the Indians strip and tie a ranger to the stake.

The Squaws cut Pieces of Pine, like Scures [skewers], and thrust them into his Flesh and set them on Fire, and then fell to pow wawing and dancing round him; and ordered me to do the same. Love of Life obliged me to comply. . . . With a bitter and heavy Heart I feigned myself merry. They cut the poor man's Cords, and made him run backwards and forwards. I heard the poor Man's Cries to Heaven for Mercy; and at length, thro' extreme Anguish and Pain, he pitched himself into the flames and expired.

After a harrowing flight through the darkness in the snow, Rogers and his men came out of the forest on the western shore of Lake George some miles south of the French advanced post. The wounded slowed the retreat. Stark and two others were sent ahead up the lake for aid. That evening they wearily stumbled into Fort William Henry and gasped out the news. A sleigh started down the lake and met Rogers prodding his party along at the First Narrows. The wounded were placed in it; the others trudged on through the cold to their base.

It was the first large-scale engagement in which Rogers had participated. Undoubtedly he aged during these few days in a way that only the leaders of small combat units can comprehend: for the first time he had failed to bring back all his men. Out of the seventy-four engaged, thirteen had been killed, nine wounded, and seven taken prisoner. Like any conscientious commander he was concerned, but Captain Abercrombie quickly reassured him: 'I am heartily sorry for Spikeman and Kennedy . . . as likewise for the men you have lost, but it is impossible to play at bowls without meeting with rubs.' He regretted not being there. '. . . I am certain . . . it is better to die with the reputation of a brave man, fighting for his country in a good cause, than either shamefully running away to preserve one's life, or lingering out an old age, and dying in one's bed, without having done his country or his King any service.'

British officers offered no criticism. Major Eyre wrote General Abercromby on the very day when Rogers came in that the rangers had 'behaved gallantly. . . .' He praised Rogers' choice of position on the battlefield. General Abercromby reported to Loudoun that Rogers' 'behaviour upon this late Occasion intitles him to marks of your Lordship's favour and Countenance. His relation by way of journal is very modest

. . . .' He pointed out that if the hostile Indians 'had not been this roughly handled they would have certainly pursued him, and at least prevented his carrying off his wounded men.' Secretary at War Fox received copies of Rogers' report; all newspapers carried accounts—the distant *Virginia Gazette,* for example, describing 'the late Action with the brave Captain Rogers.'

Rogers received word of the official reaction through Captain Abercrombie.

. . . The General . . . returns you and your men thanks for their behaviour, and has recommended both you and them strongly to my Lord Loudoun. . . . We . . . recommended, for Spikeman's company, your brother (James) for a Lt. . . . Please send me the names of officers you would recommend for your own company, and also to fill up the vacancies in the others. . . . You cannot imagine how all ranks of people here are pleased with your conduct and your mens behaviour; for my part it is no more than I expected.

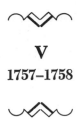

V
1757–1758

'Without Him These Four Companies Would Be Good for Nothing'

WITH restored confidence Rogers sent in his recommendations and offered to increase his companies to one hundred men each with the privates to be paid slightly less than they were receiving. Loudoun agreed and Abercromby's orders to Rogers dated 26 February 1757 officially brought the other two companies under his command. The officers were to have the same pay as British officers of the same rank. John Stark had been recommended to command Speakman's company at Fort William Henry. Captain Hobbs had died of smallpox in February and Robert proposed Lieutenant Charles Bulkeley as his successor. James Rogers became a first lieutenant when Bulkeley received his new appointment.

Rogers had gone to Albany for treatment of his wounds. Here he received disappointing news from Richard, returning from New England. On 11 December the latter had presented the muster-roll of the '55-'56 company to the New England Committee of War, but the latter had rejected the claim apparently on the ground that each province should pay its respective units. Under contemporary practice the commanding officer was personally liable to the men for their pay and Robert's position was embarrassing. He at once wrote Loudoun requesting payment from the British government or at

least assistance in obtaining payment. Circumstances inter-
vened to prevent a follow-up of this serious situation: on 5
March he was taken ill with smallpox and confined until 15
April. Then the ensuing campaign claimed his entire attention.

Believing 'it is impossible for an Army to act in this country
without Rangers,' Loudoun took Robert's, Stark's, and Bulkeley's companies with him to Nova Scotia for his planned
offensive against Louisbourg on the southeastern tip of Cape
Breton. Richard Rogers' company was left at Fort William
Henry. Little was accomplished by the expedition. Most note-
worthy was the first authentic description of the appearance
of Robert's command penned by an observant British officer:

A body of rangers, under the command of Captain Rogers, who
arrived with the other troops from the southward, march out every
day to scour the country; these light troops have, at present, no
particular uniform, only they wear their cloaths short, and are
armed with a firelock, tomahock, or small hatchet, and scalping
knife; a bullock's horn full of powder hangs under their right arm,
by a belt from the left shoulder; and a leathern, or seal's skin bag,
buckled round their waist, which hangs down before, contains
bullets, and a smaller shot of the size of full green peas: six or
seven of which, with a ball, they generally load; and their officers
usually carry a small compass fixed in the bottoms of their powder-
horns, by which to direct them, when they happen to lose themselves in the woods.

The presence of French forces at Louisbourg too strong to
challenge induced Loudoun to give up the proposed attack.
Just as the expedition was turning toward New York, news
arrived of the fall of Fort William Henry and of the massacre
of many of its defenders after the surrender. Loudoun hurried
back as fast as the winds would take him.

The reports from the Lake George front bore particularly

sad news to Robert. Richard, the one brother who seems to have been closest to him, had died of smallpox on 22 June—'no small loss to us,' wrote Major General Webb. Later Robert heard that he was one of the corpses dug up to be scalped by the maddened Indians after the fort's surrender. But the dead had their revenge—a smallpox epidemic broke out among their desecrators, who carried it back to spread death among distant tribes on the Mississippi.

Under the articles of surrender, the defeated troops were not to serve again for eighteen months. Although the British command felt that the convention had been breached by the French, the troops were dismissed. The two companies of rangers which had been at Fort William Henry—Richard's and a provincial unit under Captain Jonathan Ogden—were accordingly dissolved on 24 August.

The British fleet returning from Halifax hurried up Long Island Sound, saving the few hours an outside passage might have taken. There was a delay in New York for transportation up the Hudson but the rangers made Albany by nightfall, 14 September. Here they were met by recruits from New England enlisted by officers sent on ahead from Nova Scotia to fill ranks thinned by the fortunes of war or smallpox. In a short time all were swinging on their way to Fort Edward, where the arrival of regulars and the rangers stiffened wavering morale.

Loudoun would have been unworthy of his profession if he had not been disturbed that his army of regulars had to depend on irregulars. The Duke of Cumberland, Captain General of the British army, had cautioned: 'Teach your troops to go out upon Scouting Parties: for 'till *Regular* Officers with men that they can trust, learn to beat the woods, & to act as *Irregulars,* you will never gain any certain Intelligence of the Enemy, as I fear, by this time you are convinced

Indian Intelligence & that of *Rangers* is not at all to be depended upon.' Loudoun now began to follow the Duke's advice.

When the rangers arrived in Albany and prepared to march up to Fort Edward, Abercromby under orders from his commander issued certificates allowing cadets in regular regiments to put themselves under Rogers' orders. It was understood that upon completion of this tour of duty they would receive regular commissions in specialized companies of rangers. When Rogers arrived at Fort Edward there were approximately fifty-six of these volunteers. But Loudoun was not content to have his prospective ranger officers learn by experience. His experience with Rogers undoubtedly taught him that he had an unusual subordinate by provincial standards. Here was no farmer grudgingly donating a few months of a year to war; here was a man who had made war a career. His ranging parties were not haphazard affairs controlled by chance; they proceeded according to carefully thought-out tactics. Loudoun wanted to know these rules and put the question to Rogers.

The answer may well be claimed to be the first written manual of warfare in the New World.

Every evening, wrote Rogers, the rangers are paraded by companies. An officer of each company passes along the lines of men 'to see they are duly provided and their Arms in order so as to be ready to March at a Minute's Warning. . . .' Before dismissal guards are named and the next day's scouting assignments are delegated.

Rogers' next paragraph verbally portrayed the small—eight or ten men—patrol in the woods. Single-file, spaced 'to prevent an Enemy destroying two of us at one Shot,' the rangers cautiously move forward. ('On going over Mossy or soft ground we change our position and march abreast of each other to prevent an Enemy from tracking us. . . .') One ranger goes ahead as an advance guard; flankers about twenty yards distant constantly search for signs of the enemy.

'A private signal'—presumably the simulated call of a wild bird or animal—is arranged to warn of the approach and strength of an enemy. Rogers knew the importance of position, concealment, and surprise. 'Upon seeing an Enemy I could encounter I would endeavour for the best ground & Shelter from Trees and then make the most of it. If I have the first fire it's more than probable we gain our point for immediately after it we shall rush upon the Enemy. . . .' He had no hesitancy about retreating before a superior foe; if surrounded and outnumbered, the rangers simply broke and scattered, usually under the cover of darkness, each taking a different route back to a rendezvous 'which is every Morning altered and fixed for the ensuing Night in order to get the Party together after separation by day. . . .'

When darkness halts the march, the camping site is selected to afford the sentries the best possible observation. Half the small parties stand the first watch; the remainder take the second. When nearing their objective one or two of the rangers go ahead to select the most advantageous observation post. '. . . After Effecting our design Therein we endeavour to take what Prisoners we can and after Captivating of 'em we keep them separate till their examined and then return home in a different Road from the one we came in, taking particular care to halt only on rising ground that we may have a prospect of discovering a Party in our Rear and Be enabled to alter our Course or Scatter as the exigence of the Circumstance may require.'

Eternal vigilance was Rogers' keynote. Rangers operated in hostile territory; their guard could not relax from the moment they left their base until the gate of the fort swung shut behind them on their return.

It was still the keynote when Rogers went on to describe a reconnaissance in force—for example, three hundred men. The party is split into thirds. Rogers commands the center; 'the next Senior Officer with one hundred on my Right at twenty yards distance and the other hundred at the same distance on the Left is led by the third Commanding officer of the Party; which Divisions are marched in the Indian or single File. . . .' Ten or twelve men range thirty yards ahead of each division with two scouts leading each advance party. Forty yards to the side march flanking units of twenty-five men with two or three men thrown further out to guard against ambush. A rear guard composed of a non-commissioned officer and eight men have 'Orders to halt on all Eminencies, where any Party following us might be seen. . . .'

Rogers prepared elaborate dispositions to meet varying conditions under which a battle in the woods might be fought. Under all circumstances a battle line two deep is formed with trees as protection for the men. The flanking parties are kept out and even reinforced if necessary, for they are a source of pressure when advancing or the principal guard against encirclement when retreating. 'If I am obliged to receive the Enemy's Fire it is our Custom to fall or squat down that their Balls may go over us before we discharge at them. . . .' Constant fire is necessary if enemy pressure is great. '. . . The Front Fires whilst the Rear reserves theirs 'till the Front has discharged and then improve their Opportunity by advancing and doing the like, by which time the Front who fall back in the Rear after their first fire advance loaded and in readiness to discharge again. . . .' The maneuver is repeated to 'prevent the Enemy from coming in upon us. . . .'

'If we have the good fortune to oblige them to retreat I pursue them . . . Keeping out my Flanking Parties whilst I do the utmost in their flight to keep them off the Risings and as much as possible confine them to the Hallows that we may better surround them. . . .' If the rangers fall back, the advancing foe is to face a continuous fire. The front line of retreating rangers fires, then retires ten or twenty yards behind the second line to reload and to be ready to cover the retreat of the latter line after it fires. Constant watch is kept for favorable terrain 'the better to defend & secure our Retreat.'

If surrounded and if the position permitted, Rogers would form a square and make a stand until darkness covers his escape. But if the terrain is unfavorable to such a maneuver, 'I would retreat to a better Situation in an irregular scattering manner so as to make the Enemy conceive I was flying and when I had recovered the spot I imagined would answer our purpose I would then let them approach very close & pour in a volley upon them & immediately afterwards those nearest in front should fall in upon them with their Hatchetts and with the rest if possible surround them in their surprize.'

If camp is made, sentries are not to be relieved during the night. Six men are assigned to each sentry post 'allowing one of 'em only at a time to keep up an hour, who is to call up another to relieve him & so on 'till the whole six hours stood their Turn of duty. . . .' No noise accompanies the change of the watch.

' . . . As Soon as daylight appears I awake my People as that is the time the savages choose to fall in on their Enemies, and send out small parties to take a Scout round the Camp . . . which parties come in and join us about Sunrise. . . .' Halts for meals are 'by a Spring or Rivulet' but not before a party is sent back 'to lay by the path we came in at some distance behind us to observe if an Enemy is pursuing, besides placing Centries at all convenient places. . . .' Avoid the usual fords of rivers or the common paths on the return to base for fear of ambush; never march close to the shore of lakes for lack of protection from enemy fire. Rogers knew well the value of ambush in forest warfare. If followed, the rangers double back and waylay their own tracks. If pursuing any hostile raiders, cut ahead both to avoid an ambush set by the pursued and to lay a trap at 'some narrow passes... they wou'd go through....'

Lake George and Lake Champlain compelled Rogers to give some attention to action afloat. Boats move at night in single file, the one 'next the Sternmost waits for her & the third for That: the fourth for the third and so on to the Boat leading ahead that we may keep together to assist each other on any Emergency and prevent Separation. . . .' One man in each boat keeps careful watch for enemy fires ashore easily visible at night from a great distance. If the enemy is discovered Rogers is ready to land and attack but not before making dispositions to surprise the foe. If no enemy is discovered, rowing continues to daybreak, then the boats are concealed and the men hide in the underbrush without noise or fires.

There are many other different Methods used which cannot be so intelligibly express'd in writing As they arise in consequence of Occurrences that cannot be foreseen and are only to be Judged of and directed on the Spot by the Officer commanding the Party whose presence of mind must be his only guide to prompt him to his Duty by preserving his party or distressing the Enemy as his Situation and the Circumstances may make it requisite.

Without formal training Rogers successfully compressed the shapeless mass of backwoods fighting experiences into a simple exposition of small unit tactics soundly based on timeless principles: mobility, security, and surprise. The predawn stand-to, precautions against surprise on the march, in battle, retreat, or pursuit, covering-fire, sentry-groups, terrain selection, and other passages suggest rules from a modern manual.

No comment has been found to indicate the impression the document made on Loudoun and his staff. Impressive as it may have been, it probably did not represent exactly the key to forest warfare sought by Loudoun. There was another enemy in the North American forests which on occasion could be more terrible than the French or their Indian allies—nature. How did the rangers avoid frostbite, frozen hands and feet, snow blindness? How were freezing rains and snows survived without fires? What were the field rations? Moreover there were details implicit in the rules which the British regulars would not know. How did the rangers hide their own tracks or follow an enemy's trail? What were the signals in the woods? How were boats hidden? How were trees and bushes used for concealment? The rules have a deceiving simplicity; they actually could be applied only by expert woodsmen.

A provincial officer laboriously recorded the dissolution of the cadet company in his orderly book under 8 November 1757: 'All ye Folen tears belonging to ye Regular Troops & now with Ye Rangers are to join their Respective Corps as Soon as they can.'

The experiment was not repeated: in the meantime the decision had been made to form a regular ranger corps. Although the suggestion had been made by several persons since the regulars had appeared in North America, the move directly stemmed from a proposal by Lieutenant-Colonel Thomas Gage of the 44th Foot. The latter had had a taste of backwoods warfare while leading the advance elements of Braddock's army on that ill-fated July day in '55 near the banks of the Monongahela. He deftly combined his thoughts with a natural desire for the advancement which he had unsuccessfully sought since his arrival in America. He proposed to raise and clothe at his own expense a regiment of five hundred 'rangers' subject to reimbursement if the plan received royal approval. Unlike Rogers' units, the pay scale would be the same as that of regular troops. All this was on the condition that 'His Majesty should be graciously pleased to appoint him Colonel. . . .'

Loudoun leaped at the suggestion. He authorized Gage to choose experienced men from among the regulars (five receiving ensigncies had served under Rogers in the cadet company); permitted him to select his own officers; finally loaned him twenty-six hundred pounds from army funds to cover expenses. The regiment—eventually the 80th—was the true beginning of light infantry in the British army.

A series of incidents now occurred which could only serve to fortify Loudoun's attempt to relieve the army of its dependence on the provincial rangers.

To this date ranger discipline had been excellent. Desertions were few; trouble, if any, was smothered before it came to the attention of anyone outside of ranger ranks. Orderly books overflowing with records of courts-martial of both regulars and provincials rarely mentioned any wrongdoing by rangers. Rogers apparently knew how to control his men and when necessary, insisted on strict discipline. One ranger writing many years after the war recalled that following Rogers was a 'sore service.' Now, however, the record was shattered.

First came a scout in November 1757. A party of rangers was ordered to reconnoiter Fort Carillon and to take some prisoners. Robert was sick with scurvy; John Stark led the three hundred rangers leaving Fort Edward accompanied by Captain James Abercrombie and other regular officers. The captain may have irritated ranger sensibilities by asserting his regular rank. Whatever the cause, the rangers turned unruly. They fired at game as they went along, violating an ironclad rule. At night Abercrombie, perhaps mindful of Rogers' maxim, 'ordered that half the party should remain under arms till 12 o'clock, and the other half to relieve them at that hour' and instructed Stark about sentries. Nevertheless he found 'neither Officer or man but what a Sleep under his Blanket. . . .'

At their objective an ambush was laid in the early morning. Six men came out of the fort and two commenced chopping about three hundred yards distant from the hidden rangers. When it seemed that no more were coming out, Abercrombie ordered an officer and ten men to creep down and seize the wood-cutters. The remainder was ordered not to stir on any account. One of the Frenchmen saw the rangers sneaking down and with a warning shout he took to his heels. '. . . Upon which [later reported Abercrombie] Cap't Stark who was with me set up the Indian hollow, upon that the whole party jumped up & yelled as if Hell had broken loose & all fell a firing at a few men running away. I did every thing in my power to make them hold their tongues & behave as they ought to doe I even knocked several of them down & damned their officers for a set of Scoundrels . . . .' The withdrawal was a nightmare. 'I could not get any of them for the first few miles to form a rearguard. . . .' Three of the regulars had to perform the task. Twice on the way back Stark mistook South Bay for a beaver pond. All in all, the scout was a fiasco.

Abercrombie's report to Loudoun revealed no weakening of his faith in Robert Rogers. '. . . If Rogers had been with us we could not have failed but the rest of the Ranging Officers have no Subordination among them & not the least command of their men.' His conclusion was natural:

[The scout] has had this one good effect which is that if your Lordship should increase the number of Rangers or even keep them up to their present numbers it will be necessary to put some Regular Officers amongst them to introduce a good deal of Subordination. . . .

Within a week of this report the rangers supplied further fuel for the regulars' criticism. The whipping post was the cause. A six-foot post embedded in the ground, it was almost the symbol of discipline in the regular army. The malefactor was lashed to it and cruelly whipped across the bare back by a cat-o'-nine-tails before the assembled troops. Veterans there were who treated their scars as marks of distinction and there were some provincial officers who saw eye to eye with their opposite numbers among the regulars who believed in its efficacy. Most provincial diarists obviously recoiled with horror at the bloody sight. '. . . I was in a mortal dread of the whippings. . . ,' wrote a ranger, 'I felt that I could not survive the shame of being trussed and lashed before men's eyes. . . .'

Two rangers had been recently whipped for stealing rum from British stores. The men went around muttering that they did not like the whipping post on the Island. If the rangers were to be flogged, there would be no rangers. Rogers was ill; the other officers made no attempt to control the situation. Indeed certain ill-tempered remarks of Captain Shepherd were interpreted by the men to indicate he was in sympathy with the objectors.

During the evening of 6 December a group of grumbling rangers surrounded the post. Suddenly one seized an ax from another and with a few swift blows cut it down. In a spirit of revolt they rushed to the guardhouse holding the two whipped men. Unable to open the door, they began to rip the boards off the low roof. Captain Shepherd came running. One man pointed a musket at him, but Shepherd knocked it aside with his sword and snatched it. Realizing the seriousness of the situation, Shepherd began shouting, 'Turn out, rangers, turn out! Shoot the first man that touches the guardhouse!' Captain Bulkeley joined him and added his voice to the uproar. Most of the men seem to have reacted like Aaron Burt, a private in Rogers' company who later testified that he heard a cry, 'thought there was a Mutiny in the Camp and immediately went over to my tent and Staid there in a surprise, not knowing how to turn. . . .' Bulkeley finally dispersed the mob.

The uproar had been heard across the river in Fort Edward. Colonel Haviland of the 27th, post commandant, was not the type to leave the matter in ranger hands. (He seems to have been disliked by provincial and ranger alike. At a later date one of the former wrote in his diary: 'I heard that Col'o Haviland, going around the fort, fell down & broke his leg. Poor man! I am sorry it was his leg.') Haviland investigated, said he wanted to question the suspects but as soon as they were brought over, seized them and clapped them into the fort's guardhouse. If he had not used this ruse, Haviland assured Loudoun, 'I would have had a Battle upon the Island before they could be taken.'

Rogers got out of a sickbed to head a ranger inquiry opening on 8 December. Haviland refused to let the prisoners appear to be heard. Witnesses were evasive. Captain Shepherd admitted hearing that 'the cause of the above disorder was occasioned by two of Captain Rogers Company being punished at the Whipping Post but cannot recollect nor does he know the person or persons that uttered the Said words. . . .' No, he did not know the person from whom he had wrested the firelock. Other witnesses were generally somewhere else when the trouble started; the cry 'turn out!' seems to have been universally translated into a signal to duck into one's tent.

When a scribe had finished a draft of the inquiry proceedings, Rogers brought the papers over from the island to Haviland. It was the first time he had crossed to the fort since his illness. We have only Haviland's report of the meeting. Rogers said he hoped Haviland 'would soon put an end to this Affair for it had given him great uneasiness.' Haviland rejoined he would do nothing without orders from General Abercromby. But he was not content to let the matter rest there: he salted Rogers' wound with the taunt that he believed Rogers and most of his officers would have been happier if Haviland had not heard of the fracas and 'suppose they would have patched it up for fear of their Men.' Rogers warned of an epidemic of desertions. 'I,' reported Haviland, 'answered it would be better they were all gone than have such a Riotous sort of people, but if he would catch me one that attempted it, I would endeavour to have him hanged as an Example.'

Haviland forwarded the inquiry proceedings to Abercromby, urging a general court-martial or at least a court-martial not entirely composed of rangers 'to prevent these Mutinous fellows escaping a punishment suitable to their crime.' Fortunately for the British army Haviland had superiors who remembered there was a war with the French and that to win the army needed the rangers—riotous or not.

After reading his nephew's report of the scout with Stark and the news of the 'mutiny,' Abercromby wrote to Loudoun his suggested reform of the rangers. A regular officer should be set over them; some regular subalterns and men in whom the new commander had faith, should be mixed among them. He believed Gage's proposed regiment would soon discharge all ranger functions better than those now in the service but the latter must be kept for the present. In a later letter he demurred to increasing the number of the existing rangers. He wrote that he was 'sorry' to hear of the trouble 'because last year they were a useful and well behaved body & generally succeeded well when they went out on scouts.' Now, however, he was aware of the 'improbability of rendering them into any order and subordination.'

Rogers countered criticism with the only possible answer.

December 17th 1757. At two o'Clock afternoon marched from Fort Edward with a Party of one hundred & Fifty men to distress the Enemy at Carilon & if possible to take a prisoner. . . .

Three inches of snow covered the ground when camp was made at Halfway Brook but 'before Morning [it] fell to fifteen which made our Lodging disagreeable. . . .' (All quotations are from Rogers' report unless otherwise indicated.) Frostbite disabled eight men who were sent back. The others trudged forward and camped on the west side of Lake George. The following days they went through the forest crowning the mountains on this side, averaging only about seven miles a day. A ranger recalled many years later that 'it was heavy footing.' '21st Northwest Bay—. . . Sent back some of my people that tired and fell sick which reduced my party to one hundred & twenty three Officers included with whom proceeded. . . .'

Rogers carefully prepared for every eventuality. Camping in 'the Notch of Mountains' on the night of 21 December he ordered that each man cache a day's provisions for their return. On the 24th within six hundred yards of Fort Carillon, he 'appointed three places of Rendezvous to repair to in case of being broke in an Action & acquainted every Officer and Private Soldier that I should rally my People at the nearest to the Fort first and if broke there retreat to the second and so in like Case to a third and there make a stand till the darkness of the Night would give us the opportunity of getting off. . . .' The silent men knew that their leader expected stiff opposition; the fight of the preceding January must have flashed across their minds.

Rogers prepared an ambush along the road from the fort used by the woodchoppers. Late in the morning an advance party of twenty rangers silently watched a solitary French sergeant walk down the road, past them, and into the arms of the main party. Rogers questioned him for intelligence about Carillon and Crown Point.

About noon a French hunter was discovered coming down the path toward the fort. Rogers decided to use him as a decoy to draw the French out. A small party of rangers pretended to chase him and attracted the attention of the fort's garrison by firing a gun and giving 'the Indian Halloo.' But the French did not stir outside the fortification. Disappointed, the rangers 'went to killing their Cattle and destroyed seventeen head of them And at night set fire to their wood and consumed five piles of it.' Cannon roared from the fort's walls but did no damage. While flickering orange and yellow flames glowed in the winter gloom, Rogers turned for home: 'The twenty-seventh I arrived at Fort Edward at two o'Clock in the Afternoon with all my party in health.'

One incident, unmentioned in Robert's official report, endeared him to the English officers and men and perhaps even the French although they officially condemned it as 'an ill-timed and very low piece of braggadocio.' General Abercromby told Loudoun how 'after killing all the live stock but three Bullocks, he [Rogers] left a Receipt for the Commandant as a Voucher to pass his Accounts, with the Agent Victualler; and stuck the same in a Cleft Stick in the Path; and by the two Deserters who followed him, he learnt that this Receipt came to the Commandants hand who was much provoked at it.' Regulars on both sides, harried by the red-tape of receipts and army accounts, chuckled.

Rogers left for Albany as soon as possible after his return from the scout. On New Year's Day, 1758, General Abercromby unsealed a letter to announce that 'After the Packet was sealed Capt. Rogers arrived, fatigued with a Severe but successful Scout, and about as bad a March from Fort Edward to this place, by the sudden thaw.' He saw Rogers at once, and the story about the receipt obviously tickled the general's fancy. It was difficult to look with disfavor on a man who displayed such spirit.

Doubtlessly the rangers' dilemma had occupied Rogers'

thoughts during the trip to Albany. How could he explain the 'mutiny'? Should he beg pardon? Colonel Haviland certainly had not helped the situation. Whether Rogers decided simply that the offensive was the best defense or that the rangers were more sinned against than sinning, will never be known. He took Abercromby by surprise: he offered no apology. He insisted that Haviland had exaggerated the whipping-post incident; that Haviland was prejudiced against the rangers. He was incensed about Haviland's imprisonment of his men in Fort Edward. He demanded assurance that the rangers would be tried by their own officers as were regulars. He warned of wholesale desertions if the high command insisted on severe punishment of the 'mutineers'; there had been nine since his last return of company strength. He was ready to resign his command: he had an offer of a colonelcy in a provincial unit. If the British command wanted him to stay, he either wanted rank as a regular officer or at least to be made 'Captain Commandant of the present Rangers.'

He completely bowled over Abercromby. The latter started a report of the interview to Loudoun by describing their discussion as containing 'a good share of nonsense.' But, for example, where he formerly recommended no increase in the rangers, he now spoke of men in New England ready to recruit 'if your Lordship is for Augmenting that Corps. . . .' He concluded with a burst of praise for the ranger leader. 'With Regard to Rogers himself, I do think him so necessary and useful a Man, that I should be extremely Sorry to part with him, and rather than that, to give him some Encouragement to Continue diligent and hearty in the service. Without him these four Companies [of rangers] would be good for nothing.'

Rogers had carried his first objective; he now left for an interview with Loudoun in New York.

On 9 January Rogers reported to his commander in chief.
Loudoun started by criticizing the rangers' lack of discipline. This, he said, made him hesitant about augmenting the corps as planned. Rogers stood his ground and blamed his troubles on Haviland. Loudoun capitulated; perhaps the general had some inkling that Haviland was prejudiced against the rangers. He dropped all pretense of censure and the talk shifted to the rangers' future.

Rogers had proposed during the previous October to increase the rangers to one thousand men. Loudoun now agreed that five new companies—one to be of Mohegan Indians from Connecticut—could be formed and Rogers could propose their officers. The rangers were to receive uniforms, the cost of which was to be deducted from their pay. The six 'mutineers' were to be returned to the rangers for action by the latter. Loudoun hesitated over only one point: Rogers' desire for an advance in rank. An offer of more pay was brushed aside. Finally Loudoun promised to give his request serious consideration and Rogers wisely let it rest there.

He had won a tremendous personal victory. In an army only too ready to echo Wolfe's famous words: 'the Americans are in general the dirtiest, the most contemptible cowardly dogs you can conceive,' he had been recognized as indispensable. In a contest with a regular for authority, he had won out. In the face of a movement to halt the growth of the rangers and perhaps even to disband it, he had emerged with a doubling of his corps, his nominees by and large accepted by Loudoun as the new officers, and a bright prospect of an advance in rank for himself.

VI
1758

'A Hot Ingagment Such as Scarce Ever Was Knowed in Ye Country'

ROGERS wanted to begin the year 1758 by justifying Loudoun's faith in him. He proposed the capture of Fort St. Frédéric by a stratagem. With four hundred men he would slip down behind the mountains edging the western shore of Lake George and come out above Crown Point to intercept one of the sleigh convoys plying between St. Jean and Fort St. Frédéric. Some French-speaking rangers would disguise themselves as French drivers, proceed into the fort, and open the gates to the rest of the party, who would dash in and compel the weak winter garrison to capitulate.

To Rogers' disappointment, Loudoun showed no enthusiasm over the proposal. Actually he was annoyed: he was secretly planning a winter attack on Carillon. But he concealed this fact, merely telling Rogers to take his plan up with Abercromby. 'I am bound,' wrote Loudoun in a crabbed hand in his diary on 13 January 1758, 'to do this as he will break into my Plan of taking Ticonderoga if the Frost Permits.' As Loudoun probably expected, Abercromby allowed Rogers' scheme to go in one ear and out the other. But it is amusing to find the general sending Loudoun a scheme by his nephew for the capture of Crown Point on the very day Rogers arrived in Albany.

Rogers did not lose a minute's time in Albany. Orders were issued for raising the new companies and recruiting for the old; arrangements were made for the new uniforms. Yet he managed to be back at the Island on 25 January. Here he learned that the Hudson had been on a rampage. On 3 January a provincial diarist recorded the sweeping of the water into the ranger encampment: 'In ye Morning ye River was So High that it Ran into Many of their Hutts and Drove them out . . . some of their Hutts were Waist Deep in the Water . . . This was also a Stormy Day & Vary Slippery.' Colonel Haviland reported 'most of the Rangers on the Island were floated out of their Hutts, and the greatest part of the firewood that was there Carried off. . . .'

Men and matériel began to concentrate at Fort Edward; an attack was obviously afoot. Command fell to Brigadier General Lord George Augustus Viscount Howe who had come to America in mid-1757. He seems to have been genuinely loved by both provincial and regular soldiers. Perhaps the notes of a provincial carpenter reveal why: 'Lord How was the Idol of the Army, in him they placed the utmost confidence, from the few days I had to observe his maner of conducting, it was not extravagant to Supose that every Soldier In the army had a personel attachment to him, he frequently came among the Carpenters, and his maner was So easy and fermiller, that you loost all that constraint or diffidence we feele when adressed by our Superiours, whose manners are forbiding.'

Howe enjoyed a high reputation as a military genius. Much of this may simply have been the result of his great popularity, but his obvious desire to improve the effectiveness of the British fighting-man in American campaigns impressed everyone.

He was probably the only officer of rank higher than a captain to go out with the rangers 'to learn [wrote Rogers] our methods of marching, ambushing, retreating &c.' His mere presence began to be taken as an assurance of victory in any undertaking.

In the bitterly cold February weather an army engineer went up to Lake George with a party of rangers. About mid-lake, about two miles from its head, he found seventeen inches of dry snow over six inches of solid ice. Along the shore were between four and five feet of snow. He reported that an adequate path could not be stamped down for a military expedition by forty or fifty men on snowshoes.

It was then revealed that there were not enough snowshoes. This was blamed on Rogers. Without telling him the true reason, Loudoun had told him the preceding November to make six hundred pairs of snowshoes and as many more as time would permit. In December the rangers were supposed to make seven hundred pairs of ice-creepers and a number of hand sleighs. The abandonment of the project was therefore laid at Rogers' door.

Rogers never offered any excuses for not having them ready. It is possible to explain his failure. This was not a regular function of the rangers and probably not something that would be done without his personal supervision. But when did he have time? He was ill in early November, then occupied with the 'mutiny' and its aftermath, out on scout in mid-December; in Albany and New York during January in conference with Abercromby and Loudoun. It must be remembered that he had no knowledge that the equipment was needed for an offensive; surely what he did seemed more important than preparing snowshoes for possible new ranger companies. When in New York he had told Loudoun that two hundred pairs were ready and wood 'ready bent' for four hundred more. Undoubtedly the January flood at the Island washed most of this away.

After the first rash, criticism of Rogers disappeared entirely. Howe admitted that no assault could have been made in the deep snow nor could a battery have been erected to batter down the walls. The plan contemplated four or five hundred men stamping down the snow on snowshoes and the regulars following in the beaten path. A raid early in February by French-led Indians on snowshoes revealed the dangers of such a scheme. The raiders forced a party of woodchoppers under a guard of regulars without snowshoes off the cleared road into deep snow and killed the floundering English 'like so many Sheep or Cattle' in sight of horrified observers in Fort Edward. Abercromby admitted this possibility to Loudoun. Rogers' failure to supply the snowshoes has hidden the basic weakness of the planned expedition, but Generals Howe and Abercromby were aware of the latter and they made no effort to make any undue criticism of the ranger leader.

In the meantime fur flew whenever Rogers' and Haviland's paths crossed and everybody at Fort Edward was aware of the fact. One observer gleefully recorded on 19 February: 'Som of ye Rangers Went a Hunting & Fired Several Guns in Hearing of ye Garrison—About which Col. Haviland & Maj'r Rogers Had Som Diference &c.'

On the evening after the cancellation of Howe's winter expedition, Haviland made public that Major Putnam of Connecticut would take a scouting party to Ticonderoga followed by an expedition of four hundred men under Rogers against Crown Point. Rogers was aghast. Putnam's reconnaissance, which was specifically for the purpose of taking a prisoner, would put the French on their guard. Any deserter or prisoner from Putnam's party would be sure to tell of the expedition to follow. Robert was on pins and needles awaiting Putnam's

return and undoubtedly irked by the carefree attitude of
Haviland, who 'with a Number of Off'rs made them selvs
Much Sport in Sliding Down ye Bank in a Sley & in Danceing
on ye Ice &c.'

On 6 March Putnam came in. One man was missing—lost
'in a Very Strang Manner.' It seemed certain he had deserted
to the French. To add to the tenseness of the situation a party
of French Indians intercepted a sleigh convoy between Fort
Edward and Saratoga and captured a sutler's servant.[1] In a
desperate effort to retake the man, Rogers and his men 'with
Snowshoes, arms and ammunition, most of them stripped to
their shirts, were out of Sight of the Fort in less than a quarter
of an hour, after the Alarm arrived there.' In vain—the limitless
forest had swallowed the enemy and their prisoner. Haviland
then capped the situation by ordering Rogers' party to be
reduced to one hundred and eighty men. All thoughts of an
attack on Crown Point were given up. In fact the move seemed
to Rogers an invitation to disaster.

One hundred and eighty-one men filed out of Fort Edward
in the long shadows of the late afternoon of 10 March 1758:
eleven ranger officers, eleven sergeants, one hundred and
fifty men from the four companies, a corporal from Putnam's
provincial rangers, three regular officers, three cadets, a
regular sergeant and private. Rogers was in charge, heavy
with a foreboding of doom.

The rangers may have been clothed in their new uniforms.
Green marked them as woodsmen. The outer coat was a short
jacket without sleeves, whose armholes were covered and
strengthened by wings similar to those worn by regular
grenadiers and drummers. Underneath was a waistcoat whose
sleeves, passing through the opening in the outer garment,
became part of the outer uniform. Both jacket and waistcoat
were lined with green serge so that collars and cuffs contrasted

against the outside coarse woolen 'frieze.' Under all was worn a shirt. Buttons on front and on the cuffs were of white metal. Officers were brave with silver lace cord or looping on button-holes and edges—at once a distinguishing mark and a strengthener of the cloth at points of extra wear. Below, linen or canvas drawers were covered by a 'skirt or short petticoat of stuff, made with a waistband and one button; this is open before, and does not extend quite to their knees.' Brown leggings reached up to the rangers' thighs. They buttoned 'from the calf of the leg downwards . . . like spatter dashes.' Their footwear was moccasins.

Officers on parade wore tricorns with white silver edging, but on party had hats cropped to leave only a skull covering and a flap in front. A feather or evergreen bough jauntily stuck on the side or in back announced the owner a proper cock-of the-walk. The men wore plain tricorns on parade but preferred the flat Scotch bonnets on a scout. In many ways they resembled the Scotch soldiers in their 'little kilts' and the ancestral pride of many may have intentionally brought about this result.

The tools of their trade remained unchanged. The regulars' cartouche (or cartridge) box had replaced the pouch hanging in front; under the right arm was a powder horn suspended from a belt looped over the left shoulder. A leather sling at the left side, hanging from a belt that ran over the right shoulder, held bayonet and tomahawk. At the waist was a sheathed knife. Another sling over the right shoulder carried the canteen, probably the regulation metal type, hanging over the left hip. Muskets were strictly regulation issue. Haversacks carried rations; blankets were carried in rolls unless worn for warmth while on the march.

Cautiously the party crept northward. The lake proved clear of snow; the men wore ice-creepers. From a camp at the First Narrows a party probed down the lake; all was quiet. Scouts on lake and shore stood a cold and lonely watch; none was disturbed. At first light the entire party stood dawn alert; no attack came. Again they went on, flankers probing ahead and to the sides. Three miles up the lake a dog suddenly scampered across. The party halted while patrols investigated; again nothing. Rogers could not shake off the feeling he was being watched. He halted at Sabbath Day Point and lay by until nightfall while small parties went ahead 'to look down the lake with prospective glasses which I [Rogers] had for that purpose.' After dark the slow, cautious march was resumed. A party under Lieutenant Phillips skated in advance. Suddenly word came back that an enemy camp lay ahead. All parties were called in; packs and hand sleighs were hidden on the west shore. With three men left behind as guards, the rest advanced to attack. No encampment was found. Rogers concluded 'it was some bleak patches of Snow, or pieces of Rotten Wood (Which in ye Night resemble fire at a distance) . . . .' The party returned to the packs and huddled there the remainder of the night without fires.

Rogers, still feeling enemy eyes on him, held a council of war the next morning (13 February). Detection was too easy on the lake. The decision was to don snowshoes and proceed, 'keeping back of the Mountains that overlook ye French Advance Guards.' Near noon—about two miles west of the French advanced post on the west shore—Rogers halted until midafternoon to permit the French day scouts to withdraw to the fort without bumping into him. Then he planned to slip down during the night and prepare an ambush for the morning.

At length it was time to push on: equipment was slipped on, moccasins were thrust into snowshoe thongs. The party divided into two divisions: the first under Captain Bulkeley and the second under Rogers. A steep mountain guarded their right; a frozen stream ran along its foot, on which Rogers kept a careful watch. The enemy might be expected there 'as the snow was four feet deep and very bad travelling on snow-shoes.'

It happened as he foresaw: an enemy was reported approaching on the frozen stream. How many? About a hundred. Swiftly the rangers stripped for action. Their column faced left; the advanced guard became the right flank guard. Quickly they marched to the river bank and spread out, seeking cover behind tree and rock. The rangers waited, every second an eternity. Then the enemy appeared: painted savages with daubed blankets drawn around their heads with a scattering of hooded Frenchmen in white woolen capotes. They were permitted to pass until their advance elements were opposite the rangers' left flank. Then Rogers fired his musket as a signal. A ranger volley scythed the French line, killing—according to Rogers—'above forty Indians.' Now the ranger right flank broke cover to head the retreating enemy, but they broke through with Captain Bulkeley's men in yelling pursuit.

Suddenly there was a new crash of musketry and an outburst of savage war whoops. Bulkeley and about fifty of his men fell. The attacked enemy had been only an advance party; the retreat had drawn the rangers into unexpected contact with the main body. The remnant of Bulkeley's division, rallied under fire by two mortally-wounded officers, fell back on Rogers as the French now became the pursuers. The rangers fought from tree to tree—to quote Rogers—'with the greatest Intrepidity & bravery imaginable.'

A party of French and Indians slipped through the trees around the ranger line to attack in the rear. Then with wild whoops echoing in the chill woods amid smoke and the staccato of musket fire, the French drove home an attack from both sides. Fighting desperately, the rangers threw them back. Again the attack was pressed home. Lieutenant Phillips was

sent to secure some rising ground on the right; Lieutenant
Crofton swung to the left on a similar mission. Now the fighting became hot and close; often the lines intermingled, none
knowing from which side the death-dealing bullet or
tomahawk blow would come. About an hour and a half after
the first shot was fired, as darkness came on, Rogers' center
collapsed under overwhelming enemy pressure. Only thirty-
odd men were still alive. About twenty with Rogers fell back
on Crofton and Phillips. The latter was dickering for surrender
terms; Rogers' group only paused to fire a volley and then fled
on, scattering into the vast labyrinth of the wilderness. Phillips and his men surrendered on assurances of 'good quarter.'
They were then tied to trees and many hacked to pieces 'in
a most barbarous and shocking manner. . . .' Phillips managed
to cut his bonds and escape.

Rogers, like many another, had a narrow escape. In the
heat of the pursuit he threw off his uniform jacket with his
original commission from Shirley in its pocket. The Indians
claimed his death and exhibited the coat and commission as
proof. There was rejoicing in Fort Carillon: 'Saint-Saveur
says his favorite phrase is—"Rogers is killed completely,
clothes, coat and breeches!"' Exactly what happened is not
known. He may have lost his pursuers near the steep, rocky
precipice now known as 'Rogers' Slide' and made the lake at
about eight o'clock.[2] He met some of his men and marched
them to where the packs and sleighs had been stored. Two un-
wounded men were sent ahead to ask aid from Fort Edward;
eight others were also sent on, drawing four severely wounded
men on the hand sleighs. The rest huddled around Rogers
without fire for the rest of the night. As expected, more rangers
came in and finally Rogers decided to turn back up the lake.

High excitement gripped Fort Edward about noon on the
14th: '. . . Som of Maj'r Rogerse Scout Came in & Inform yt
they Have Had a Hot Ingagment such as Scarce Ever was

Knowed in ye Country & Most of His Party is Destroyed.' Captain Stark and rangers hurriedly left with three horse-drawn sleighs. They met Rogers some six miles north of the lake's head but night had fallen. The next day—'a Vast Cold & Tedious Day Especially for ye Wounded Men'—the remnants of Rogers' command began to straggle into Fort Edward. A provincial observer jotted down a terse, unforgettable picture: 'About 5 o'Clock I se ye Maj'r Com in Him Self Being in ye Rear of ye Whol—.'

Rogers had suffered a severe defeat. Only fifty-four (including the seriously wounded) out of the original one hundred and eighty-one came back to Fort Edward. He manfully shouldered the blame: 'I now imagined the enemy totally defeated'; there was no attempt to blame the dead Captain Bulkeley for the reckless pursuit by the latter's division which ran into the main body of the enemy. Rogers claimed no credit; praise was reserved for others. His report contained a long roll of names of those who 'behaved exceedingly well.' But there was no need for comment on his behavior. No one at Fort Edward would lose the memory of the man who came trudging in, last of all, in the gathering gloom of that cold March day. A regular officer turned historian pronounced the general verdict: 'both the Major and those under him did everything that could be expected from good officers and soldiers.'[3]

Lord Howe, now commanding the northern forces, summoned Rogers down to Albany. (Abercromby had gone to New York to succeed Loudoun, whose recall had finally reached America.) Howe gave Rogers a warm reception, raised his spirits, advanced him cash to recruit more rangers, and gave him permission to go to New York. There was only one bit of disagreeable news: four of the five new ranging companies were destined for the Louisbourg campaign.

At New York Rogers asked Abercromby for the promised advance in rank. (Indeed he was already called 'Major.') The new commander in chief questioned Loudoun and the latter admitted his promise to give it serious consideration. The detailed instructions from home told Abercromby 'to raise as Considerable a Number of Rangers, as may be practicable. . . .' and he considered Rogers the only officer of value. There was only one possible answer to Rogers' inquiry. On 6 April 1758 he commissioned Rogers 'Major of the Rangers in his Majesty's Service, and likewise Captain of a Company of Rangers. . . .'

VII
1758

'Believe Me D'r Sir, I Do Not Exagerate This Affair'

EARLY spring, 1758, was the season of preparation for the offensive which would restore British military prestige. The main thrust was to be at Louisbourg, but besides a blow at Fort Duquesne in western Pennsylvania, plans also contemplated an invasion of Canada by way of Ticonderoga and Crown Point.

On 12 April Rogers conferred with Howe, who had charge of the preparation for the northern push, 'concerning the methods of distressing the enemy and prosecuting the war with vigour in the ensuing campaign.' The ranger leader then returned to Fort Edward to put into operation 'a comprehensive, continuous patrol plan that would gain the approval of any modern intelligence officer.' Four parties went out, each under a captain: the first along the west side of Lake George as far as Ticonderoga; the second along the east side; the third covered the mountains between Lake Champlain and Lake George while the fourth, with no geographic boundaries, had the task of taking prisoners. The patrols served both to conceal British preparations and to reconnoiter French positions.

In late April and early May, Rogers himself slipped by Carillon to Crown Point via the east bank of Lake Champlain and
took three prisoners. French officers sadly concluded that the
news of his death had been—to say the least—premature.

The rangers operated according to precise plans and training. It was not the traditional haphazard high adventure in
the field and careless repose in camp. Provincial diaries attest
to the drills which spelled survival in the turmoil of wood
fighting. When, for example, Lieutenant Samuel Thompson
of Massachusetts arrived at Fort Edward on 25 June 1758, he
was alarmed by 'a very smart firing half a mile in ye wood.'
Then he learned that 'ye General had given leave for four or
five hundred Rangers to go out and hold a bush fight for ¼ of
an hour.' A doctor recorded on another occasion: 'Major
Rogers this Day exercised his men in Bush Fiteing which drew
a great Number out of ye Camp, to view them.' On another
day the doctor watched 'the Rangers exercise in Scout marches
& Bush fighting which make a very pritty figure.'

The orderly book of Captain Monypenny, General Abercromby's aid-de-camp, for May and June attests to the fact
that Abercromby and Howe were trying to adapt the British
regulars for fighting in the forest, following the ranger model.
Officers were to carry only minimum equipment—a tent, port-
manteau, blanket, and bearskin; they were to get only one
ration a day. 'Whenever the men march they are to put their
provisions in their haversacks and roll them up in their blankets like the Rangers.'

Slowly the grand army that was to carry Ticonderoga collected at Fort Edward. In June all ranger leaves of absence
were cancelled; the units were to be at full strength on 10
June. Rogers at this point had four ranger companies, one
Stockbridge unit, and one of Connecticut Mohegans.

Lord Howe moved up to Fort Edward at the beginning of

June. He ordered whaleboats up to Lake George and directed Rogers 'to take a plan of the landing place at the north-end with all possible accuracy, and also of the ground from the landing place to the French fort at Carillon, and of Lake Champlain for three miles beyond it, and to discover the enemy's number in that quarter.'

During this scout Rogers and two or three others pressed ahead of the main body to reconnoiter the fort. Returning, they found that the French had attacked the remainder of the party, which had scattered. Following ranger tactics, all gathered at the previously selected rendezvous and count taken: five were dead, three were French prisoners. But Rogers had a map for the landing and a report indicating some four thousand men at Carillon.

Following the scout, the rangers continued to throw out patrols although they were more in the nature of a screen for the expedition now preparing to embark on Lake George. French raiders were not idle, delivering sharp, slashing thrusts. An entire party of nineteen rangers sent to probe down the lake never returned.

Drums beat reveille at daybreak, 5 July. An army of over fifteen thousand men stirred from its blankets, ready for embarkation. It moved with precision. First to get under way was the advance guard of rangers, bateaux men, and light infantry in whaleboats. Then the main body embarked. By 7:00 a.m. the lake was black as far as an eye could see with 135 whaleboats, 900 bateaux, and two floating batteries, all moving northward under threatening skies. Late in the afternoon the army went ashore at Sabbath Day Point, in part to allow laggards to catch up and in part to throw the watching enemy off guard. If the French believed that this was to be the British landing, they would be less likely to have an effective defense prepared at the actual landing place. About ten

o'clock in the evening orders were passed to re-embark and
the expedition was soon under way, the dark lake pricked by
twinkling lanterns.

On order of Lord Howe one of the ranger whaleboats forged
ahead to reconnoiter the landing place; at gray dawn it rejoined the van, reporting enemy fires. A reconnaissance by
Howe accompanied by Rogers and Colonel Bradstreet ascertained that the enemy was weak. They returned; Abercromby
ordered the landing to proceed as planned.

The ranger whaleboats pulled into a bay (now Hearts Bay)
and their occupants leaped ashore at the foot of a mountain on
the west shore of Lake George, about a mile and a half south
of the principal landing place of the expedition. A small
French force was quickly put to flight. The remaining part of
the van rowed on to the general point of disembarkation. No
opposition was offered; the French, apparently caught by
surprise, fled in confusion from their posts on the western
shore across the bridge to the portage road. All they could do
of value was to destroy the bridge after themselves. As the
main British force came majestically down the lake, elements
of the Connecticut forces separated from the mass and landed
by the side of the rangers.

The entire army was ashore by noon: not a single casualty
had been suffered.

Rogers sent an officer to ask for orders: he was told 'to gain
the top of a mountain that bore north about a mile from the
landing-place, and from thence to steer east to the river that
flows into the falls betwixt the landing and the saw-mill, to take
possession of some rising ground on the enemy's side, and there
to await the army's coming.' He was apparently expected to
flush out any hostile ambushers waiting to rush out from the
rising ground to the west of the general line of march. The
rangers immediately got into motion; no enemy was found
and it was simply a hike through familiar territory. Their

MAJOR ROBERT ROGERS

From one of the original edition issued by Thomas Hart in London on 1 October 1776. The notation identifying this edition, 'Ioh Martin Will excudit Aug. Vind.,' is omitted on later copies. (From author's collection)

ELIZABETH BROWNE ROGERS

From a portrait by Joseph Blackburn. According to tradition she is shown in her wedding gown. (Courtesy of Mrs. Kenneth Roberts)

A PLAN OF THE CITY OF ALBANY

From 'A Set of Plans and Forts in America' published by Mary Ann Rocque in 1765. This small town was the center of all British activity in the northern sector of the French and Indian War. The wide central street is the east end of the present State Street; the fort was located approximately where the present Capitol Park begins. (Courtesy of the trustees of the Boston Public Library)

PLAN OF FORT ST. FRÉDÉRIC (1752)

This portion of the plan shows the fort as it probably existed during the French and Indian War until its demolition in 1759. The buildings at the top are a portion of a proposed extension of the fort which was never made. (Courtesy of Arthur S. Hopkins and Inspection Générale du Génie, Paris)

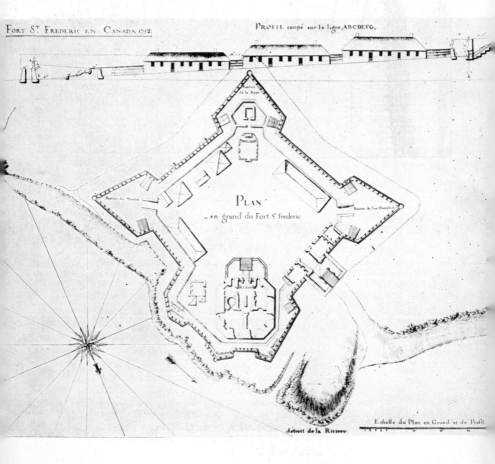

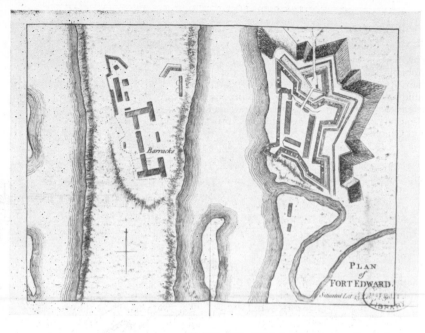

Barracks

PLAN
of
FORT EDWARD

PLAN OF FORT EDWARD (1759)

This plan from the Rocque's set shows the fort and its outworks. On the left is a portion of the Island with the barracks in which the rangers were quartered. (Courtesy of the trustees of the Boston Public Library)

A VIEW OF FORT TICONDEROGA (1759)

A portion of the drawing made by Lieutenant Thomas Davies after the capture of the fort. The full drawing also shows more British encampments and the defensive lines stretching across the peninsula. (Courtesy of New-York Historical Society)

A NORTH EAST VIEW OF CROWN POINT (1760)

From a drawing made by Lieut. Davies. On the opposite shore in the center is a heap of rubble, the remains of Fort St. Frédéric's citadel, while to the right rise the ramparts of new Fort Crown Point. (Courtesy of the Public Archives of Canada)

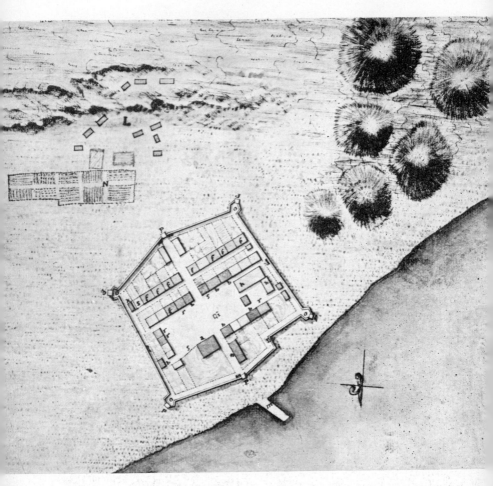

SKETCH OF THE FORT AT MICHILIMACKINAC (1766)
This plan was drawn by Lieutenant Perkins Magra in the spring
or early summer of the same year in which Robert Rogers arrived
at the post. (Courtesy of Clements Library)

objective was reached expeditiously and without incident. Ranger patrols probed to the east: the main body of the French was about a quarter of a mile distant.

Abercromby and Howe had made their first major error: they expected Gage's Light Infantry and special units of the best marksmen of each regiment, to whom special 'Rifled Barrelled Guns' had been issued, to replace the rangers as guides through the forest, aided by the provincials.

By two in the afternoon columns were ready to push into the forest. On the extreme left were Connecticut provincials, next Rhode Island forces, regulars made up the center, then the New York, Massachusetts, and New Hampshire forces. The left was commanded by Gage, now a brigadier general, and the right by Lord Howe. The march began.

The forest quickly destroyed the beautiful marching order. '. . . The wood being thick,' Abercromby later wrote, 'impassable with any Regularity to such a Body of Men, and the Guides unskilled, the Troops were bewildered, and the Columns broke, falling in on one another.' The one man who knew the locality intimately, and in whom all had confidence, was not at hand; the regular light infantry and provincial guides were miserable failures.

It took about two hours for most of the army to cover a mile. Then a French unit of about three hundred blundered into the British left front. 'When the firing began on part of the Left Column, Lord Howe thinking it would be of the greatest Consequence, to beat the Enemy with the Light Troops, so as not to stop the march of the Main Body, went up with them, and had just gained the Top of the Hill, where the fighting was, when he was killed. Never Ball had a more Deadly Direction . . . I was about six yards from him,' wrote an eye-witness, 'he fell on his Back and never moved, only his Hands quivered an instant.'

Part of the extreme left of the columns—Connecticut men—
had come up to Rogers and informed him of the army's approach. When the firing was heard in its rear, they immediately pulled back as did part of the rangers. Caught between two
fires the small French party was wiped out. The skirmish
revealed how the shadow of the forest drained away the courage of the regulars. An officer noted uneasily that the com-
paratively 'little firing threw our Regulars in to some kind of a
Consternation . . . .' In the confusion 'part of ye 55th and
the 42nd had returned to the Landing place. . . having lost
the rest of the Army, during the Skirmish, with a great Number of the Provincials.'

Generals Abercromby and Gage—the latter now second in
command—seem to have been helpless in the woods. The remainder of the army tried to press on to Rogers' position. '. . .
As the Heads of the Columns were descending a low ground,
A fire Was heard in the front . . . .' Gunfire increased, then 'a
loud heidious Yell.' Panic gripped regular and provincial alike.
'. . . No intreaty could prevail with the men for some time, but
in about an hour's time after this, we found out, the fire that
began this Confusion in the front was from Our Selves . . . by
this time it was almost Dark, we were separated & had som
difficulty to Join Afterwards; but in a very irregular Way, the
Reg'ts intermix'd with each Other, And as it appeared to me
in a most wretched situation . . . .'

And so they spent the night, fifteen thousand scattered
between the landing place and Rogers' position, recently so
brave and gay, now their favorite leader dead, their morale
badly shaken, their leaders once more obviously unable to
cope with forest warfare.[1] '. . . Believe me D'r Sir,' protested
the British officer whose observations of the march have been
quoted here, 'I do not Exagerate this affair.'

In the early morning of the 7th, Abercromby ordered all

forces back to the landing place for regrouping. Rogers was now sent forward with four hundred rangers to the west bank of the stream he had crossed the previous day; others were incorporated into the command of Colonel Bradstreet, who seized the portage road on the east bank, rebuilt the bridge at its northern end to the sawmill, and crossed to the northern bank. The army, with its morale perking up, followed under dark skies, and Rogers was brought up from the west.

The sun on 8 July seemed to augur good fortune. A reconnaissance by the army engineer and Captain Abercrombie guarded by a detachment of rangers revealed that the French were planning to give battle outside the fort's walls from behind a breast-work on a low hill about a thousand yards from the fort.[2] The decision was to attack at once. The rangers led the advance, driving in the French outposts. Gage's light infantry formed on Rogers' right; Bradstreet's bateaux men on his left. Together they poured a fire on the barricaded enemy that Montcalm, the French commander, later described as 'most murdering.'

Then out of the woods behind them came 'the heavy red masses of the British troops advancing in battle array . . . .' The remainder of the story of that sad day in British army annals is not that of the rangers. Assault after assault failed to pierce 'the bristling mass of sharpened branches' lying in front of the breastwork while the French poured volley after volley into the exposed attackers, who suffered appalling losses. The British had men and courage, but no over-all command. The rangers covered the rear of the disorganized retreat—no difficult task since the French attempted no pursuit—and on the evening of 9 July their whaleboats nosed into the beach at the south end of Lake George.

Abercromby, cowering at the head of Lake George expecting Montcalm to mount an offensive, spread panic with his fear. Confusion and death from wounds and disease gripped the camp.

Except for Bradstreet's successful thrust at the small but important post at Cadaraqui, all activity in the Champlain area was left to patrols in strength attempting to defend the British lines of communication—against which the French had unleashed a series of devastating attacks. Abercromby tried to counter with defensive measures: strengthening the Lake George camp, placing a Massachusetts regiment at Halfway Brook, installing an alarm system between the lake and Fort Edward; doubling-up of supply trains and escorts. He did not see the only effective answer: to carry the raids to the French through the rangers.

This the French soon made clear. A patrol from Halfway Brook was cut to pieces; the men in the pursuing party deserted their officers. At Fort Edward a New Hampshire colonel refused to supply additional guards for a convoy composed of slow ox-carts bound for the lake. French and Indians intercepted it, claiming '110 scalps . . . 84 prisoners . . . of these, 12 are women or girls . . . Some baggage and effects belonging to General Albercrombie [sic]; as well as his music, were among the plunder.'

A few terror-stricken fugitives found their way back to Fort Edward. A relief party was formed and the alarm cannon boomed. When it was heard at the Halfway Brook post, part of the garrison marched out and fell in with the rear of the foe which had become intoxicated with the liquor taken as plunder. But the provincials refused to attack. Abercromby got the news by nine o'clock in the evening. Major Rogers and Major Putnam were ordered to assemble seven hundred men for the pursuit. The anxious general stayed up to two o'clock in the morning to see them off. Later he dispatched one thousand men under Colonel Haviland with orders to support

Rogers. Then he nervously awaited news of the result.

On 30 July a message came in from Haviland: the enemy had been far down the lake when Rogers came up. But there were signs of other war parties. Accordingly, Haviland was ordered to send Rogers and Putnam on a sweep of the country in the Wood Creek area, coming in at Fort Edward. They were to have seven hundred selected men. Besides the rangers and Connecticut men so selected there were sixty regulars and light infantry under Captain James Dalyell.

The group prepared an ambush near the junction of Wood Creek and South Bay, but premature challenges by Connecticut provincials scared off hostile parties. On 7 August one hundred and fifty of the party was ordered ahead to Fort Edward: no enemy of any size seemed near.

That night camp was made near the rotting, fallen-in stockade of old Fort Anne on the southerly bank of Halfway Brook near its junction with Wood Creek. In the morning the expedition moved westerly. Vigilance relaxed: three muskets were discharged—some later said at game; others, at marks. The reports attracted hostile ears; Indians and French under an able partisan leader, Marin, quickly prepared an ambuscade. Putnam in the lead marched directly into enemy arms; he was made a prisoner as the first shots rang out. 'The enemy rose like a cloud and fired a volley upon us . . . the tomahawks and bullets flying around my ears like hailstones,' recalled a participant years later. The Connecticut provincials broke, but the regulars following stood their ground. Rogers tried to move up his men, to rally the provincials, and to guard the rear. For a moment the fighting was intermixed, every man for himself. Then Rogers managed to bring up his rangers; the British line stiffened and threw back the enemy. An Indian leaped on a fallen tree, 'kill'd two men himself upon which a Regular Officer . . . Struck at his head with his Fusee, but could not knock him down though he made his head bleed, and as he was going to kill the officer with his Tomahawk he was Shot by Major Rogers . . . this Sachem was 6 foot 4 inches high proportionable made, in short he was the largest Indian ever Rogers saw.'

After an hour's fight the enemy broke and fled. Rogers laid it to the 'vigour and resolution' of both men and officers. But Captain Dalyell knew who made the difference between victory and a rout and reported that Rogers 'acted the whole time with great calmness and Officerlike.'

The French minimized their losses on this occasion but their raids slackened.

The experiences of this campaign halted all talk of the rangers being replaced by Gage's new light infantry and re-affirmed the indispensability of Rogers. When regulars now made proposals to resume an offensive, Rogers and his rangers were assigned a major role. Nothing of course was done. Abercromby's recall arrived in mid-November; tall, thin-nosed Jeffery Amherst, '58 victor at Louisbourg, was named as his successor. Army headquarters in New York City welcomed him from Halifax on 12 December.

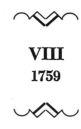

VIII
1759

'Rogers Is a Good Man in His Way but . . .'

AT the beginning of February 1759 General Gage replaced General Stanwix in Albany as commander of the northern district. His official correspondence during this period reveals a burning desire on his part to alter the status of the rangers in the army and to replace Rogers by a regular officer.

Criticism of the rangers was not new, but earlier officers had found fault in an attempt to improve the service; Gage now seemed chiefly interested in destroying confidence in the corps. When word went out by letter and advertisement that ranging officers on recruiting service were to forward all volunteers immediately to meet a pressing need at Fort Edward, Gage told Colonel Haldimand, commander of Fort Edward that, 'from the Experience I have had,' he doubted if many would appear before mid-March. In view of the season, the poor circulation of colonial mail and newspapers, and the slowness of travel, this date would not seem an unreasonably long time. Gage spelled out his criticism in a letter to Amherst: 'No Rangers are Yet arrived, nor do I Expect to see many till towards the Middle of next Month, notwithstanding Your Letters and Advertisements; when You are better acquainted with them, You will find them not very alert in obeying orders, especially when at a Distance & at home.' From this patronizing tone one might assume that Amherst was fresh from Europe. Actually four companies from Rogers' corps had served under him at Louisbourg in 1758.

Gage appointed himself Amherst's tutor about the rangers. When the general expressed a hope that maurauding Indians would be cut off by rangers, Gage quickly corrected him: '. . . I despair of this being done by Rangers only, Judging from the many pursuits of those people after Indians during my Service in this Country, in which they have never once came up with them.' This was true, but the fault was not in the rangers' discipline. Gage, the 'regular,' said: 'The Light Infantry of the Regiment headed by a brisk Officer, with some of the boldest Rangers mixed with Them, to prevent their being lost in the Woods, will be the most likely people to Effect this Service.' The rangers, he told Amherst, 'have never been on a proper footing, & want to be new Moddell'd.'

Ranger officers had tacitly been given the same status as provincial officers: only regular officers of their own rank or higher were superior to them. Gage ventured to disturb this delicately balanced solution, which could cause great trouble, without consulting Amherst. He wrote Haldimand:

The Rangers have, strictly speaking, no Rank at all, but as the Provincials had Rank, the Rangers assumed it, & were suffered to enjoy it the last Campaign: You may very well remember that Rogers Commanded in the Affair near Fort Anne, when Cap't Dalyell was present. You will avoid all disputes on this Subject as much as possible, for fear of disgusting the Rangers, but if You are forced to a decision, You must decide against the Officers of the Rangers as They have certainly no Rank in the Army.

Gage well knew who would probably be 'disgusted.' Inevitably it happened: during a scout to Ticonderoga Rogers asserted his rank over a regular captain who on his return complained to Haldimand. The latter hesitated to follow

Gage's instructions: Rogers may have been merely a brevet major but he was too important to brush aside as abruptly as Gage indicated. Instead Haldimand referred the matter to Gage. The general, too, when he found that something more than a hypothetical problem was on his hands, decided to submit the question to his superior: 'There was some Dispute between Rogers, & Cap't Williamos . . . about Rank . . . The Matter is loose & wants to be fixed. I must say, They [the rangers] much better deserve Rank than the Provincials.' It was a strange retreat from his previous instructions to Haldimand.

In late March, while Rogers was in Albany, ranger officers objected to going out on scouts ordered by Haldimand because of the weak forces sent out. Haldimand again turned to Gage, who took a strong position in the matter. Any ranger officer objecting to marching with the numbers designated by Haldimand was to be confined on the charge of mutiny; anyone trying to resign his commission was to be arrested and tried as a deserter. From the point of view of army discipline Gage was correct although rather harsh. Yet, during the '59 campaign, he himself was to disregard a specific order from Amherst to attack the French fort of LaGalette because he considered his force too weak.

When Rogers recovered from an illness and prepared to return from Albany to Fort Edward, Gage gave him directions to put his corps into order. At about the same time he instructed Haldimand to have a regular officer do this duty as soon as Rogers arrived. This duplicity lays Gage open to a charge that he was deliberately trying to cause trouble: what could Rogers' reaction be when he learned that his function had been turned over to a regular? His standing with his men would be seriously impaired. Anticipating an explosion, Gage casually referred to his action in a letter to Amherst:

. . .Major Rogers . . . left this Place a few Day ago, with Orders to put his Comp'ys in some order, but as I know him to be a true Ranger & not much addicted to Regularity, I had before sent Directions on this head to Col'o Haldimand. . .

He did not explain that he had told Haldimand to have a regular officer take over Rogers' duty. But he tried to instill further distrust of the ranger leader in Amherst's mind: 'Rogers is a good man in his way, but his Schemes are very wild, & He has a new one every Day.' Then if there was trouble from the rangers and as Amherst now would not trust Rogers, Gage wanted the commander in chief to know what to do: 'I inclose you a Scheme for putting the Rangers in some better order, which I have got Major Moneypenny [sic] to write out; if you approve of it send your Directions, many Things more may be added.'

There was no trouble. Rogers had the sense to hold his peace. Only rumor told of any dissatisfaction. Possibly he restrained himself because he had hints that Amherst had confidence in him in spite of Gage's efforts. Robert Townshend, the Deputy Adjutant General, had written him that 'You may depend upon General Amherst's intentions to have you. . . .'

Furthermore he had concrete evidence of Amherst's trust in him. He had wanted to discuss the enlistment of Indians with Amherst, but the shortage of rangers had held him at Fort Edward and compelled him to forward his ideas in writing. All correspondence passed through Gage's hands and he held up Rogers' letters while writing Amherst for instructions on the matter. As usual he clearly indicated that be disapproved of Rogers' idea: 'These Indians were last Campaign a great Nuisance to the Army & did no Manner of Service. . . .' He told Haldimand how he tried to suppress Rogers' proposal to use Indians: 'I never desire to see them any more.'

However, Gage's letter crossed one from Amherst indicating that he had faith in Rogers' opinion:

Captain Jacobs of the Stockbridge Indians was with me some time since—, I sent him with a Letter to Major Rogers, to give in his proposals to him and directed Major Rogers to report to me his opinion of their Services.

Actually Amherst was no admirer of Indians. He admitted to Gage that 'I know what a vile brew they are and have as bad an opinion of those lazy rum drinking Scoundrels as any one can have. . . .' But he believed that the French feared them 'and I shall for that reason engage as many of them as I can. . . .'

Captain Jacobs arrived in Albany and Gage could not satisfy him: he would talk only with Rogers. So Gage summoned Rogers down from Fort Edward even though a horse had to be supplied him because he had been badly frost bitten on his March scout. Jacobs was satisfied only when Rogers finally arrived in Albany. Then Rogers had no doubts about his standing with Amherst.

What Amherst thought about Gage's barrage against the rangers will never be known except what might be implied from the fact that he did not even bother to comment on it in his correspondence with Gage. Possibly he wondered at its cause: the rangers had given no reason for the outburst. At the same time the commander in chief had proof that generals of more standing in combat than Gage felt differently about Rogers and his rangers. General Wolfe, preparing for an assault on Quebec, asked that Rogers and his own company of rangers be included in the forces supplied him. This request, from a man whose contempt for American soldiers was notorious, did not fail to impress Amherst.

The commander in chief wrote Rogers on 1 April. The ranger's recommendations concerning the Indian companies were accepted by the general. Welcome balm to Rogers' wounds was Amherst's assurance: 'I shall always cheerfully receive Your opinion in relation to the Service you are Engaged in.' When the general came to Albany in May, he had Rogers come down, listened sympathetically to his problems, and assured him that he had rank and that it would be publicly announced in the army orders.

It scarcely needs be added that Wolfe did not have his request granted; Amherst kept Rogers and his own company at Fort Edward to assist him in his personally directed attack on Fort Carillon.

What was behind Gage's attack on the rangers? Undoubtedly he would claim that he only wanted to improve the army. But his fault-finding at a time when the rangers had done nothing to deserve it combined with his actions reveal clearly that he had personal reasons for his attack. As innovator and commander of the light infantry Gage wanted no rivals in the service. The '58 campaign had undoubtedly whetted his desire to wipe out the rangers. There the light infantry had failed miserably in the Ticonderoga woods and Gage had clearly shown 'his ineptness in wilderness fighting.' On the other hand Rogers had emerged with a burst of glory from the fight near old Fort Anne—and Gage still remembered it, galled by the fact that Rogers was in charge even though a captain of his light infantry was present.

Gage's inward feelings can be imagined when Amherst issued orders that were directly contrary to what Gage had told Haldimand:

Major Rogers is on all detachments to take rank as Major according to the date of his commission . . . as such, next after the Majors who have the King's Commission, or one from His Majesty's Commander-in-Chief.

Events were to prove that Rogers had gained a powerful enemy for life.

The scout carried out by Rogers in March had been one of the most gruelling in his career. In severe winter weather he had led a strong reconnaissance party of rangers, Indians and volunteers to reconnoiter Fort Carillon. He had marched and fought continuously for twenty-one hours in enemy territory and emerged with prisoners and only three dead and one seriously wounded. An idea of the rigors of the weather may be gained from the fact that more than two-thirds arrived back at Fort Edward with frozen feet. The whole party was 'so fatigued on their arrival, that Col'l Haldimand could [get] no particular Acc't.'

Though frostbitten, Rogers was soon en route to Albany, as already recounted, to settle matters with Captain Jacobs the Elder. He was continually shuttling back and forth between his post and army headquarters. On this occasion he was taken ill, spent the latter half of March in Albany; was back on the Island in early April; again in Albany in May to see Amherst.

British plans for the northern New York region again contemplated an offensive down Lake George and Lake Champlain: Fort Carillon at Ticonderoga was the first objective.

Amherst moved slowly, fortifying as he went. When the army was finally at Lake George, after a gruelling march on the excessively hot 21st of June, he hesitated so long that doubt assailed the troops. Was Carillon enchanted, as rumor had it? Morale sagged: 'Jonathan Corbin confessed that he was afraid to go to Boges [camp slang for Carillon] Set his name down for a coward.' Desertions increased; threats and punishment had no noticeable effect. A searing heat wave followed by torrential rains accompanied by violent thunder and lightning seemed heaven's prediction of disaster.

Finally the army embarked on 22 July and spread down the lake. That night was spent afloat in 'a disagreeable tumbling sea' while freshening winds and driving rains threatened disaster. The weather moderated toward dawn; the signal to proceed was given; the flotilla finally neared the foot of the lake.

The rangers led the van into the shore of a bay on the eastern side (now Weeds Bay) and were the first to go in. There was no opposition. Rogers then swung his men forward to outflank any enemy planning to oppose the general landing, which was at the southern end of the portage road. No enemy was found; Rogers went forward to the bridge leading to the sawmill across the stream connecting the lakes. Finding it still intact, he dashed across and took a position on the slope just in time to beat off the first French attack. He did this so easily that he thought it merely a rear-guard action. Actually it was a sally led by Carillon's commander in person who had hoped to meet the British 'on vantage ground.' (It was fortunate that Rogers moved with such dispatch. Captain Monypenny, Amherst's aid-de-camp, thought the terrain 'so immensely strong by nature, that an inferior force of veteran troops, if vigorously determined, would probably defeat the utmost efforts of five times their numbers.') The regulars and provincials followed; that night the army laid on its arms near the sawmill, 'an event at which the General expressed great satisfaction.'

Early the next morning Amherst successfully ringed the fort on land, Rogers being sent northeasterly to Lake Champlain. Siege operations occupied Amherst's attention: artillery was brought up, approach trenches begun. Rangers got a taste of European-type warfare when they were sent into the approaches to keep up a fire on the French to cover the workmen. Amherst curiously left open the possible retreat route by water. Rogers had scouts watching Crown Point and received hourly reports from that region.

A bateau and two whaleboats were carried over land and Rogers was ordered out on the night of 26 July to cut a log boom which the French had thrown across the lake. When he was halfway there, the fort on the western shore erupted like a volcano, splitting the darkness with a violent flash; cannons boomed madly when prepared fuses flared; then flames from the burning fort sent their eerie light glinting over the lake. Under cover of the explosion the French garrison took to their boats to flee downstream. Rogers did remarkably well with his small fleet: he forced ashore ten boats 'with a considerable quantity of baggage, and upwards of fifty barrels of powder, and large quantities of ball.'

Instead of pursuit, Amherst stopped to repair the fort and sent the rangers back to the sawmill to guard against possible raiders. Ranger scouts on 30 July watched the French blow up the citadel of Fort St. Frédéric and sail down the lake. Amherst had the news at least by noon of the following day. But he sent forward neither army nor reconnaissance until 3 August when a ranger unit was ordered up. The army finally moved on the next day. Almost immediately the force was occupied with the construction of a new fort on the point. Again the campaign paused, but Rogers found some compensation, as Amherst noted in his journal for 5 August: 'I . . . sent Mr. Rogers on the other side the Lake to see for the best Place for cutting timber to erect the Fort, gave him leave to shoot Deer; he killed three and seven Bear . . . .'

IX
1759

'Take Your Revenge'

AMHERST wanted to know what was happening to Wolfe's assault on Quebec. On 7 August Ensign Hutchins of the rangers was dispatched to carry a message via the Kennebec River. But this roundabout route would be too slow; on the next day two regulars, Captain Kennedy and Lieutenant Hamilton, were sent directly northward to follow the St. Lawrence to Quebec. One of the Captain Jacobs and four Stockbridge Indians accompanied them. As a pretext they carried a flag of truce, purporting to be carrying a peace offer to Indian settlements en route. One solitary report came back from them—then silence.

On 10 September an undated letter from General Montcalm was brought in under a flag of truce. It disclosed that Kennedy and Hamilton were prisoners; a hunting party of St. Francis Indians had captured them. Amherst went into a passion, claiming that a flag of truce had been violated. (Actually he was misusing it.) Two days later Rogers was ordered to organize an expedition of two hundred and twenty men. Secrecy shrouded the project, Amherst taking care that no one except Rogers knew why or where the party was going. Rumor said the objective was 'Suagothel.' Where that was nobody knew; perhaps the sound of the word caused some to scratch their chins and grin. Volunteers from regulars and provincials were carefully screened. The next day the camp buzzed with the news that thirty days' rations were being issued.

The target was the Indian village at St. Francis. Rogers had proposed such a blow to the succession of British leaders under whom he had served. His arguments concerning an offensive had had no effect; nor did the bloody and butchered bodies of the Indian victims; nor did the fear gripping the New England frontier. What finally convinced the British command that this nest should be wiped out was the effrontery of 'the enemy's Indian scoundrels'—to quote Amherst—in seizing two British regular officers. Surely Rogers had a sardonic grin when he later described how 'exasperated' Amherst was by the capture; certainly irony flowed from his pen when he wrote: 'this ungenerous and inhumane treatment determined the General to chastize these savages with some severity . . . .'

Rogers was to be his rod. On 13 September the major was ordered to proceed 'this night . . . to Missisquey Bay, from whence you will march and attack the enemy's settlements on the south-side of the river St. Lawrence in such a manner as you shall judge most effectual . . . . Remember the barbarities . . . committed by the enemy's Indian scoundrels on every occasion, where they had an opportunity of shewing their infamous cruelties on the King's subjects, which they have done without mercy. Take your revenge, but don't forget that tho' those villains have dastardly and promiscuously murdered the women and children of all ages, it is my orders that no women or children are killed or hurt . . .'

The immediate hazards faced by Rogers were not the Indians. Between Crown Point and St. Francis yawned one hundred and fifty miles of primordial wilderness. The terrain was blank on British maps save only for information from former Indian captives or reconnaissance parties tentatively probing at the northern end of Lake Champlain. Not only was the course unknown; it was held by an unbeaten foe.

French vessels controlled Lake Champlain. In his solitary report Captain Kennedy had described sighting a brigantine, a schooner, a topsail schooner, and twelve small boats. If discovered, the ranger whaleboats would be blown out of the water.

Once by the French lake navy, a long trek loomed. This was no tip-and-run attack on a frontier post where a quick retreat brought the comparative safety of no-man's-land of mountain and forest. Here stood Fort Isle aux Noix, more than seventy miles south of the target, and beyond it to the north were a series of posts, all ready to pour forth eager soldiers. Montreal itself was only slightly west of the route. The rangers might slip by these danger points through the unpatrolled mazes of the wilderness but the attack on St. Francis would sound the tocsins. Word would spread like wildfire along the St. Lawrence to Montreal, then southward to the forts—Chambly, St. Jean, and Isle aux Noix. In no time intercepting parties would stand athwart Rogers' return route. He could only foresee a hard fight at the best.

After nightfall, 13 September, Rogers and two hundred men shoved off into the encompassing dank darkness from the shallow beach at Crown Point. Once afloat, each whaleboat waited on the one following to prevent separation. Rogers, in the van, stared into the blackness, the men at the oars sporadically hushed and motionless—all listening, straining for sight or sound. Ahead were the French vessels. Captain Kennedy had reported them near 'Corlears Rock,' some seventeen miles north of Crown Point. That was a month ago. Where were they now?

Dawn sent the rangers into the protective shore—possibly at Button Bay. Boats and men were quickly hidden in the greenness and scouts hurried overland to the north, constantly peering out at the blue waters of the lake. Only a few miles to the north they found the French boats cruising off the projecting mouth of the Otter River. Just south of this point, where the lake narrowed, was an ideal spot for a French defensive patrol. While some scouts watched the endless tacking of the French, others hurried back to Rogers. He could only sit tight, waiting for a dark night or a French retirement northward.

Here mishaps rapidly decimated his party. First, a sick Indian was sent back to Crown Point. Then seven more sick men were led back by Captain Butterfield of the provincials. Hard on his heels went Captain Willyamos of the regulars with four regulars, three rangers, two provincials, and thirteen Indians. Willyamos had been burned in a gun powder explosion; some of the others were hurt in the same accident, others were sick. Shortly afterwards seven rangers carried back two regulars wounded by an accidental firelock discharge. One died the day he was brought into Crown Point. Rogers had been out only six days and had lost one-fifth of his force.

The weather had turned cold and rainy. In the reduced visibility the whaleboats managed to slip by the French vessels during the night, never knowing when a cannon blast would blow them out of the water. Now the broader reaches of the lake spread before them; flat shores slowly unrolled on either side. Probably they turned into the narrow corridor (East Bay) lying between the east shore and Grand Isle, hoping the shallow bar between island and mainland would hamper any French pursuit.

East Bay ended in the irregular, swamp-fringed shoreline of Missisquoi Bay, at the extreme northern end of the lake.

Rogers swung into a short stretch of solid ground on the northeast side of the latter bay at about the location of present-day Philipsburg; whaleboats and provisions against his return were cached in the underbrush. Early on 23 September the rangers filed northeasterly into the wilderness, leaving behind two Indians 'to lie at a distance in sight of the boats, and there to stay until I [Rogers] came back, except the enemy found them; in which case they were with all possible speed to follow on my track.'

In the evening of the second day of the march, the two Indians stumbled wearily into the rear guard. They had been running for many hours: some four hundred French had found and burned the boats; half were in hot pursuit of the rangers. Rogers later described the situation:

This unlucky circumstance . . . put us in some consternation . . . Being so far advanced in their country, where no reinforcement could possibly relieve me, and where they could be supported by any numbers they pleased, afforded us little hopes of escaping their hands. Our boats being taken, cut off all hope of a retreat by them; besides the loss of our provisions left with them, of which we knew we should have great need at any rate, in case we survived, was a melancholy consideration.

In total darkness the officers held a hushed council of war. After their objective was destroyed, the only chance of escape lay in making a wide sweep southeasterly, following the St. Francis to its forks, then following its southerly branch down and past Lake Memphremagog, then still pushing southerly, finally following the valley of a river, the Passumpsic, into the Connecticut just above the latter's junction with the Wells River at the upper end of the Lower Coös. Rogers decided to chance it. Lieutenant McMullen, who had lamed himself, was sent back to Crown Point the next morning with six rangers. He bore Rogers' request that Amherst send provisions up the

Connecticut from No. 4 to the Wells, 'that being the way I should return, if at all. . . .'

On the ninth day after leaving Rogers, McMullen came into Crown Point. He estimated that he had left Rogers 'about forty miles beyond Mischiscove Bay'; perhaps he meant to the northeast, but his listeners seem to have taken it to mean north of the bay. If Rogers was that close to his objective, speed was necessary. Amherst at once ordered Lieutenant Samuel Stevens of the rangers, whom Rogers had recommended for his knowledge of the region around No. 4, to proceed at once. 'Herewith you will receive a Letter from me to Mr. Bellows at No. 4 . . . Who is thereby directed to furnish You, Provisions sufficient to Victual MAJOR ROGERS and his party . . . and with said Provisions, and a competent number of men, which Mr. Bellows is likewise ordered to furnish you with, to be aiding . . . in Conveying them to Wells River, You will proceed thither, and there Remain with said Party as long as You shall think there is any probability of Major Rogers returning that way. . . .' Amherst, too, had his doubts.

The orders were dated 4 October; the same day saw Stevens en route to No. 4.

Even the wilderness seemed to raise its hand against Rogers. He and his men were now crossing 'wet sunken ground; the water most of the way near a foot deep, it being a spruce bog.' For nine days they splashed through cold muddy water. Feet were sore, tender from constant immersion; they suffered from chilblains; clothes were soaked. They struggled through swamp thickets, tripped over submerged fibrous roots, and fell headlong into the bogs. There were no fires to dry out clothes; a thin damp blanket was poor protection against the chill dampness of fall nights. Beds were spruce boughs laced together in the branches of standing trees. They were up in the cold before dawn; they marched until it was quite dark before making camp. Meals were cold nibblings of dried beef, sausage, corn meal—and perhaps not even that for everyone: one member of the expedition later recalled 'Three days without provision. . . .'

Finally the ground became firm; a short distance beyond, they stood on the west bank of the St. Francis River. Their objective was on the east side; the river must be forded. The icy water was about five feet deep and the current was swift. By putting the 'tallest men up the stream, and then holding by each other, we got over with the loss of several of our guns. . . .' The latter could not be spared: the best swimmers stripped and dove for them; several were recovered. Now St. Francis was only fifteen miles downstream; and 'we had now good dry ground to march upon. . . .'

From a vantage point high in a tree Rogers spied gray swirls of smoke slowly rising into darkening skies. Through bare but interlaced branches a few slanting roofs could be seen. Darkness soon blotted out all; it was early evening, 5 October 1759.

At eight o'clock, the main body hidden, Rogers and two officers stole forward to reconnoiter the Indian town. After creeping near the rough cabins, they lay motionless in the brush, watching the Indians 'in a high frolic or dance,' howling drunkenly over the thumping of small water-drums and the whirring of pebble-filled turtleshell rattles. They were obviously unaware of the presence of any enemy. Satisfied the ranger officers left their hiding place shortly after midnight as silently as they had arrived.

At three in the morning of 6 October Rogers marched his one hundred and forty-one officers and men to within fifteen hundred yards of the now silent settlement. A hushed command: packs were slipped off and stacked; guns were loaded, bayonets softly slid over the muzzles and locked; tomahawks and knives were loosened. Slowly, quietly, a thin, long line of dark figures crept to the edge of the clearing surrounding the town. Damp mists still swirled around the haphazardly placed dark blobs which were the huts. Then—half an hour before dawn—Rogers gave the signal and the line surged forward.

The surprise was complete.

The Indians, in a stupor from the night's orgy, were still on their pallets when hut doors crashed in under the butt ends of muskets or the weight of yelling rangers wielding bayonets, knives, or tomahawks. Some had their heads split open before ever waking. Others, sleep-befuddled, stumbled out and were shot or bayoneted as they emerged. A few escaped to the river and took to canoes. Forty rangers had been detailed to cut off such a line of retreat: muskets roared from the shore. Stricken Indians overturned in delicately balanced canoes; others struggling in the current were shot in the gathering morning light.

A few Indians made a half-hearted resistance from some of the cabins, shooting through doorways or windows. Rangers encircled them; torches tossed on the roofs soon converted them into bonfires. Some perished in the flames singing quavering death-chants; others were slain as they darted from flame-encircled doorways. There was the smell of blood and the stench of burning flesh as flames and smoke poured into the sky. Among the huts stood a chapel into which rangers broke their way. Some emerged, leading the resident Jesuit missionary, Pierre Joseph Antoine Roubaud, with a rope around his neck; others inside swung hatchets with iconoclastic zeal. On the altar stood a small silver image of the Virgin Mary, weighing about ten pounds; one ranger slipped it under his shirt.

All the town was now given to the torch except three huts holding a store of corn. It was only seven o'clock in the morning when all resistance ceased. Rogers at once paraded his men and took stock: one Stockbridge Indian had been killed, Captain Ogden was seriously wounded, six others were scratched. They had no idea of the St. Francis casualties; guesses ran as high as two or three hundred, but the losses were probably less. About twenty women and children huddled together stolidly eyeing the rangers ringed around them; five English women captives ran from man to man, seeking some one with news of their home.

The smoking funeral pyre which had been the Indian settlement of St. Francis now became only smoking embers. The rangers, too, lost the blood lust which had gripped them when they had seen scalp-festooned poles by the huts. The St. Francis Indians had lived by the sword and they died—men, women, and children—as they had lived, but no harder than had died hundreds of families on the New England frontier.

Prisoner interrogation revealed that this blow had been expected at an Indian settlement on the Yamaska River ('river Wigwam Martinic'); three hundred French and Indians were supposed to be near by. A council of war briefly considered the return route: it approved the trail to the Connecticut. No time was lost. All captives except five young girls and boys were sent scuttling. Packs were recovered; corn was distributed from the Indian warehouses. Some rangers surreptitiously gave valuable space to loot—the silver image, wampum, and even worthless documents. Later there was talk of gold and silver—one newspaper stated that 'one Ranger is said to bring off 170 Guineas.' How much was truth and how much idle rumor cannot now be told.

The rangers now filed southeasterly up the St. Francis, each man carrying in his haversack his fate: the corn from the village. The forks of the river were some seventy miles away;

forty more must be covered to bypass Lake Memphremagog.
Inevitably the corn began to give out—more quickly for some
than others. For eight days the expedition trudged along while
north winds whipped the men with freezing rain. Game disappeared before them. Somewhere near Lake Memphremagog another council of war was held. It was decided to split
into small parties; perhaps they would come on game more
quietly than the detachment. The rendezvous was on the Connecticut at the Wells River where the provisions from Amherst
were expected. The units scattered. Some turned southeasterly
toward Crown Point—those with the captives took this route.
Others turned east. There were 'many days tedious march
over steep rocky mountains or thro' dirty swamps, with the
terrible attendants of fatigue and hunger. . . .'

There was also the enemy.

'Two days after we parted,' wrote Rogers, 'Ensign Avery, of
Fitche's, fell in on my track, and followed in my rear; and a
party of the enemy came upon them, and took seven of his
party prisoners, two of whom that night made their escape,
and came in to me next morning. Avery, with the remainder
of his party joined mine. . . .' Two of the five remaining prisoners were later exchanged. Frederick Curtiss, one of them,
briefly described the ordeal:

. . .After nine days travail in an unknown Wilderness . . . [we]
were at the close of the Ninth Day Surprised by a party of Indians
about Twenty or Thirty in number that had pursued us & watching
an opportunity when we were Resting our Selves being much
Enfeebled by travail & destitute of provision save mushrooms &
Beach Leaves for four or five days then past Came upon us unper-
ceived till within a few foot of us. Some with their guns presented
while others Seised upon us that we had no opportunity for defense or flight & So made us all prisoners Stript us of our Cloathes
& tyed us to trees save one Ballard whom after binding they
stabb'd & killed. afterwards they loosed us from ye tree & carryed

us about two mile: Camped for that night. Two of ye prisoners Escaped vis. Hewet & Lee. The rest of us was Carryed back & we travail'd together or in Light ye next Day to the place they went about building their Canoes which was the last place that I saw my fellow prisoners Excepting Moses Jones. as they Got their Canoes Ready they went off one Canoe Load after another, ours was the Last . . . at the End of five days we got Back again to St. Francis at night, having lived nine days on mushrooms and Beach leaves. These prisoners that was Carryed in the day Time was killed outright five of whom Lay there dead on the Ground . . .

Another section of eighteen men under Lieutenant Dunbar of Gage's Light Infantry with Lieutenant Turner of the Indians as a guide was also attacked. Both officers and ten men were slain; the remainder escaped.

Starvation was a specter more menacing than pursuing Indians. Thomas Mante, who served in the army and was later a historian of the war, has told the story of Lieutenant George Campbell's section—and by so doing, has told the story of all:

. . .These were, at one time, four days without any kind of sustenance, when some of them, in consequence of their complicated misery, severely aggrevated by their not knowing whither the route they pursued would lead, and, of course, the little prospect of relief that was left them, lost their senses; whilst others, who could no longer bear the keen pangs of an empty stomach, attempted to eat their own excrements. What leather they had on their catouch-boxes, they had already reduced to a cinder, and greedily devoured. At length, on the 28th of October, as they were crossing a small river, which was in some measure dammed up by logs, they discovered some human bodies not only scalped but horribly mangled, which they supposed to be those of some of their own party. But this was not a season for distinctions. On them, accordingly, they fell like Cannibals, and devoured part of them raw; their impatience being too great to wait the kindling of a fire to dress it by. When they had thus abated the excruciating pangs they before endured, they carefully collected the fragments, and carried them off. This was their sole support, except roots and a squirrel, till the 4th of November, when Providence conducted them to a boat on the Connecticut River, which Major Rogers had sent with provisions to their relief.

Rogers' party seems to have had the least trouble although like the others, fatigue, cold, and starvation were at its side. His exact route is unknown; his path possibly ran southerly from the south end of Lake Memphremagog along the Barton River to Crystal Lake, then a short distance overland to the Passumpsic and down its valley to its junction with the Connecticut about ten miles north of the Wells River. When the Connecticut was reached the emaciated, ragged men found a new reservoir of strength in hope and hurried southward.

20 October 1759. Were those gunshots that Rogers heard in the distance? The Wells River was near: it could only be the relief party. Answering shots rang out from his party.

Lieutenant Stevens had obtained men and provisions at No. 4 and had gone up the Connecticut. But he thought the river too dangerous to ascend above the Lower Coös Intervales (about three or four miles south of Wells River) and elected to make camp there. He and some of his party went daily overland to the Wells River and fired their guns as a signal.

20 October 1759. There were answering shots. But soon a bateau appeared with two hunters. Yes, they had fired some shots. Stevens and his men lost hope and turned back to their camp.

Rogers found only a fire at Wells River; shots and calls had only hollow echoes as answers. Despair seized the men. 'Our distress upon this occasion was truly inexpressible; our spirits, greatly depressed by the hunger and fatigues we had already

suffered, now almost entirely sunk within us, seeing no re-
source left, nor any reasonable ground to hope that we should
escape a most miserable death by famine.'

These were Rogers' later words; at the time he hid such
thoughts. The men were set at digging up groundnuts and lily
roots, which, after being boiled, were edible—the 'wretched
subsistence as the barren wilderness could afford.' Rogers
ranged as far as he could in the stormy, cold weather to find
the other parties and to lead them to the place of rendezvous.
But finally he realized that aid must be obtained from No. 4
if any were to survive; the river must be his life-line.

A raft was laboriously made from dry pine logs and floated.
Lieutenant Grant was given command of those remaining and
told to expect provisions in ten days. There was no mention of
what to do if they did not show up. The men watched while
Rogers, Captain Ogden—miraculously recovered—a ranger,
and one of the Indian boys took their places on the crude craft
and shoved off. The current seized the raft and sent it swirling
and dipping into the middle of the river. The crudely hewn
paddles of the crew jabbed into the foam made no impression.
The following day the crew was unable to send the craft into
shore before it was in the rapids above White River Falls.
They were lucky to tumble off with their muskets. The precious craft went bouncing among the foam-crested waves
into the rocks and soon only separate logs were racing down
the river.

Our little remains of strength however enabled us to land, and to
march by them [the falls]. At the bottom of these falls, while Capt.
Ogden and the Ranger hunted for red squirrels for a refreshment,
who had the good fortune likewise to kill a partridge, I attempted
the forming a new raft. . . . Not being able to cut down trees, I
burnt them down, and then burnt them off at proper lengths. This
was our third day's work after leaving our companions. The next

day we got our materials together, and completed our raft, and floated with the stream again till we came to Wattockquitchey Falls, which are about fifty yards in length. . . .

Here the raft was hastily paddled into shore before the current caught it. Rogers went to the bottom of the falls, stripped, and swam out into the rough, icy water to catch the raft while Ogden tried to lessen the force of its descent by letting it down on a rope made of hazel withes. Later, Rogers said of his part simply, 'I had the good fortune to succeed . . .'

Leaden skies were threatening snow the next morning as they re-embarked. The next day, 31 October, they saw men cutting trees. The raft was shoved into shore; the woodchoppers gave the starving men what food and drink they possessed. No. 4 was near by.

Within an half hour after Rogers' arrival at the post, provisions were on their way up the Connecticut to Grant's party. They arrived four days later—the tenth after Rogers had left.

On the day after his arrival, after watching two more provision-laden canoes start up the Connecticut, Rogers turned back to the fort to pen his report to Amherst. Apparently his daily notes had been lost; everything is dated by its relation to the day he left Crown Point; the first sentence marked his arrival at the St. Francis River. After that was finished, he penned notes to the New Hampshire authorities. Some of his parties may have gone southeasterly into the northern reaches of that province; would relief parties be sent north with provisions?

After a brief rest, Rogers himself went back up the river on 2 November: 'to seek and bring in as many of our men as I can find. . . .' More provisions accompanied him; he also had men hired from No. 4 to beat the woods for missing detachments. The latter began to show up: Lieutenant Farrington's section, Sergeant Evan's unit and the men remaining from Dunbar's and Turner's parties.

7 November 1759. Snow and hail were pelting down on the frozen camp at Crown Point when a rumor spread like wildfire: Rogers had come in at No. 4! He had only lost one man! St. Francis was destroyed! Captain Ogden had arrived with Rogers' report of 1 November, and exaggeration had supplied the details.

That afternoon an Indian unobtrusively slipped into camp and, Indian-style, allowed a proper interval to elapse before casually mentioning that he had left sixteen of Rogers' party at the mouth of the Otter River. Amherst immediately dispatched rangers in whaleboats to the spot. The next day they brought in four Indians, two rangers, one of the released prisoners, and two Indian girls and an Indian boy who were from St. Francis. All were loaded with wampum and trinkets plundered from that village. Four days later three more rangers came in, reporting two others five miles off.

Amherst wrote Rogers on 8 November: 'I . . . assure you of the satisfaction I had on reading it [Rogers' report] as every step you inform Me You have taken, has been very well Judged, and Deserves my full approbation.'

New England hailed the stroke with joy. The same blasphemous utterances which had echoed in that land since the landing of the Pilgrims were repeated: '. . . A just Providence never design'd that those blood thirsty Heathen should go down to the Grave in Peace.'

The march from St. Francis cost Rogers three officers—only one of whom actually belonged to any ranger company—, forty-six sergeants and privates. Only two of the men taken captive by the French and Indians are known to have survived.

Lieutenant Stevens was arrested at the end of the year although he protested to Amherst that 'Your Excellancys Commands I endeavored to Comply with, in Every Respect, as far as my weak Judgment did permit. . . .' Difficulties in locating witnesses or obtaining depositions delayed his court-martial until 23 April 1760. Some discrepancy as to dates and some doubt as to whether he actually heard the shots of Rogers' party developed at the trial. Furthermore it was true that Amherst had left to his judgment how long he should wait for Rogers. But there was no doubt that he had been ordered to take the supplies to Wells River and that he had failed to do this. Found guilty, he was dismissed from service.

In the army some criticism was heard, particularly of the men who used precious space for loot rather than for provisions. Rogers had Sergeant Lewis of Gage's unit confined 'for aspersing my Character by Spreading a Fake Report that I took away from Dunbars party Provisions and gave it away to others who had loaded themselves with Plunder after the place was destroy'd.' Amherst thought Rogers unduly sensitive—'from anything I have heard of the Affair, it is not in the power of that Serjeant to hurt your Character. . . .' But it was a serious charge in the eyes of men who ranged the woods. If unchallenged it might well have destroyed the willingness of volunteers from among the regulars to follow Rogers into the wilderness.

Legend has taken over the story of the St. Francis raid. Human—and probably other—bones discovered in areas where the expedition may have passed have been immediately identified as remnants of returning rangers. Loot is always said to have been found near rotting cloth, bones, and rusty muskets. There are stories of enough gold and silver candlestick-holders to equip the most elaborate Old World cathedral. Old rangers are said to have been constantly going back to find buried loot—particularly the silver statue (which actually seems to have been brought into Crown Point). The tale usually runs that they could not find what had been hidden—the identifying brooks or other landmarks had changed.

Better still is the legend of a lone hunter who 'a number of years ago' wandered far into the White Mountains. At night while rain beat down and the thunder roared and echoed in the mountains, he sought shelter in a cave. There, as lightning shed an eerie, momentary light, he saw a vision of a church with a line of Indians worshiping at the feet of a glittering silver statue floating at the head of the procession. Then darkness blotted out the scene.

The tales of the raid which entwined in the rising smoke from campfires at Crown Point have flamed eternally in the campfires of New England.

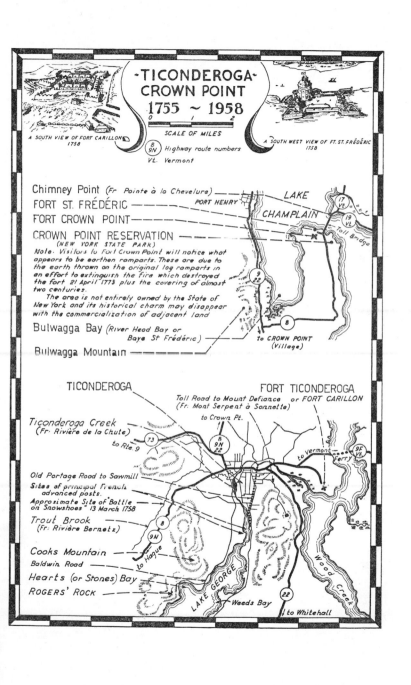

-TICONDEROGA-
CROWN POINT
1755 ~ 1958

0   1   2
SCALE OF MILES

A SOUTH VIEW OF FORT CARILLON 1758

A SOUTH WEST VIEW OF FT. ST. FRÉDÉRIC 1758

8 9N — Highway route numbers

Vt. — Vermont

Chimney Point *(Fr. Pointe à la Chevelure)* ———

FORT ST. FRÉDÉRIC ———

FORT CROWN POINT ———

CROWN POINT RESERVATION ———
(NEW YORK STATE PARK)

Note: Visitors to Fort Crown Point will notice what appears to be earthen ramparts. These are due to the earth thrown on the original log ramparts in an effort to extinguish the fire which destroyed the fort 21 April 1773 plus the covering of almost two centuries.

The area is not entirely owned by the State of New York and its historical charm may disappear with the commercialization of adjacent land

Bulwagga Bay *(River Head Bay or Baye St. Frédéric)* ———

Bulwagga Mountain ———

PORT HENRY

LAKE CHAMPLAIN

Toll Bridge

to CROWN POINT *(Village)*

TICONDEROGA

FORT TICONDEROGA or FORT CARILLON

Toll Road to Mount Defiance *(Fr. Mont Serpent à Sonnette)*

to Crown Pt.

Ticonderoga Creek *(Fr. Rivière de la Chute)* ———

to Rte. 9

to Vermont Ferry

Old Portage Road to Sawmill

Sites of principal French advanced posts.

Approximate Site of "Battle on Snowshoes" 13 March 1758

Trout Brook *(Fr. Rivière Bernetz)* ———

Cooks Mountain ———

Baldwin Road ———

Hearts (or Stones) Bay ———

ROGERS' ROCK ———

to Hague

LAKE GEORGE

Wood Creek

Weeds Bay

to Whitehall

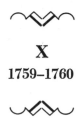

X
1759–1760

'At Length . . . the End of the Fifth Campaign'

HOPE held Rogers at No. 4 until late November 1759. Finally despairing that any more survivors would appear, he set out for snow-covered Crown Point and reported to Colonel Haviland, post commander, on 1 December. Bad weather had beaten back Amherst's belated thrust down the lake in mid-September. Leaving only a skeleton garrison, including two ranger companies, at the new unfinished fort, the commanding general had started for winter headquarters on 25 November.

Robert Rogers spent the next two months waging a campaign in Albany and New York to have his accounts paid. He was more helpless here than the rawest British regular in the North American forest. John Appy, Judge-Advocate and Secretary to the Commander in Chief, was his opponent in the wilderness of legal technicalities. Amherst referred these matters to Appy, a born accountant, who could readily produce the record of what he spent five years previously on a certain day for a pineapple-ice, to whom it was paid, and

who his companion was. He could not understand people who
failed to keep similar accounts. He was an ideal protector of
the Royal Purse. Every claim was probed for weaknesses;
when he found one, he charged valiantly, riding roughshod
over defenses or explanations. He was, it seems, often able to
salute his commander in chief with the accounts limply im-
paled on his terrible pen. Rogers was no match for him. From
the time when he first served Loudoun as judge-advocate,
Appy knew the poor bookkeeping of the rangers. They were
ignorant of the paths of army tradition; they stumbled over
the slightest mathematical entanglement; they were as awk-
ward with quills as Appy was with a tomahawk. He had a
field day with Rogers' '59 accounts. Objection after objection
covered sheet after sheet.

From a strict point of view he was right. For example,
Rogers claimed pay due to rangers now dead in order to
reimburse himself for advances to these men. How could the
army pay him without proper releases from the heirs and
personal representatives of each ranger? Rogers could not
possibly get all these papers. Yet he had borrowed in order to
make these advances and his creditors looked to him for repayment.

Rogers finally got most of his accounts in order although
some, notably those of the Indian companies, were not settled.
He went down to New York to settle with some creditors but
was back in January 1760 still trying to collect the remainder.
Finally on 6 February he left with what money he was given,
bound for Crown Point.

At Fort Ticonderoga—the Indian name had under British
rule supplanted the French 'Carillon' or 'Vaudreuil'—a convoy
of sutlers' sleighs were preparing to move down the lake to
Crown Point. There was a small ranger escort made up of
recruits under Sergeant Thomas Beaverly. Rogers entrusted

his money to Beaverly's care as he did not plan to move until later and would be alone. There was a trifle over six hundred and ninety-two pounds to pay the rangers at Crown Point and about four hundred pounds of his own money.

Shortly after the convoy left, Rogers set out in his own sleigh over frozen Lake Champlain. At about midway to Crown Point he overtook the rear of the convoy. This was where he had waylaid French sleighs in January 1757. Any such memories were suddenly interrupted by war whoops as Indians broke out from cover on the east shore and instantly overran the convoy. Rogers smashed through the enemy cordon, and his steaming horse had hardly halted on the parade ground of Fort Crown Point when he was asking permission to form a pursuit. Haviland refused: he had no men to spare. The major must have dispiritedly withdrawn, to stare glumly across the water at the woods in whose depths the Indians were jubilantly retreating northward without molestation, shaking the money bags with glee and derision before the eyes of captive Sergeant Beaverly.

After a reconnaissance of the French fort on Isle aux Noix in early May, Rogers was ordered down to Albany where on the 23rd he conferred with Amherst. He was disturbed by his financial difficulties and Amherst listened sympathetically, promising to look into the matter. Then the general broached the real reason why he wanted to see him: Rogers was to lead another offensive patrol in strength into enemy territory.

The French were reported laying siege to Quebec; a diversion was necessary. 'Major Rogers, you are to take under your command a party of 300 men, composed of 275 Rangers, with their proper officers, and a subaltern, two serjeants, and twenty-five men of the Light Infantry regiments; with which detachment you will proceed down the lake, under convoy of the brig. . . .' Two hundred and fifty men were to land on the west shore of Lake Champlain, slip by Isle aux Noix and strike at the posts at St. Jean (St. John to the British) and Chambly. '. . . Distress the enemy as much as you can. This will soon be known at the Isle au [sic] Noix, and you must take care not to be cut off . . . I judge your best and safest retreat will be, to cross the river and march back the east-side of Isle au Noix.' Fifty rangers attacking 'Wigwam Martinique' would heighten the furor. Rogers also received a letter for General Murray at Quebec, written 'upon a very small piece of paper.' It was to be forwarded as Rogers judged best.

Crown Point, 30 May 1760. Rogers lacked the specified strength but Haviland refused to allow him to fill the gap from volunteers from the regulars. There was no time to appeal to Amherst; Rogers loaded men, provisions, and whaleboats onto the four sloops and the one brig available on Lake Champlain. Anchors were weighed the following morning, sails set, and prows headed north. Soon garrison idlers sitting on the tumbled gray rocks, once the citadel of Fort St. Frédéric, saw only five white specks disappearing down-lake.

Two days later one sloop bore off into the shallow northern reaches of Missisquoi Bay. Boats were lowered and Lieutenant Holmes led fifty rangers ashore for the thrust against Wigwam Martinique. Four men with him were to bear off by themselves to carry the message to Quebec; one was Sergeant Beaverly who had escaped his captors. The remainder of the squadron sailed to the west. On the morning of 4 June Rogers put his whaleboats over the side. The rangers, muskets slung across their backs, haversacks loaded, blanket-rolls in place, clambered into the boats. Oars were shipped; soon the boats were gliding into a shallow beach, a few miles south of the entrance into the Richelieu River.

How to slide by Isle aux Noix? Two sloops were ordered to make a diversion in the direction of the Richelieu River, but a heavy rain pinned down the expedition on the 5th. In the afternoon French boats appeared; Rogers ordered the sloops back. But his landing had already been discovered. Ranger scouts, who had been concealed in the brush opposite Isle aux Noix, reported that three hundred and fifty troops were rowed over from the island fortress to the west shore. There they had formed into ranks and had pushed southerly to meet Rogers, who had less than two hundred men.

Rogers, forewarned, selected his terrain carefully, anchoring his right flank against a swamp. The French attacked his left as expected. Lieutenant Farrington with seventy men slipped around the bog along the lake shore to hit the French from the rear. When he opened his attack, Rogers 'pushed them in front.' Only a heavy downpour which allowed the enemy to scatter saved the French from annihilation. Rogers lost sixteen men and a regular ensign; ten men and a ranger captain were wounded. He estimated forty French dead. Fifty French flintlocks were recovered.

The dead and wounded were laid in the boats. All returned to the Isle la Motte, where the small English flotilla was waiting. Rogers penned an interim report to Amherst; it was carried to Crown Point in a ship carrying the wounded ranger captain who was dying and the corpse of the ensign. The dead men were buried on a near-by island.

Careful arrangements were now made with Captain Grant, fleet commander, in preparation for a second landing. The vessels were to sail down to Windmill Point at the entrance into the Richelieu to divert French attention from a landing by Rogers on the west shore in the mouth of the Chazy River. He would then march north in accordance with Amherst's orders. If unmolested he hoped to come back on the east side and be picked up at Windmill Point or south of it. '. . . But if the enemy should attack me on my march before I get to the place I am ordered, which I believe they will do, in case I am worsted I shall be obliged to come back on the west-side, and shall make the before mentioned signals betwixt the Isle a Mot [sic] and the place where I had the battle with the enemy on the 6th instant. . . .' The signals were 'a smoak and three guns, at a minute's interval each from the other, and repeated a second time, in half an hour after the first. . . .' Rogers knew the French were on guard; a fight was almost inevitable.

In the blackness of midnight, 9 June, Rogers with two hundred and twenty men (having been reinforced by Stockbridge Indians) pulled into the appointed landing place. Immediately they marched northwesterly. Rogers' superb leadership and Grant's co-operation ('I,' wrote Rogers, 'cannot but observe with pleasure, that Mr. Grant, like an able officer, very diligently did all that could be expected of him. . . .') got the party safely by Isle aux Noix. Five days later the expedition turned easterly and came out in the evening on the road between St. Jean and Montreal, about two miles north of the fort. Late at night the rangers marched to attack, but their scouts discovered that the garrison was alert. Rogers wasted no time on futile gestures. He turned and marched northerly to St. Thérèse—described later by a provincial as 'a Little Snugg Fortress . . . [with] a Butifull Little Trench Round it' —some six miles distant.

Daylight found Rogers concealed in the underbrush carefully reconnoitering the post. There was a stockade around two large storehouses; about fifteen houses stood outside the wooden walls. Early-risen Frenchmen were carting hay into the fort. Rogers formed a typically daring plan; he called his officers together and issued instructions. 'I waited for an opportunity when the cart had just entered the gate-way, run forward, and got into the fort before they could clear the way for shutting the gate.' At the same time others swooped down on the houses. The French were completely surprised and the rangers won a total victory without firing a shot. Before the dust had settled, twenty-four soldiers and seventy-eight inhabitants were their prisoners.

Rogers learned that some young men had slipped through the ranger net and had fled northward to Fort Chambly. The countryside would be aroused. Rogers moved fast: women and children were sent toward Montreal; the fort and houses were fired; wagons, provisions, cattle, and boats were destroyed—except for eight used to transport the rangers and twenty-six male prisoners to the east bank of the river. Now Rogers turned southerly.

He tried to give Isle aux Noix a wide berth, but the French were waiting for him. His advance guard fell in with a van of eight hundred French, but the enemy main body failed to back up its advance party. Rogers continued his march; as he neared the shore, advance parties went ahead to signal the vessels, which were ready when the main body appeared. 'We directly put on board, the enemy soon after appeared on the shore where we embarked.'

The next day (21 June) Rogers picked up Lieutenant Holmes who had failed to find his objective. All turned back to Crown Point, arriving two days later. Rogers went into his camp which was pitched on Chimney Point, the east shore opposite the old French fort. Rogers had returned from the second landing without the loss of a single man. Amherst told him that he saw 'with pleasure . . . that you had done every thing that was prudent for you to attempt with the number of men you had under your command.' The general told Haviland, 'Major Rogers has done very well.'

It still rankled some regular officers to see Rogers given rank and it was claimed that the '59 orders were only for the campaign in the field. Amherst sharply wrote Haviland: 'the order I gave last Year was not to any limitted time, & it of Course

Susists now . . . and You will be so good as to give in publick orders that Major Rogers is to Enjoy the Same Rank as was granted him last Year.'

The 1760 offensive contemplated three thrusts against the French. Amherst was to lead one northeasterly down the St. Lawrence; Murray was to move southwesterly from Quebec; Haviland was to smash through the Isle aux Noix defenses into Canada's interior. Rogers with the largest contingent of his ranger corps was part of the latter expedition. The sands were running out for the French, but the defeated must go down fighting. There was time for death yet to claim many a life.

Regiments concentrated at Crown Point even later in the summer than in prior campaigns. Discipline suffered among those waiting for tardy units. Regulars and provincials freely traded blows; there was a duel; various difficulties arose with the camp 'ladies.' Rum was a diversion: 'At night we concluded by drinking to wives & sweethearts which is as constantly observ'd as any duty we have in camp.'

Finally, with the boom of a cannon and a ruffle of drums sounding 'General Beat' at sunrise on 11 August, the expedition got under way. A grand fleet of small craft spread wings against the wind and set off down-lake. On the fourth day a heavy squall hit them. 'We were obliged every one to shift for themselves; a prodigeous sea & hard wind obliged us to make a harbour on ye north side of . . . Scuylers Island.' One canoe holding ten rangers split open and all drowned. All craft were off the next morning and although the wind was 'not so Boistrous as Yesterday Yet Several Boots was Cast away & Some Stove on the Shore we Came about 35 miles & Encampt on Isle La Motte.' Sunrise on 16 August saw them again afloat; the boats, wrote an observer, 'form'd the line, 2 boats abrest. I believe the whole reached 4 miles & made a very beautifull appearance. The weather quite pleasant. . . .' French vessels appeared as the flotilla entered the Richelieu River but fled after a brief skirmish.

The landing was on the east shore of the river; the advance guard under Colonel Darby and Rogers immediately marched over the wet, low land and seized without opposition ground opposite the fort. The army moved up; batteries were erected. There was a pause in the mid-afternoon of the 23rd before the first firing. First, massed drums beat 'a point of war'; then bands blared martial music, 'followed by all the provincials singing hyms.' After this salute to the god of war and the Prince of Peace, the shelling began.

The French had two tartans—small vessels with lateen sails—a schooner, a large radeau or barge carrying four cannon, and some smaller boats anchored within pistol shot of Isle aux Noix. Two companies of regulars, four of rangers, together with Captain Solomon's Indian company, hurried off through the woods, hauling behind them two howitzers and one six-pounder. Opposite the craft the cannons were loaded, then run out of the forest shadows. The first balls were skimming over the water before the French discovered what was afoot. The first shot from the six-pounder cut the radeau's cable and it drifted into the eastern shore under British muzzles. The other vessels hurriedly hoisted sail and beat a retreat down the river. Excitement increased to fever point among the British when one after another were observed to go aground on a point of land about two miles down the river. Darby immediately sent Rogers after them.

Coming out on the shore opposite the grounded boats, Rogers found that they were still off-shore. The best swimmers among his rangers were immediately ordered to strip. With the slender handles of their tomahawks gripped in their teeth, they plunged into the water while the remaining rangers kept up a steady covering fire from the shore. The naked, dripping rangers were soon pulling themselves aboard one of the

French tartans, whose terror-stricken crew offered no resistance.

In the meantime Colonel Darby came up in the captured radeau. The French in the other vessels surrendered without a murmur. Haviland was notified of the good news and sent men to man the craft. In the meantime the regulars and rangers hurried back to rejoin the army.

About midnight, 27 August, the French slipped out of the fort and, making the mainland safely, hurried northward. British besieging forces—at least in the Champlain sector— seemed to hesitate to surround an enemy fort on all sides; apparently they believed in giving the foe a sporting chance to escape.

Haviland cautiously waited until 29 August before sending Rogers in pursuit. His advance was strictly limited to St. Jean, only twenty miles distant.

Rogers immediately ordered his entire force—six ranger companies and two Indian units—into bateaux and embarked. The first faint light of 30 August revealed ahead of them rolling clouds of black smoke rising to the heavens. They found the fort at St. Jean in crackling flames; the French were gone. A reconnaissance detail managed to bring in two captives who revealed that the French had fled toward Montreal the preceding evening.

Pausing only to repair quickly the loghouses near the river to enable a portion of his force to guard the boats against any French attack, Rogers set out with four hundred rangers and the Indians to make the French 'dance a little the merrier.' He managed to overtake the French rear guard which he threw back on the main body. The French hurried on, crossed L'Acadie River, and destroyed the bridge. Rogers was forced to turn back to St. Jean to meet Haviland. On Sunday, 31 August, reported a diarist, 'Major Roggers Took & Brought

in 17 Prisoners amongest which was one Major & 1 Cap't of
yt French army.'

Haviland cautiously ventured down as far as St. Thérèse
'and made a strong breast-work, to defend his people from
being surprised.' In the meantime the rangers began rounding
up the inhabitants to swear fealty to the King of England.
Rogers then joined Colonel Darby to attack the stone fortress
at Chambly, but its small garrison surrendered without a
struggle. The rangers began spreading stories about the
French girls which made the others ache to get further into
Canada. 'Our rangers keep bringing in the best of the inhabitants, as they take their choice of them; they also inform
us the ladys are very kind in the neighbourhood, which seems
we shall fare better when wee git into the thick setled parts
of the country.'

Haviland sent Rogers on to Montreal where Murray and
Amherst were converging. French Canada was doomed.
Reported a French officer: 'On the morning of the 7th the
town of Montreal was invested by three armies consisting
of more than 32 thousand men. . . . Never was seen more
beautiful military combinations or so many troops reunited on
the same point and in the same instant, against a body already
expiring. 8th M. de Vaudreuil concluded a general capitulation for the Colony. . . .' The next morning the British flag
was snapping in the breeze over the French capital.

'Thus at length,' wrote Robert Rogers, 'at the end of the
fifth campaign, Montreal and the whole country of Canada
was given up, and became subject to the King of Great Britain;
a conquest perhaps of the greatest importance that is to be met
with in the British annals. . . .'

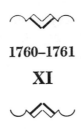

'The First English Officer That Ever Came into Our Country'

THE French capitulation in 1760 called for the surrender of the western posts at Detroit, Michilimackinac, and elsewhere. No British force had ever ventured west of Fort Pitt. The route from Montreal was perilous, particularly in this late season; the intervening Indians were hostile to the British; there was always the possibility that the western French commandants might refuse to recognize the Montreal surrender. Amherst did not hesitate in his choice of a leader to carry Britain's flag into the West. On 9 September, while British regulars were tramping through Montreal's gates, Robert Rogers was told this was to be his final duty as ranger commander.

The assignment offered Rogers a new lease of life. Five years of war had brought no permanent rank. Peace meant the dissolution of the ranger corps and with that the end of his career. He could not even look forward to the retirement pay allowed regular officers. His service had involved him in debt; creditors were pressing him closely. But Montreal was buzzing with gossip: fortune awaited the first man arriving at the French posts. Furs stacked sky-high could be bought for farthings. The golden lure of the West now beckoned.

On 12 September Rogers received written orders from
Amherst. With two ranger companies, a regular army engineer, and a former Detroit resident as a guide, Rogers was to
ascend the St. Lawrence, skirt Lake Ontario's northern shore
until opposite Fort Niagara, cross over, and then enter Lake
Erie via the portage and the Niagara River. The boats were
to follow Erie's southern shore to Presqu' Isle where Rogers
was to leave the rangers and find General Monckton 'wherever he may be'—presumably at Fort Pitt. From him Rogers
would receive orders concerning the relief of the French
garrisons, collecting the arms of the inhabitants and admin-
istering the oath of allegiance. 'When this is done,' concluded
Amherst, 'and that you have reconnoitered and explored the
country as much as you can, without losing time unneces-
sarily you are to bring away the French troops and arms, to
such place as . . . directed by Gen. Monckton.' Finally, march
back 'to Albany, or wherever I may be, to receive what further orders I may have to give you.'

Rogers was entrusted with the general's orders to Monckton to dispatch regulars to garrison the Detroit fort. Sir William Johnson, then with Amherst, gave Rogers an order to
George Croghan, his Indian commissary at Fort Pitt, direct-
ing the latter to join the expedition and to assist in pacifying
the Indians.

Now there was no need to slip away under the cover of
darkness. At high noon, 13 September, fifteen whaleboats
pulled away from the Montreal wharves, turning their prows
upstream to face 'a passage of seventy leagues with fearful
rapids to mount, which wears out the best men. . . .' For the
next few days the rangers battled the St. Lawrence's current
as the water rushed madly to the sea through a narrow chan-
nel over a succession of falls and rapids. Rogers drove his men

where possible: the lateness of the season put a premium on each hour. At the end of the rapids, by the evening of the 19th, Rogers was forced to halt a day to repair the boats and to send ten disabled men overland to Oswego.

Then strong winds held him to camp. Impatiently he bided his time: at midnight, 22 September, the wind abated. Camp was struck by starlight and the boats were under way. The rangers rowed throughout the night and the following day until Lake Ontario opened before their eyes. Camping on the site of ruined Fort Frontenac, Rogers was halted by bad weather: wind, snow, and rain. Afloat finally on the 25th the rangers drove on two days and a night, following compass through fog and darkness along an unmapped shoreline in order to take advantage of relatively good weather. Then again storms halted them on the 27th. On the succeeding days, following the northern bank of the lake, Rogers met Mississauga, former French allies, now anxious to ingratiate themselves with the victors. Conferences were held in the traditional manner: presents and speeches were exchanged.

On 1 October Rogers led his flotilla directly southward across Lake Ontario. When darkness fell, the boats were off the south shore some five miles west of Fort Niagara. Some were leaking and in bad shape from the rough voyage. In the morning Rogers ordered all to proceed in a line, ready to help the following boat. This precaution saved the lives of the men in Lieutenant Caesar McCormick's boat when its seams suddenly opened and it sank in a swirl of water.

Soon the rangers were turning into the landing at the mouth of the Niagara River. They could see the old stone 'castle' of Fort Niagara on the east bank, with its tall chimneys reminiscent of those on Fort St. Frédéric's citadel at Crown Point. Time was then spent furnishing the expedition with blankets, clothing, provisions and new boats.

The post was jammed with English traders aching for

permission to go west. Rogers was a means to their end and doubtlessly all pressed him with attractive offers. He and Lieutenant McCormick formed a trading partnership with Edward Cole and Nicholas Stevens. Goods were purchased from the partnership for the expedition and other merchandise of the group became part of the expedition's cargo. While Rogers' action was no violation of any law and was accepted practice, it was a poor move for a person in a responsible position, and he was a true son of the frontier which was noted for the thinness of its standards of conduct. Dishonest or not, Rogers now laid himself open to accusation and innuendo.[1]

In spite of warnings from Frenchmen wise in the navigation of the lakes not to set out so late in the season, particularly along the southern route where shelter from Lake Erie's notoriously sudden storms was rare, Rogers decided to press ahead in a bark canoe with two officers and eight rangers. He would find General Monckton and have the regulars up to Presqu' Isle by the time the main body of rangers under Captain Brewer arrived. For the latter he commandeered all bateaux at the fort. The traders jumped at the chance to man them in return for passage to Detroit for their goods and themselves. Names famous in the early fur trade such as Alexander Henry and James Sterling were among them.

Although hampered by bad weather Rogers was at Fort Pitt late on 16 October and delivered his orders to Monckton who took immediate action. Rotund, near-sighted Captain Donald Campbell was selected to head a company of Royal Americans under orders to prepare to march at once. Monckton gave Rogers orders to be followed in taking over Detroit. The ranger handed Johnson's instructions to George Croghan who immediately sent Iroquois and Delaware emissaries to Detroit to summon some of the chiefs to meet the expedition at the mouth of the Detroit River. Then on the 20th Rogers was off again, back to Presqu' Isle.

Captain Brewer, 'in a most shattered condition,' had finally made Presqu' Isle. Rogers was back on the evening of the 28th; with him were all the available carpenters from Fort Pitt, who immediately began to repair the damaged craft or to build new ones. Captain Waite was sent back to Niagara for more supplies to be brought to Detroit via Erie's northern shore. On 3 November Brewer, with forty rangers and ten or twelve Indians headed by Andrew Montour, Croghan's half-breed interpreter, was dispatched overland with forty oxen —fresh meat for the expedition when it reached its destination. Then at seven o'clock in the morning of 4 November the expedition set sail in nineteen whaleboats and bateaux. Two whaleboats—Rogers' and Croghan's—led the way, then came the regulars, with the rangers bringing up the rear.

The first of the western Indians were met the following day at noon; thirty Ottawa hailed the flotilla from the shore with the customary ragged fusilade of shots into the air—the 'feu de joie.' Rogers pulled into shore, held a short council, and then reimbarked, to land early in the afternoon at Crooked Creek (the present Ashtabula).[2] The Indians had followed and a series of conferences took place during the late afternoon and evening. The Indians professed 'satisfaction in exchanging their Fathers the French for their Brethern the English . . .'; gifts were given the Indians and the council closed with the smoking of the calumet or pipe of peace. Rogers was still careful: 'The peace thus concluded, we went to rest but kept good guards.'

The expedition pressed on. A sudden storm—with waves 'Mountains high' according to Croghan—hit them on the morning of the 12th and drove some boats ashore, damaging flour cargoes. The ammunition boat was almost broken to pieces. Haven was found in the mouth of the Cuyahauga Creek (now the Cuyahoga River). Here more Ottawa appeared, but there was no council of importance. Now and then bad weather pinned them down as on the 16th and 17th, but as soon as possible they hurried on. Rogers saw the country with the enthusiasm of every explorer who had felt the tug of the western star:

The land on the South Side of Lake Erie from Presqu' Isle puts on a very Fine Appearance. The Country level, the Timber tall, and of the best Sort. Oak, Hickory and Locust. It is well Watered and for Game, both as to plenty and Variety perhaps exceeded by no part of the World.

On 20 November from his camp on the western end of Lake Erie, Rogers sent the British engineer, Lieutenant de Brahm, and Médard Gamelin, a Detroit inhabitant who joined him at Fort Niagara, ahead to Detroit under a flag of truce. Brahm carried a letter to the French commandant informing him of the Montreal capitulation and Rogers' orders to take over the post. The expedition followed after Brahm. En route it met some Huron who informed Croghan that his messengers had reached Detroit. The Indians there had appointed representatives to accompany Croghan's envoys back to meet Rogers at the portage between Lake Sandusky and Lake Erie. Rogers then put in at the present-day Portage River, where high winds kept him from proceeding on 21 November. In the evening a canoe full of Indians came into camp announcing their arrival with three discharges of their guns. They proved to be Croghan's envoys with the deputies from the Detroit tribes.

According to Rogers the latter were Huron, who said that there were four hundred warriors gathered at the entrance into the Detroit River to bar passage to the British and that the French commandant had urged them to defend their country. They wanted to know if it was true that Canada had been conquered. Rogers confirmed this. The next morning at a conference—'though several of their People were in liquor'—the Indians formally assured the English of their welcome. Both Rogers and Croghan returned assurances of English good intentions and with a belt of wampum, the former sealed a promise of a Detroit conference.

The Indian deputies then left to return to the leaders encamped at the entrance to the Detroit River and the expedition followed. On the 23rd it camped on Cedar Point where there was a large encampment of Huron and Ottawa, including some from Detroit. After crossing Maumee Bay in a fog on the following day, Indians came into the camp to report to Rogers:

. . .Mr. Brehme and his party were Confined, & that Mr. Besleter [M. Bellestre, French commandant at Detroit] had Set up a high flagg Staff with a Wooden Effigy of a Man's Head on the Top, & upon that a Crow, that the Crow was to represent himself, the Man's Head mine [i.e. Rogers'], and the Meaning of the Whole that he would Scratch out my Brains.

In compliance with a request from the Indians the expedition halted on the 25th near the entrance into the Huron River to allow the Indian leaders waiting at the mouth of the Detroit River to be called in. The next day was spent in council with these men who most likely included Pontiac, one of the war chiefs of the Ottawa living near Detroit. Formal greetings were exchanged; the whites explained the purpose of their coming. This was followed by an adjournment while the chiefs gravely considered the news. Then they returned with speeches accepting English rule, the pipe of peace was smoked, gifts were distributed, and finally rum sealed the new friendship pact.[3]

On the 27th, as the party proceeded to enter the Detroit

River, two different parties from the French fort appeared with messages from Captain Bellestre. Rogers halted, and on the next morning sent Captain Campbell ahead with the terms of the Montreal surrender, a letter from the French governor to Bellestre, and a formal written demand for the post's surrender: '. . . I am determined Agreable to my Instructions from General Amherst Speedily to relieve your post. I shall Stop the Troops I have with me at the hither end of the Town, till four oClock, by which time I expect your Answer. . . .'

The party slowly followed in Campbell's wake, stopping at either the Potawatomi village on the northern bank of the river or the Huron settlement on the opposite side. In the evening Captain Campbell returned, reporting that the post would be surrendered peaceably on the following day.

The cold midday sun of 29 November found the green-clad rangers and the Royal Americans in red coats and blue breeches drawn up on a field of grass at the western entrance to the small stockaded French village, on the northern river bank. Hundreds of Indians bedecked in all their finery, feathers waving, ornaments jingling, painted to the tips of their hair, crowded around. Over the tall stockade showed sloping roofs, dormer windows, and cross-topped church steeple, while the breeze whipped the French flag, golden fleur-de-lis sparkling. The western gate opened and a French officer smartly marched out, faced Rogers and saluted. Captain Bellestre's compliments to the major; he was at the latter's command. Rogers snapped out an order. Lieutenants Leslie and McCormick with thirty-six Royal Americans disappeared into the gate. Inside on the small parade ground on the eastern side the French garrison was drawn up under arms. The newcomers halted and stood stiffly under attention. Captain Bellestre barked an order and the golden fleur-de-lis gave a final flash and then became only a design on a piece of limp cloth dropping into the hands of a waiting soldier. Swiftly the British colors went up. When the new flag became visible to those outside, the British force cheered. Thereupon 'about 700 Indians gave a shout, merrily exaulting in their prediction being verified, that the crow represented the English.' The French soldiers and those few inhabitants who dared to venture outside to view the feared invaders were silent. The French reign at Detroit of some fifty-nine years had ended.

The destiny of the West was now in British hands.

Captain Campbell described the fort as being 'very large and in good Repair, there are two Bastions toward the water, and a large fast Bastion towards the inland, the point of the Bastion is a Cavalier of wood on which are mounted the three pounders and three small Mortars, or cochons. The Pallisadoes are in good order. There is a scaffolding round the whole which is only floored towards the Land for want of Plank. There are seventy or eighty houses in the fort laid out in regular streets.'

Detroit had not witnessed for many years the activity which followed the surrender. On 30 November Captain Brewer arrived with the welcome cattle. By noon of the next day all of the French militia had been brought in, disarmed, and given the British oath of allegiance. On 2 December Lieutenant Holmes and thirty rangers were sent to escort Bellestre and the French garrison back to Fort Pitt together with twenty English prisoners brought in by the Indians.

The Indians were streaming into Detroit from all points of the compass. On 3 December Croghan opened a three-day conference with representatives of the Huron, Ottawa, and Potawatomi with Major Rogers, Captain Campbell, the remaining officers, and the principal inhabitants of Detroit in attendance. There were the expected exhortations by the English that the Indians become 'faithful Allies' and the return promises of friendship, amid the usual trappings of Indian diplomacy. Rogers used the opportunity to request Indian guides to the other French posts which were to be occupied. Forty-two more English prisoners were surrendered during the proceedings.

On 7 December Lieutenant Butler, Ensign Wait, and twenty rangers left to take over the French posts southwest of Detroit. On the following day Rogers boldly set out for Fort Michilimackinac. Thirty-five rangers, five or six French inhabitants, Montour, and four Indian guides accompanied him. Heads of the old inhabitants shook discouragingly. 'Every body here,' wrote Captain Campbell, 'says he will find great Difficulty to get himself to Mackilemakinac even with a small Detachment they doubt even its possible to be done.'

Two days later Rogers was camping at the north end of Lake St. Clair; the next evening he was at the west end of the strait at the entrance of a large river where many Indians were hunting. By 12 December he was twenty miles further along the shore of Lake Huron; three days later he was seventy-five miles further. But winter had set in. Ice floes were steadily increasing and hampering progress. On the 16th a strong north wind jammed the ice together and halted all progress. The native Indians declared it was impossible to go by water and there were no snowshoes for overland travel. 'To our great mortification we were obliged to return to Detroit. . . .' It took every ounce of his great leadership to get the party back safely by the 21st.

Either at Detroit or en route to Michilimackinac Rogers met Jean Baptiste Cadotte, a French fur trader who lived at Sault St. Marie and wielded great influence over neighboring

Chippewa, some of whom Rogers also met. From him Rogers may have heard of rich copper mines, an attraction to the French from the beginning of penetration into the area. Once back in Detroit Rogers entered into an agreement with Cadotte and Alexander Henry, one of the traders who had come out with the expedition, who probably advanced the goods for the proposed deal. Cadotte probably spoke to the Chippewa. On 23 December four chiefs of this nation signed two deeds of land: one to Rogers, Henry, and Cadotte which has never been found, and one to Rogers alone which is still in existence. The latter's phrasing shows the hand of an English scriviner but has a sonorous quality reminiscent of Indian oratory. The chiefs were acting 'in the Presence of God and with Regard to his Angels. . . .' It was their 'Free will and Pleasure' to make the conveyance to Rogers 'in Consideration of the Love and Good Will we have to him as also a Desire we have To Convince the World that we will Grant him our Bounty for Being the First English Officer that Ever Came into our Contry with Troops. . . .'

The consideration recited in the deed was impressive. ' . . . One hundred White Blankets Fifty Stroud Blankets Twenty Barrels of Rum forty Pounds Vermillion Twenty thousand Wampum and three hundred Pounds of Gunpowder Two hundred weights of Shott & Ball. . . .' It seems probable that there could only have been a token payment and a promise of the remainder in the future.

The conveyed tract comprised an estimated twenty thousand acres of land on the south side of Lake Superior and 'in the Bounds that God has Given us to Inherit and, the Which we have Posses'd, under God for Many Generations Back, Long Before any White People Came Amongst us and we Look to the Starrs when We Attempt to Count the Years wee have own'd it. . . .' It was bounded on the north by Lake Superior; on the east by the Ontonawyon River; on the west by the Copper River and on the south by 'a Streight Line from the head of the one River to the head of the other River.' The Indians reserved 'Hunting and fishing on said Lands to ourselves when we Please. . . .'

Across the bottom of the deed was affixed a belt of black wampum. On either end and in the middle were strips of white beads representing rivers. A 'Memorandum' is written below the signatures. It explains that the belt was presented by the 'head Warriors & Young Chiefs with all their Village' and that 'they will ever acknowledge' the authority implied by the wampum. 'The Belt must always be shown when the deed is presented. . . .'

With this deed in his pack Rogers left Detroit on the same day it was executed, for a quick march overland to the east. By 2 January he was on the south side of Sandusky Bay, writing with undiminished enthusiasm of his 'good opinion of the Soil from Detroite to this place. It is timbered principally with Black and White Oakes, Hickory, Locust and Maple. We found Wild Apples all along the West End of Lake Erie, Some Savannas of Several Miles in Extent without a Tree, but clothed with jointed Grass Six feet high which Rotting every year Adds to the Fertility of the Soil.'

Rogers then cut southeasterly through what is now northern and central Ohio. His prosaic recording of the direction of march is interspersed with a paen of praise for the countryside. Here was 'a very remarkable fine Spring . . . rising out of the Side of a Small Hill, with such force that it Boils above the Ground in a Column three feet high. . . .' Game was plentiful: 'This Day we killed plenty of Deer and Turkies on our March'—'this day on our March Kill'd three Bears and two Elks besides other Game'—'went a hunting for Beaver killed same.' 'Fine' springs or 'very fine' rivers were the camping spots. ' . . . All the way from Lake Sandusky, I found level land & a good Country; No Pine Trees of any Sort, the Timber is White, Black & Yellow Oak, Black & White Walnut, Cypress, Chestnut, & Locust Trees.' Hills were 'abounding with Chestnut and Oak.' Indian towns 'had plenty of Cows, Horses, & Hogs &c.' Here was the Golden West of 1761.

Near Fort Pitt he sent his rangers under Lieutenant McCormick overland northeasterly to Albany and then crossed the Allegheny to the fort on 23 January. After three days of rest he headed east on what he called the 'common road' to Philadelphia. He arrived there on 9 February. The *Pennsylvania Gazette* reported that 'As soon as the Arrival of this Gentleman was known the People here, to testify their Sense of his distinguished Merit, immediately ordered the Bells to be rung, and Shewed him other Marks of Respect.'

Two days later he was on his way to New York. He strode into British army headquarters on 14 February 'in perfect Helth,' as he exuberantly wrote, and even Amherst probably lost his customary cold reserve in greeting the major. Rogers became the topic of the hour.

Well might the bells ring. With the skill of a natural woodsman he had taken an expedition in open boats over eight hundred miles into a region totally unknown to him, in a perilous season of the year with only one casualty. It was done so simply that only the disasters of other expeditions make it seem other than a pleasant Sunday afternoon row. On his return he followed the trails through the woodland of a new region as if he were in his native New Hampshire.

At this triumphant moment in his career he could have written—as he did years later to Lord Hillsborough:

From the Time at which I was first called to the Service of the King, to the End of the French War, my Career through Difficulties, Perplexities and Dangers, of every Sort was uninterrupted and Successful . . . and if there was any Reward in the universal Elat of the day, I certainly had a most ample Proportion.

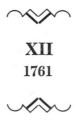

XII
1761

'That I Might Pay My Creditors'

ROGERS could view his brief span of twenty-nine years with pride. From an unsophisticated farmer tempted into crime for a few counterfeit notes, he now was the army's most famous colonial fighter, to whom all society was open. He had challenged the wilderness and enemy alike and had won his position by unique ability. In the eyes of the public he epitomized the virtues of an American frontiersman: physical vigor, independence, and, above all, a flinty self-reliance. He stood, heroic and shining, in the warm sun of fame while welcoming bells pealed.

But the clamor soon died out, the silence of peace succeeded the alarms of the past half-decade, and he faced the decision imposed on young men since the beginnings of organized warfare. His entire career had been the army; in it he possessed power and command. Civilian life offered no such opportunities: he was trained for nothing; no family offered him shelter, stability, and position. The forest? A taste of civilization had made the struggle for existence on a wilderness farm even more unpalatable. He had little choice but to stay in the army.

At first this held great promise. He possessed the favor of the commander in chief. General Amherst proffered a captain's commission in the regulars and an opportunity to fight with Lieutenant-Colonel Grant against the Cherokee. He accepted and took command of a South Carolina Independent Company, replacing Paul Demere who had been killed by the Indians after the surrender of Fort Loudoun in August 1760.

The press eagerly heralded his moves. On the very day Rogers arrived in New York, a Charleston newspaper was assuring the worried populace that more troops and 'the famous Major Rogers' with Indians were being dispatched from the north. As a matter of fact papers had predicted that when he entered the wilderness on his way back from Detroit, he would reappear in Charleston. Nothing seemed impossible or improbable when combined with the magic name of 'Major Rogers.'

There was one matter to be settled before Robert could sail: the settling of his accounts with the Crown. It was not merely the payment of remaining obligations to his men but, most of all, the repayment to the money-lenders of Albany of the funds borrowed not only for his own subsistence but for loans to his men against their pay. Amherst was aware of this situation and patiently waited for Rogers to conclude the matter. It took several weeks to prepare and present the claims. On 8 May Rogers was thunderstruck by the news that a good portion of his account had been denied. Three days later he wrote to Amherst explaining his situation. He had drawn bills of exchange for six thousand pounds for money disbursed for army service since the beginning of the war and his creditors were daily importuning him. The only money available was what was due from the government.

To explain the maze of eighteenth-century army finance

and to examine Rogers' accounts in detail, repeating the arguments pro and con, would require a volume in itself. A few details may give some insight of the system which had Robert in its toils.

He had renewed his claim for pay of the company raised for the '55-'56 winter campaign. The Provincial Committee for War, Massachusetts Bay, and New Hampshire had each denied liability. Both Loudoun and Abercromby denied that it was a Crown expense, but had promised that the amount would be stopped from the money given by Parliament to the colonies. But nothing had been done. Rogers, on perpetual duty, had little time to press the matter and his men had sued him: there were thirty-eight attachments on his New Hampshire property. Amherst had looked into the matter in 1760 but had done nothing. Now Rogers' claim was definitely turned down. Technically Amherst and his Judge-Advocate John Appy were correct: the Crown had not employed Rogers to raise the company. Amherst was ready with sympathy: 'The non-payment of your Comp'y in 1755 I think is a hardship on You. The Provinces should be Accomptable to You; I can't Remedy it.' That his company's services were as much for the Crown as they were for the colonies meant nothing.

It is easy to shrug off Rogers' claim on narrow legal grounds but the situation had permitted the first damaging blows to his reputation: the claims of unpaid soldiers. His credit was sacrificed. Rogers put in a claim for guns lost by the rangers; he had procured special firearms for his men in 1759. Amherst exploded: it was 'a most Extraordinary Claim; no allowance of this Sort ever having been made.' Rogers reminded him of an occasion when such an allowance was made. The general was forced to rejoin that the instance was an 'Act of Charity' and refused to consider it a precedent.

Rogers claimed money advanced to Captain Solomon for

his Indian company. Amherst was quick to point out that although the claim was for £278:8:0, there were vouchers for only £118:8:0. Moreover, he said, the claim should have been presented when the Indian company was paid off; Rogers' agent Burbeen had had notice of this event. Rogers' answer was a quiet reminder how Amherst had failed him. He told the general, 'The Article of Cash Delivered to Captain Solomon, is to my small Fortune a Very Interesting one. . . .' Amherst had approved the advancement of funds: ' . . . That part for which I produce no Voucher was Delivered to Solomon by your Approbation, in the Secretarys office at Albany by Mr. Appy in the presence of Mr. Mair, and myself; I gave a Receipt for it and it has since been deducted out of my Pay.' Everyone knew that the only way to be repaid by the Indians was to stop it out of their pay before they got it: 'I intreated Your Excellency at Montrial Just before my Departure for Detroit not to pay off the Rangers till my Return, as they were Indebted to me on Recruiting their Companies, and your Excellency was as good as to Promise me in the presence of Sir Wm. Johnson that you would not. when these things are recollected—and Your Excellency also Considers that Burbeen had in truth no Notice of Solomons being Paid till the Money was Actually passed the pay Masters hands, I Persuade my self this Article of my accounts will readily be Allowed me. . . .'

He was mistaken. Amherst refused to say another word about the subject. Appy in a 'Reply to Major Rogers' admitted the truth of Rogers' remarks but explained that the Indians had 'just' received their pay when Burbeen was informed. He thought that the latter might have recovered the debts from them but failed to explain how. Obviously Rogers was foolish to have depended on Amherst's promises.

One of the largest items claimed by Rogers was for pay to rangers taken prisoner by the French. The claim was for the period from the time of their exclusion in the pay warrants

to the time of their return from captivity. It totalled £2268-
6-5½. Amherst and Appy had no difficulty in finding objections to this item. Rogers must prove that they were captured
and released on the days specified in the claim; Rogers must
prove they were not included in other abstracts; Rogers must
prove the French government did not subsist them; if ranging
officers subsisted the men, Rogers must produce the receipts;
Rogers must prove that none of the men worked for compensation for the French during their captivity; Rogers must prove
whether the bills of exchange offered by him as evidence of
being drawn on for funds by captive ranger officers were for
themselves or for the men—if for the latter, Rogers must
produce receipts from the men. Finally he must prove that
none of the prisoners voluntarily stayed in Canada longer
than was necessary!

Rogers struggled to meet the objections. For example, he
had no receipts to show that the men had received the pay.
Why? Consider the deposition of Lieutenant Nathan Stone,
prisoner from 25 June to 14 September 1759, 'that the French
did not permit himself or any other Officer, to his knowledge
to take Receipts for the Money they did advance to the Men
to purchase them cloathing and other Nessasarys, and when
the Money was delivered to Prisoners by himself, the Interpreter took down the Mens Names, the Corps they belonged
to, and Carried out the sums opposite to their Names, and
that it was the Manner he delivered the Prisoners the Money
and at the time of the Delivery of this Cash he was not allowed
Pen and Ink in his hands. . . .' Amherst and Appy obviously
considered that the French should have run their prison
camps to take better care to assure perfect British bookkeeping.

Let there be no doubt: Amherst tried to be fair to Rogers.
He appointed three officers—Major Scott, Captain Wilkens,
and Captain Pringle—to meet at Appy's house to review the

whole state of Rogers' accounts and to report 'if anything appeared to be yet due to Major Rogers, that with justice to the publick could be allowed him.' Scott had commanded units of Rogers' rangers in '59; Pringle had been out on scout with Rogers on the occasion of the famous 'Battle on Snowshoes' in '58. But they were regulars and could see things no differently than Amherst. Moreover it would be difficult for them to find in Rogers' favor when their commander in chief had decided to the contrary. Their inquiry only turned up some errors in Rogers' claims.

Amherst resolved the problem by offering an amount in complete settlement. This placed Rogers in a quandary: his creditors might be put off by part payments but the offer would leave him in debt. But he had no choice; he could not afford to turn down the offer.

For the moment his creditors were appeased. But the debts were not wiped out. Where could he get other funds?

There was the trading partnership formed at Niagara. Edward Cole was said to be holding the profits in Niagara. On 17 March Robert gave his partner John Askin, former ranger sutler turned trader, a power of attorney to collect his share. At the same time he formed another trading partnership with Askin.

All considered land a great creator of wealth. Rogers applied to New York for a grant of an estimated twenty-five thousand acres of land lying along the westerly side of Lake George with the site of destroyed Fort William Henry as its southeast corner. In May the petition was read in the provincial council and a warrant for a survey was issued.

Never did Rogers make a worse mistake: it brought him face to face, with the biggest landowner in Northern New York, Sir William Johnson, who brooked no rivals. Communication may have been slow in his day, but Johnson was soon aware that 'Major Rogers has put in a Petition for a tract of land near Lake George.' He was ready when in early June Rogers' representative innocently came to his residence asking for advice about the survey. Lake George was within the boundary of territory claimed by the Mohawks; Johnson suddenly became solicitous. He 'sent for the Chiefs of the Mohawks to come to my house in order that I might assist this Gentleman who is unacquainted with such affairs.' The chiefs knew what was expected of them. In sonorous tones and with dramatic gestures they protested that the tract in question was in their best hunting ground. ' . . . They cannot apprehend his Majesty would (after the many assurances given them from time to time of his resolution to protect them and their Lands) encourage or at any Rate allow, their Lands to be now taken from them without their consent. . . .' If this perfidious survey were permitted, 'they could then have no further dependence on any thing has been promised heretofore, and must look upon themselves from that time, in danger of being made slaves, and haveing their Lands taken from them at pltasurt [pleasure?], which they added, would confirm what the French have often told the Six Nations. . . .' Rogers' representative was probably only too happy to accept Johnson's advice to postpone the survey.

Johnson solemnly reported the incident to Cadwalader Colden, New York's lieutenant governor:

. . .I cannot Sir Consistent with the duty I owe His Majesty and the good of the Service I am by him employed to avoid acquainting you, I am verry apprehensive that pressing the Indians so much to dispose of their Lands and that in such great Quantitys contrary to their Inclinations at present, will give them great umbrage and alarm all the Nations, and probably produce consequences wch may be verry prejudicial to his Majestys Interest and stop the settling of the Country. . . .

Johnson's high-minded concern about preserving the Indians' land might have been impressive except for the fact that he was trying at the same time to obtain approval of his acquiring from the Canajoharie Mohawks a mere forty-five thousand acres of land—not in the distant mountainous reaches of Lake George, but carved out of the very heart of the Mohawks' lands, along the fertile rich banks of the river bearing their name.

Rogers was not in New York when the survey was halted. In late May after settling his accounts, he had left for New England on a thirty-day furlough and arrived in Portsmouth on 3 June. He tried to receive payment for his '55-'56 company from the New Hampshire legislature but it had no time for a soldier in peacetime seeking to collect an old debt.

Rogers' eternal torment had begun. He was to be followed to his grave by the ceaseless dunning of creditors. There would be the ever-growing burden of obligations, the struggle for relief against resistance from adversaries, the malicious gossip that damns a debtor whenever he tries to hide his condition with a brave front, the growing internal desperation as moral disintegration threatens to follow financial doom. 'A Debtor's Progress' is a commonplace but none the less bitter series of vignettes true of any age and worthy of the brush of a Hogarth.

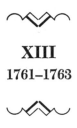

XIII
1761–1763

'Hir Who So Sudenlly Made Me a Prisonar to Love'

ALTHOUGH Rogers' financial affairs were not going well, there was a happy side to life. He was in love—suddenly, desperately in love. The girl was Elizabeth Browne, the youngest (about twenty) and, of course, the most beautiful daughter of the Reverend Arthur Browne, the rector of Queen's Chapel in Portsmouth.

Little is known of the courtship. Betsey—to use her common name—was only fourteen when Robert became a member of the Masonic lodge of which her father was chaplain. Then he probably never noticed her; now she was grown up, graceful, attractive. In a letter to her shortly after their marriage Robert left the best available description of what happened: 'O could I but be where I now wish with you Betsy, once more to feast my Eyes on hir who so sudenlly made me a prisonar to Love. . . .'

As dashing on the field of love as on the forest battleground, Robert carried all before him: the heart of his desired, probable parental opposition to a hasty marriage. In the evening of 30 June Betsey—even the newspaper used this name—married Robert in a ceremony presided over by her father in Queen's Chapel as candles flickered in the breeze from the near-by star-sprinkled Piscataqua River.

The honeymoon was brief; he had already overstayed his leave. On 6 July he kissed his bride good-by at her father's Portsmouth home and turned southward. He paused in Boston to borrow money to finance his way to Charleston and to write his excuses to Amherst. (He blamed his delay on his attempt to clear himself from debt, a reason to which Amherst was sympathetic.) On 23 July he sailed from New York for Charleston.

For the first time in his army career he failed to do the spectacular. While Rogers was attending to the affairs of his heart, Lieutenant-Colonel Grant had whipped the Cherokee in a whirlwind campaign. Robert arrived at Cape Fear on 10 August to face only the annoying problems of reorganizing and filling the depleted ranks of his company.

The Independent Companies—regular units set up in South Carolina and New York—were notorious for their poor condition. Recruiting for them was not easy, particularly in a strange province. Yet on 19 October Robert was able to report to Amherst a strength of four sergeants, four corporals, two drummers, and fifty-eight privates. He wanted to come north, presumably to recruit, but he dared to confess: 'Another motive that Induces me Humbly to ask Leave to go to New England this Winter, My Spouse whom I lately married is Still att New Hampshire, I should be glad of Liberty to go there and bring my family to this Place. . . .'

A packet of ancient letters tells of Robert's love and longing for his Betsey. When her first letter arrived on 9 November, he answered it the same day. Humbly thanking her for it, he told her of 'the Satisfaction I had in Reading it many times over and kisst the name of my Dearest Lady . . . it is Betsey

that is my pride, O could I but be . . . with you Betsey. . . .' She
wanted an organ:' Buy the organ by all means, Dearest . . .
When I go home I shall hear how fine you play. . . .' He told
her that he even had the camp parole on one occasion 'Betsey.'
His next letter told her that he was not allowed to come north.
'I could heartily wish I had brought you with me—prepare for
coming hear—.'

Military life in peacetime palled: Robert looked elsewhere.
An opportunity beckoned: Edmund Atkin, Superintendent
of the Southern Indians, died. On 24 October Rogers was
petitioning Amherst for the position. But he needed an influential patron. Governor Thomas Boone of South Carolina
already had a candidate; Robert moved swiftly to North Carolina on a pretext of recruiting. It was a tribute to his amazing
personality to find him readily winning the support of the
governor, Arthur Dobbs, and his council. On 9 December
1761 a petition was sent to Pitt: 'We the Governor and Members of His Majesty's Council . . . being satisfied of Major
Rogers' Zeal and Attachment to His Majesty's Service, his
Knowledge and Experience in Indian Affairs, his Activity and
Resolution, beg leave to recommend him to your favor, and
request you solliciting His Majesty for his succeeding Mr.
Atkins.'

Rogers did not get the appointment: Governor Boone's
nominee, John Stuart, obtained the position. But the meeting
with Dobbs changed the whole course of Robert's life.

Arthur Dobbs—then seventy-two years old—had been
interested in exploration. About twenty years previously the
lodestar of the Northwest Passage, which had drawn explorers
into the interior of North America for centuries, cast its fatal
light on him. Convinced that there was a water passage
around or through the northern end of North America to the

Pacific which would offer a short approach to the trade of the Orient, he sent out an expedition to Hudson Bay, the supposed eastern end of the passage. When the search failed, he blamed the Hudson's Bay Company, claiming that it blocked the expedition for fear the discovery would endanger its fur monopoly.

His efforts gradually deteriorated into ink battles. Finally he gave up and his last words appeared in a pamphlet:

The Person who had promoted this Discovery, after it had been so long dormant, to which he applied his Thought and Time for eighteen years, in order to improve the Wealth, Trade and Navigation of Britain, hopes it won't be taken amiss of him, that after so many Years Trouble and Attendance at a Great Expence to his Private Fortune, and Loss to his Family, that he should hereafter retire and leave the Prosecution of the Discovery of the Passage and the Extension, of the British Trade to some more happy Adventurer.

The erstwhile ranger became the 'Adventurer,' but he was fated not to be the 'happy Adventurer' for whom Dobbs hoped. No document attests to Dobbs' influence on Rogers but the conclusion seems inevitable. An advertisement dated at Charleston, 27 February 1762, now appeared in the press: subscriptions were asked for a four-volume set of Major Rogers' memoirs. The first was to contain the journals of his scouts and expeditions since 1755; the second, a description of the British colonies in North America; the third, a brief account of Canada; and the fourth, a description of the Indians and 'Some Reflections on the great Advantage that would accrue by regulating a proper Trade with them, and the great Value of the interior Country and the Ohio, and betwixt that and the Country of the Illinois, and great Lakes northward to Hudson's Bay and some proposals for the Discovery of the North-West-Passage by Land.' Rogers knew his chance to find the passage depended on his extraordinary ability to find his way cross-country. Dobbs had sought it by water; Rogers now gave the idea his own twist.

Rogers had pleasant moments in the South: he described to Betsey his 'fine house there and a very pretty orange garden' where he hoped to walk with her. Later he glowingly wrote how South Carolina abounded 'with cattle and swine . . . and its forests are stored with deer . . . and many other kinds of wild game; nor are its rivers and seas destitute of fish and fowl . . . in short, this is a very rich and fertile province, and is peopled by many wealthy inhabitants, who live in great ease and splendor.'

But he had an affliction which possibly he had picked up during his expeditions through the swampy shores of Lake Champlain or acquired since coming to the South: malaria. The summer season was a veritable hell for him. It was really his own experience he was describing when he later wrote:

. . .From May to September, and sometimes longer, it is excessively hot, with a thick sultry air in the forepart of the day, which those who are not used to it can scarcely breathe in; when the sun breaks out, it is with the most intense heat; . . . very sudden changes and alterations in the weather, which render the inhabitants and natives themselves to fevers, dysenteries, and various distempers: add to all these the miriads of musquetoes, which are enough to devour one during the summer-season. It is difficult to sleep without a smoak in your bed-chamber, to expell them, or abate their impetousity. You cannot otherways avoid being either stifled by the heat, or dinned and tormented by these animals.

In the early spring of '62 he told Amherst, 'I have had the fever and ague almost ever since I arrived in Charlestown. . . .' In another letter he confessed that 'I am scarcely able to walk, and having used all means to get rid of this disorder as yet without success . . . [fear] whether I shall ever obtain relief from the same in this warm clime.' He did not want to 'complain about my station, yet if permitted by Your Excellency should be glad to exchange for an Independent Company elsewhere.'

Betsey, too, wanted him home. Without telling her the reason, Robert answered that he had asked Amherst for a change of post. She suggested that he sell his commission, then buy another in New York. Rogers wanted to satisfy her —his letters reveal how completely in love he was—but he hesitated to make any move without Amherst's approval: the general had gone to great lengths to get Rogers his present commission.

With his heart in Portsmouth, malaria seizing him as the summer season began, Rogers could accomplish little. Miserable, desperate, he begged Amherst in July for a brief leave northward:

The fever and ague which I have been afflicted and have now upon me together with the heat of this climate have sunk my spirit and broke my constitution beyond anything I have ever suffered or cou'd conceive, owing partly to my having been used formerly to a cold climate and an active life, and, being now as it were to one so accustomed, shut up in an oven and deprived of motion. . . . I do most earnestly beg your Excellency's leave to go for a few months to some of ye northern colonys where I may have a chance of recovering my health and (if I may obtain Your Excellency's approbation for the purpose) exchanging my company with one of the New York Independent Captains. . . .

Amherst finally gave his consent provided that Governor Boone had no objection. The latter readily consented and reported to Amherst: 'You have made poor Rogers sincerely happy. Never lover pined more for his mistress, than he for a little northern air.' On 9 October Robert sailed for New York; on his arrival Amherst gave him permission to go to New England. Betsey was soon in his arms.

Robert's return brought him face to face with his creditors. They were waiting for him when he landed. In New Hampshire he learned of judgments being obtained by former members of his '55-'56 company. His associates in the proposed land grant from New York had dropped the matter when it appeared that Sir William Johnson refused to join with them. He had to reveal his situation to his wife and her family. Her father became worried about his daughter's future; Robert, too, wanted to protect her. He had been acquiring land in Rumford where he apparently intended to reside. On 20 December 1762 he transferred all his property to his father-in-law; in turn the latter transferred it to his son Marmaduke for the sole and separate use of Elizabeth and after her death, for the use of any children by Robert.

There was one small rift in the clouds. On 1 February 1763 the New Hampshire legislature allowed Robert a little over two hundred and thirty-five pounds for his '55-'56 company. It covered only a portion of the claim and of course made no allowance for the costs added to Robert's burden by both his attempts to collect it and the suits against him.

Rogers grasped for any straw to pull himself out of the morass of debt. He tried desperately to interest the New Hampshire government in a lottery in order to build roads from Rumford to No. 4 and from Canterbury to 'Cohass,' which, he later wrote, 'for its beauty and fertility, may be deservedly stiled the garden of New England.' It would bring fur trade into New Hampshire; new settlements would be encouraged. But his efforts were in vain. In the middle of February he left for New York taking Elizabeth with him. While there, he hurried to Newport in March to settle his partnership account with Edward Cole and Askin. Each received a trifle over nine hundred and seventy-five pounds. It helped a little.

Robert was still holding his commission in the South Carolina Independent Company. He had to sell this before he could buy a captaincy in a New York unit. His search for a purchaser not proving successful, he proposed forming a ranger outfit. Amherst quickly put an end to that—he had 'a very despicable' opinion of rangers in general although, he assured Robert, 'I have a very good opinion of you, and shall readily employ you when the service will permit me. . . .' Finally in April 1763 a purchaser for Rogers' commission turned up: Lieutenant James Calder of the Royal Americans. With Amherst's permission he sold out and promptly bought George Coventry's captaincy in the New York Independents. He had a bright idea and submitted it to Amherst: station his company at a frontier post where he might engage in the fur trade on the side and recoup his fortune. Amherst had a stricter concept of ethics than his contemporaries; in as gentle an answer as possible he made it clear that he thought it unbecoming for an officer to be concerned in the fur trade and would not allow the practice while commander in chief. It might be added that he was apparently blind to a widespread practice.

Then came a blow from another quarter. The Reverend Mr. Browne was upset by Robert's financial condition, a lively topic of interest in the circle of men of property who were his chief parishioners. He began to hear what he later described to Rogers as 'various and odious Reports originating at Boston, and propagated thro the Country to your Dishonour.' Rogers' misfortunes were attributed to 'Prodigality or ye Gratification of unlawful pleasure and Passion.' He wrote his daughter and urged her to leave Rogers. Then he sued his son-in-law for over twenty-five hundred pounds for lodging and support of his daughter and Rogers' servants while Robert was in the South and for Rogers' board for almost three months. The result surprised him. His beloved daughter stood loyally by her husband. She sharply reminded her father of her love for Robert and her duty to him. She accused the minister of harboring 'an indifferent opinion' of her husband, which so deflated him he did not press the action.

Robert's darkening future as creditor after creditor filed suit against him must have been lightened, at least temporarily, by this evidence of the love of Betsey for him.

Amherst received orders from home to break the Independent Companies. This meant Robert's retirement on half pay. He was not in New York at the time and Amherst sent word to him in Albany via Captain Winepress. The general was troubled by the private affairs of the young man whom he sincerely liked. He knew that creditors would soon be after him. Amherst wanted him to keep out of the way until everything was settled. It speaks well for Robert that Amherst tried to help him. Sorely troubled by opposition to him in the home government and by personal problems, the commander in chief was an unflagging worshiper of honor. Rogers would never had held Amherst's loyal support had his troubles originated from the causes attributed by gossip and believed by the Reverend Mr. Browne. Rare, indeed, was such a deep tie of affection between a high-ranking, professional English officer and a colonial of the frontier.

Suddenly, however, Rogers was granted a temporary reprieve: a widespread Indian uprising set the frontier aflame.

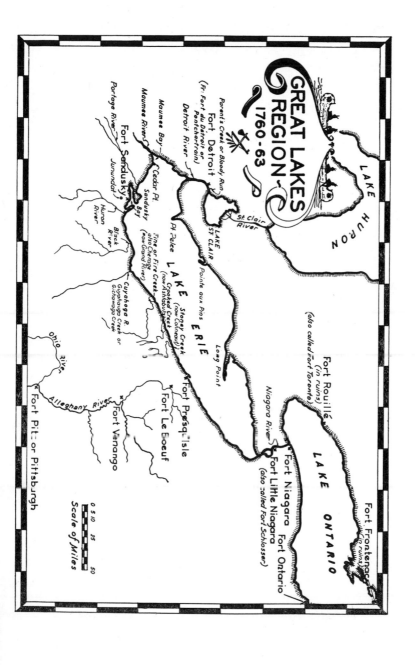

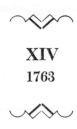

XIV
1763

'Damn'd Drubbing the Savage Bougres Gave Us the 31st'

WAVE after wave of discontent had swept over the Indian tribes along the British frontier since the ending of the war. Contrary to promises, trading goods had failed to become plentiful and cheap; settlers were encroaching on hunting grounds; British officials severely curtailed the presentation of gifts. No summary expresses the Indian point of view better than 'Ponteach's' speech in the play of the same name which appeared in 1766 and was attributed to Robert Rogers:

> Where are we now? The *French* are all subdued,
> But who are in their stead become our Lords?
> A proud, imperious, churlish, haughty Band.
> The *French* familiarized themselves with us,
> Studied our Tongue, and Manners, wore our Dress,
> Married our Daughters, and our Sons their Maids,
> Dealt honestly, and well supplied our Wants,
> Used no One ill, and treated with Respect
> Our Kings, our Captains, and our aged Men;
> Call'd us their Friends, nay, what is more, their children,
> And seem'd like Fathers anxious for our Welfare.
> Whom see we now, their haughty Conquerors
> Possessed of every Fort, and Lake, and Pass,

Big with their Victories so often gained;
On us they Look with deep Contempt and Scorn,
Are false, deceitful, knavish, insolent;
Nay think us conquered, and our Country theirs,
Without a Purchase, or ev'n asking for it.
With Pleasure I wou'd call their King my Friend,
Yea, honour and obey him as my Father;
I'd be content, would he keep his own Sea,
And leave these distant Lakes and Streams to us;
Nay I would pay him Homage, if requested,
And furnish Warriors to support his Cause.
But thus to lose my Country and my Empire,
To be a Vassal to his low Commanders,
Treated with Disrespect and public Scorn
By Knaves, by Miscreants, Creatures of his Power;

.   .   .

No, I'll assert my Right, the Hatchet raise,
And drive these *Britons* hence like frightened Deer.
Destroy their Forts, and make them rue the Day
That to our fertile Land they found the Way.

British officials brushed the complaints aside as the vaporizings of primitive orators; warnings were disregarded.

What followed was one of the last struggles of the north eastern woodland Indians against white supremacy: the uprising still popularly known as 'Pontiac's Conspiracy.' Fort after fort fell into Indian hands until by 22 June not a single post in the western Great Lake area remained in British hands except besieged Detroit; in western Pennsylvania only hard-pressed Fort Pitt still flew its flag.

News traveled slowly in 1763. Not until the exhausted and frightened remnant of a force which had been surprised and cut to pieces while en route to Detroit, arrived back at Fort Niagara on 5 June was word sent easterly of the uprising. Amherst received the stunning news on 16 June. Captain James Dalyell, his aid-de-camp, left immediately for Albany. All possible reinforcements were to be collected for Niagara's protection; if necessary, he had authority to proceed to Detroit. In his pocket was a letter for Rogers: Amherst wanted him to go along with Dalyell. Robert did not hesitate. On 22 June he bussed his Betsey, sent her packing back to Portsmouth, and again turned to the west.

While Dalyell sent back a stream of letters to Amherst complaining of recruiting difficulties, Rogers started another series of letters to the commander of his heart. A brief two days after their parting, he wrote Betsey from Fort Stanwix. Then on the 29th, having arrived the previous evening at Fort Ontario on Lake Ontario's south shore, he was writing to 'My Dearest Dear Betsey.' The next day the love sick warrior was again writing, asking for word from her—'its needless for Me to Express my Love for you as pen and paper could not paint it in its trugh light. . . .'

Amherst decided that Dalyell was to form a relief party for Detroit. Troops were taken from the garrisons at Fort Ontario and Fort Niagara. On 10 July the expedition embarked upon the waters of Lake Erie. About four o'clock in the afternoon, five days later, the boats pulled into the east harbor formed by the curved peninsula at Presqu' Isle. Only charred timbers, burned bones, and trenches met the mens' eyes. Dalyell announced that the post had been abandoned under Amherst's orders and that the bones were provisions burned by the garrison before retreating to Pittsburgh. He fooled nobody.

Perhaps in the cool darkening light of early dusk, perhaps by the yellow flickering light of the campfires, near the sleeping bodies of soldiers quiet in their blankets, Rogers began another letter: 'Dear little Angel. . . .' After a brief reference to the fort—he correctly saw that the Indians had sent flaming arrows into it—he assured her that he would return in the fall to settle his affairs. Then he poured out the yearnings of his heart:

. . .It is my Dearest dear the greatest Hardship that I ever Suffered to be from you, and could not concive the Separation, from you for So Short a time could Have that affect on me that it Raley has—Every moment My thoughts are with you My Souls desiar is to be personaly So and am Determened never more to be from you after this War—but will As Surely as I live when I Return continue to be a more Study [steady] Husband as Ever—more loving there canot be. . . .

The thin column of boats rowed ever-further west. On the 28th the expedition landed on the south side of Lake Sandusky, where another post had stood but which had been wiped out by the Indians. A Huron village stood four miles to the south; Dalyell decided to destroy it. Rogers commanded the advance guard which found the wigwams and cabins deserted. The dwellings and neighboring corn fields were set on fire; a few packs of raccoon and beaver pelts, corn, and bear's oil were found.

Again en route, at midday on the 28th the flotilla headed into the Detroit River, and Dalyell decided to proceed immediately to the besieged fort. A dark night and a providential fog provided welcome cover. As the flotilla crept nearer the fort, it pulled too close to the west shore near the Potawatomi village and was discovered. Shots rained on the boats; eleven men were wounded, one mortally.

Detroit's garrison knew nothing of Dalyell's coming; only a schooner from Niagara was expected. One of the besieged described Dalyell's arrival on the 29th of July:

This morning at half past four o'Clock it being very foggy we heard the report of several Musquets & now & then as we thought Swivels at the Huron village which we [thought] to be some Indians firing at the Scooner . . . but in about half an hour to our great Surprize, we saw about twenty Batteaux, which upon their Coming near we found to be English Boats, with a Detach't of About 260 men under the Com'd of Capt Dalyel. . . .

Major Gladwin, garrison commander, was 'most agreably surprised,' but when Dalyell immediately asked 'as a particular favor' to be permitted to attack the Indians, he was troubled. He and two experienced Frenchmen called in for advice tried to dissuade Dalyell, but Dalyell, convinced that a single blow would send the rascals flying, refused to listen. Finally Gladwin consented, perhaps afraid to refuse permission to a man so close to Amherst.

When word went out to prepare for the attack there were long faces. Later it was said that the move was against the judgment of 'most of the Officers that were Upon the Detachment.' At about two o'clock in the morning of 31 July two hundred and forty-seven men, fourteen sergeants, sixteen officers (including Rogers), eight volunteers, and two French guides assembled in the gloom inside the fort. A half hour later columns two deep swung out of the post's eastern gate on the 'Great Road' running easterly along the river bank toward Pontiac's camp. Two boats, each carrying a small cannon, followed to cover the return to the fort and to bring in any casualties.

About a mile outside the fort orders were given to form into platoons; if attacked in front, firing would be by 'Street Firings.' Marching with the usual tramp of feet and rattle of equipment down an open road in the early dawn without flankers, the British command seemed oblivious to the possibility of dark eyes watching from neighboring shadows.

The most experienced Indian fighter—Rogers—was merely in the main body, not even with the all-important advance party. This was a regulars' 'show.'

A half mile beyond the point where platoons were formed, the advance guard under Lieutenant Brown of the 55th tramped onto the narrow wooden bridge over Parent's Creek. About halfway across the soldiers were met by a wall of fire from unobserved Indians behind cover—principally ridges of land running parallel to the stream on its east bank. Brown dropped, a bullet in his side. Most of his command crumpled to the wooden planks, dead or wounded. Dalyell and the main body were so close to Brown that several of his men were killed or wounded by the opening fire and a bullet grazed Dalyell's thigh. Momentarily there was confusion. Rallying, the soldiers charged across the bridge and rooted out Indians from behind a ridge. Darkness hampered finding the foe. Then came the sound of firing in the rear, mingled with war whoops and screams of mortally wounded men.

The rear under Captain Grant of the 80th had been fired on from a supposedly deserted French farmhouse and from behind fences. He seized the house and inside found two cowering Frenchmen who revealed that the Indians had been lying in wait for the English, that they numbered about three hundred, and expected to cut off any retreat to the fort. Dalyell appeared, but seemingly had lost all power of decision, going and returning without issuing orders. Finally he told Grant that he had decided to retire to the fort.

When the center under Captain Gray started to move back, the Indians poured in volley after volley from behind surrounding trees, hedges, orchards, and houses. Men dropped on all sides; the English had to charge to scatter the attackers. Dalyell and Gray led one charge; the former was killed, the latter badly wounded. In the confusion Dalyell's body was not recovered but Gray was removed to the one remaining boat. The other had already retired filled with wounded. Rogers had by this time taken charge of a detail and had taken over a house, driving out its Indian occupants. The column retreated and left him exposed to the full weight of the Indian attack. He pulled out of the house and began a rear-guard action. Overwhelming fire forced him to seek shelter in another house. Lieutenant Bean was dispatched to warn Captain Grant, now in command, that now was his chance to get back to the fort; Rogers would hold back the Indians and hope for aid from the boats. Grant seized the opportunity, got back inside the fort, and sent word to Rogers to come off, but the latter was pinned down.

Rogers' fight was to be the last he ever had with Indians and was as gallant a stand as he ever made. With thirty men and two officers he held off the Indians, who were trying desperately to roll up the British rear. 'Here I stood them,' he later wrote, 'for about two Hours, with only the Loss of two Men; they were in Number 200 at least, and they kept up a very brisk fire through the Windows of the House, which were very large; but I fortified them with Beaver Skins as there were many in the House, as also the Chamber, beating the Boards off the Roof, and making a Breast-Work of them and Skins.' Finally 'about 8 o'clock the two Rowboats came up, one with a 3 Pounder in her Bow she immediately threw in a Shower of Round and Grape to the Right and Left of the House, to a Barn and some Defiles which were there, and drove the Enemy back, with the Help of our Small-arms. This gave us an Opportunity of making our Retreat to the Fort, where we arrived at Half past 8.'

Sixty-one officers and men were killed or wounded; Dalyell's mutilated corpse was brought in the next day. His heart had been rubbed in the faces of the prisoners by the exulting Indians, who had suffered few losses. James Sterling, a trader, aptly summarized the encounter in a letter to his brother John: 'damn'd Drubbing the Savage Bougres gave us the 31st.'

Letters from Detroit told of Rogers' role in the battle: 'It's said that Cap't Rogers, generally call'd Major Rogers, was particularly active in covering the Retreat. . . .' Guy Johnson, secretary to Sir William Johnson, wrote Mrs. Rogers of Robert's safe arrival in Detroit and of the fight in which 'by the prudent steps taken by Major Rogers the Troops made a good retreat.'

The siege dragged on. Rogers looked into evening skies to the east and wondered when he would return to Betsey. His debts worried him; he confessed in a letter to Amherst that he could not pay them. But he wondered if he could be given command of a frontier post. Then he began to think of going to England and asked for Amherst's recommendation in return for his services at Detroit.

He fought in defense of the post by the side of new acquaintances. One was Captain Joseph Hopkins, a Marylander, commander of a unit of light infantry variously described as the 'Independent Company,' 'Hopkins' Rangers,' 'Queen's Royal American Rangers,' or 'Queen's Rangers.' It had been raised in the summer of 1762 for service at Detroit. Hopkins performed well on active service and hoped to be rewarded by advancement in an army career. His hopes were blasted by the economy forced on the military in America by the home government. On 9 September Amherst signed an order disbanding his unit. From Major Gladwin's correspondence it appears that while Hopkins was a good fighting man, he was difficult as a member of the garrison. The climax came when Gladwin was formally handed a document reading:

Sir

As Captain Hopkins has been Accused by Lieutenant Cuyler of Ungentleman like Behaviour, in selling Rum etc. at a Profit and Overcharging the Men of his Company for Necessary's furnished by him—The Officers of the Garrison whose Names, are Undermentioned do therefore refuse to do duty with him till such times as he Clears his Character.

First of the fourteen signatures appended to this statement was that of Major Robert Rogers. Of all the transgressions laid to Robert's door, he had never been accused of cheating his men. A debtor, he had loaned money to his officers to enable them to buy commissions in the army. Hopkins' actions undoubtedly offended his sense of an officer's obligations; he was first to sign although he thereby invited Hopkins' undying hostility.

Hopkins narrowly escaped a court-martial in Detroit; Gladwin was later reproved by General Gage for failing to hold such a trial. But the cloud hung over his head. After the siege was lifted he went to New York and from there to England to seek a reward for his services. Failing to obtain what he regarded as his just dues, he turned and entered the service of France. Time was to prove that he never forgot what happened at Detroit.

The siege of Detroit dragged on into late fall with more and more of the Indians becoming disaffected and coming in to beg for peace. Finally even Pontiac on 31 October buried the hatchet.

The end of the siege meant that Robert could return east. But between Detroit and the Atlantic coast lay a belt of Indian nations which had not been forced to plead for peace; moreover the season was late for traveling and early winter storms were already lashing the fort. From 13 to 16 November a series of tempests tore at the stockades, culminating in a howling blizzard on the 17th. Eight inches of snow fell while the wind drove the river up to the fort and stripped the roofs off two houses within its walls. Nevertheless three days later Rogers left the town in command of two hundred and forty men. This time authority was given where it fitted; Rogers met the challenge. In bateaux, constantly on guard, the expedition followed the north shore of Lake Erie. He drove the men on day and night with only brief halts. By midafternoon on the 27th all were safe within the walls of Fort Niagara.

The fort commander hoped that Rogers would remain at Fort Niagara for the winter as the Indian threat was still alive. But he was allowed to go on, pleading that he had had proposals to make to the commanding general. Moreover, as Niagara's commandant said, he was 'the only Guide or Person that can be of real Service' to the party then leaving for Fort Ontario if it had to march overland any part of the way.'

Robert did not go directly to New York headquarters. He hurried to New England to spend Christmas with his beloved Betsey.

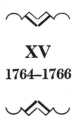

XV
1764–1766

'To England . . . To Get What Ever May Offer'

THE comfort of being again at home did not hide fresh misfortune. The Indian war had proven disastrous to hundreds of traders: the Rogers and Askin partnership was no exception. In midsummer Askin and William Gordon, a silent partner, had assembled a huge amount of goods to be taken to Detroit. Hostilities halted Gordon at Fort Niagara, where he was 'cooped up in what was called the bottom, a low point of land between the Fort and the Lake.' Becoming ill, Gordon disposed of the goods at ruinous prices and in November returned to Albany, happy that no creditor knew of his connection with Rogers and Askin. The partnership was facing bankruptcy.

After Christmas Rogers left for army headquarters in New York. While he was in Detroit, his friend and benefactor Amherst had been supplanted by Gage. No doubt mentally praying that the new commander in chief had forgotten wartime rivalries, Robert penned a memorial to him from New Haven proposing to raise a ranger corps for the coming campaign against the Indians and requesting his wages for services in '63. He followed his letter to New York, but had scarcely arrived in early January 1764 when he was arrested

by civil authorities on complaint of a creditor and thrown
into jail for debt. He was soon free, thanks to soldiers of the
First Battalion of the Royal Americans who had formed part
of the contingent returning from Detroit under him, and
Highland troops stationed in New York. Rogers was always
a favorite with the men—regulars as well as provincials. A
great many of the soldiers were debtors who had been driven
into the service by the dismal alternative of jail and it is easy
to guess at their feelings to see a favorite officer treated in
this manner: 'So this is how a man is treated for defending
his country!' A group broke into the jail on Sunday evening,
14 January, and hurried Rogers out at pistol-point while he
protested—according to the *New–York Gazette*—'Indeed I
am afraid, gentlemen, you will ruin me.' The city's bells began
tolling the alarm and local provincial soldiers hurried to the
jail. The first group of soldiers with Rogers had gone but a
second with the same aim in mind was on the scene. Soon
regulars were jostling militia amid epithets and insults. Peace
was fortunately restored before serious fighting broke out.

Robert left New York by boat and landed in Connecticut
where no New York civil process could touch him. The
creditor class in New York now were convinced of his worth-
lessness, but there was no widespread outcry. The report in
the *New–York Gazette* was sympathetic: Rogers 'behaved
with great Decency' and the only conclusion was that it was
an example 'of the too great Distrustfulness of Creditors, and
a proof that a reasonable Agreement might be preferable to
a Confinement, which by utterly ruining the unhappy Debtor,
seldom answers to the Expectation of a doubting or merciless
Creditor.'

Robert returned to New Hampshire and sent his brother
James down to New York to collect his pay. Bad news came
back: Gage claimed Rogers was a volunteer and entitled to

no pay. Here is clear proof of Gage's antipathy to Rogers. Before returning home, Amherst had left various papers and memoranda for his successor. One contained instructions about certain individuals. On the first page Amherst had tried to protect the interest of his favorite:

Captain Rogers, who is Serving with Major Gladwin, must have his Half pay made up *full pay*, so long as he is kept on that Service.

Amherst used the word 'must' and underlined the words 'full pay' so that there would be no misunderstanding. It can only be assumed that Gage made no effort to see if Rogers' claim was justified or not.

Rogers was forced to send Paul Burbeen to New York with a copy of Amherst's orders and a request for reimbursement for advances made to the men he had taken to Detroit. The next day he forwarded a memorial, asking to be allowed to raise a ranger unit, to command a frontier fort or to be given a recommendation 'home'—which to all colonists of that date meant England. Gage answered on 19 March. He finally agreed to give Rogers his full pay but denied any knowledge of any funds due to any men under Rogers. He offered no encouragement about any army service and plainly told Rogers he did not want to hear anything more about his financial troubles.

Denied an opportunity to fight in the '64 campaign, Rogers made an unsuccessful stab at civilian existence. Trying to keep up a front in keeping with his prominence and with a background of debts, there followed a year of misfortune, increasing debts, and lawsuit on lawsuit.

He tried the great American hope: land speculation. A grant was obtained from New Hampshire of a tract near Lake Champlain; rights of others in it were purchased. Another grant was secured from the same source of three thousand acres along the upper reaches of the Deerfield River. Families were being settled on these tracts when the bad news arrived: on 20 July 1764 a royal decision established the boundary between New York and New Hampshire at the west bank of the Connecticut. Any New Hampshire grant in the region was worthless. Another 'Instance of hard fortien Amongst Others of the Like Kind,' was Rogers' wry comment.

Others had sought rewards in London directly from the government; he was convinced that this might be his salvation. Possibly to forestall the forwarding of any claims to London, he began to spread the story that he intended to go to the East Indies. Then he slipped away in March 1765 without even his wife's knowledge. From shipboard he sent her an apologetic note addressed to 'My only Life.' Confessing his lack of money, he told her: 'I am going to England as fast as I possibly can to get what ever may offer—if aney thing valuable So much the better—if not its my Intentions to take Even a Company and dispose of it together with my Books and Return to my own and Dear Betsy as soon as ever I can—.'

Its needless to say more than this that you are the only Joy of my heart and the pleasant thoughts I have of Seeing you again when in a better Cituation Revives me and believe me my Dearest your Ever Faithfull and loving Husband while Life Remains. . . .

Rogers landed in Dublin, crossed the Irish Sea in a packet-ship, passed around Land's End and up the River Thames to the heart of the English-speaking world, London. There he slipped into metropolitan life as if bred in it. There is a wisp of tradition that Rogers led a wild life in London. No contemporary comment or allusion has been found on this subject. He had neither money nor time for extravagant revelry.

Rogers had two books published at his expense to attract

attention to his cause. Undoubtedly he was assisted by his secretary, Nathaniel Potter, a Princeton graduate and former minister, who had been hired in Boston during 1764. Perhaps he had a London mentor in Dr. John Campbell, an unflagging writer on many subjects. Rogers' publisher—who advanced him credit—was J. Millan, 'Bookseller, near Whitehall,' whose current list of books ran from 'Inigo Jone's Designs for Chimnies, Ceilings, Temples &c' to 'New Prussian Field Regulations for Foot, with 19 large fine Plates.'

First to appear was the *Journals of Major Robert Rogers.* It contained, according to the subtitle, 'An Account of the several Excursions he made under the Generals who commanded upon the Continent of NORTH AMERICA, during the late War. . . .' It also promised a description of the most important events of all campaigns, but the text failed in this respect.

Contemporary journals were generous in their reviews. *The Monthly Review* said in part: 'from the speciman of the work before us, it appears, that the accounts . . . may be depended upon by the public: they are undoubtedly as authentic as they are important and necessary, to those who would acquire a thorough understanding of the . . . late military operations in North-America. The Author writes like an honest, a sensible, and a modest man; and he has given, throughout his whole conduct, undoubted proofs, that he is a brave and skilful officer.' The reviewer in *The Critical Review* was more cautious, remarking that the *Journals'* credibility depended on Rogers' 'moral character,' but added: 'We perceive he has strenthened his relation by the military authorities to which he was subjected, and the communications which he sent to his superiors.' The reviewer found 'the fatigues he underwent . . . almost incredible, were they not confirmed by the unquestionable relations of persons in the like circumstances.' That one of Rogers' aims was widely known is evident from the concluding sentence: 'If the author has obtained a government in the country he was so instrumental in reducing, we very heartily wish him joy.'

Its companion volume was—to judge from the reaction in the press—far more popular: *A Concise Account of North America*. It contained a description of not only the different British colonies but (to quote the subtitle) 'Also of the Interior, or Westerly Parts of the Country, upon the Rivers ST. LAURENCE, the MISSISSIPPI, CRISTINO, and the Great Lakes. To which is subjoined, An Account of the several Nations and Tribes of Indians residing in those Parts. . . .'

Where the *Journals* had been designed to attract public attention to Rogers, this volume was primarily intended to interest the British in the interior of America. It caused considerable comment. Several journals gave it an extraordinary amount of space. The comment in *The Monthly Review* began:

> Few of our Readers, we apprehend, are unacquainted with the name, or ignorant of the exploits, of Major Rogers; who, with so much reputation, headed the provincial troops called *Rangers,* during the whole course of our late successful wars in America. To this brave, active, judicious, officer, it is, that the public are obliged for the most satisfactory account we have ever yet been favoured with, of the interior parts of that immense continent which victory hath so lately added to the British empire.

What author's heart would fail to expand with pride at these words?

The volume began with summaries of the history and situation of the British colonies, largely culled from other books and containing only scattered traces of Robert's own experiences. Although this section took up slightly over half the book, it was—as the commentator in *The Monthly Review* stated—'chiefly intended to form an introduction to the Major's description of our late conquests in that part of the world; and which must, undoubtedly, be considered as the most valuable part of his work.' In his section on the interior Rogers constantly hammered at the value of the country to Britain. Around Lake Superior: 'nor do I see any reason why this should not become a rich and valuable country, should it ever be inhabited by a civilised people.' Lake Huron: 'this country . . . seems to be destitute of nothing that is necessary to supply the natural wants of the human species.' The land around Green Bay 'wants nothing but civilised industrious inhabitants to render it truly delightful.' Near Lake Sandusky 'the soil is not exceeded by any in this part of the world; the timber tall and fair; the rivers and lakes abound with a variety of fish, and here is the greatest plenty of wild water-fowl of any where in the country. The woods abound with wild game. In a word, if peopled, and improved to advantage, it would equal any of the British colonies on the sea-coast.'

This enthusiasm carried through to the last paragraph of the book:

It hath been sufficiently remarked, as we have travelled through this extensive country, that it everywhere abounds with fish, fowl, and variety of game, that in its forests are most kinds of useful timber, and a variety of wild fruit; and, no doubt, every kind of European fruit might be cultivated and raised here in great perfection. In a word, this country wants nothing but that culture and improvement, which can only be the effect of time and industry, to render it equal, if not superior, to any in the world.

Equally interesting was Rogers' treatment of the manners, customs and character of the Indians. It was totally different than what might have been anticipated of a frontiersman, yet no surprise to a careful observer of Rogers' treatment of his Indian companies and of the Indians met on his trips to the West. The book presented a thoroughly sympathetic and understanding portrayal of the Indian, not hiding his weaknesses nor faults but emphasizing his good points—at times with an eloquence which, to judge from the reviews, struck a responsive chord in every reader:

In short, the great and fundamental principles of their policy are, that every man is naturally free and independent, that no one or more on earth has any right to deprive him of his freedom and independency, and that nothing can be a compensation for the loss of it.

The *Concise Account's* emphasis on North America's interior created a favorable atmosphere in which to cast Rogers' proposal to discover the Northwest Passage. It was now filed with the government as a plan 'for the benefit and Advantage of the British Interests in that Wide-Spread Empire, which the Glorious Successes of the Late War added to His Majesty's Dominions.'

Robert's petition stated that he 'had obtained a Moral certainty' that there was such a passage but he was vague about its location. His proposed three-year trip contemplated penetration of the interior to the head of the Mississippi 'and from thence to the River called by the Indians Ouragon, which flows into a Bay that projects North-Easterly into the Country from the Pacific Ocean. . . .' This bay 'and also the Western Margin of the Continent' were to be explored 'to such a Northern Latitude as shall be thought necessary.' At the end he would know 'whether there is, or is not, such a passage. . . .' If none, then there would be an end to the repeated hazardous and expensive undertakings; if there was a Northwest Passage, it would establish communication with the countries of the East and open a new and valuable commerce. This was, of course, the centuries-old dream of the magic western way to the silk, spices, and gold of the East.

Command of the expedition would obviously give Rogers needed employment. His personal interest was frankly admitted; he needed relief from his financial dilemma which had resulted, he claimed, from expensive law suits incurred on account of his army service. The road to royal preferment would be smoothed by recommendations from the powerful and influential. Rogers, relying on the coin of his reputation, importuned anyone who might help him. Benjamin Franklin, perhaps the most influential American in London, had offered to write him a recommendation the previous fall; while en route to London Robert wrote to ask his aid, particularly for the plan to discover the Northwest Passage. Robert won new friends through acquaintances made in the army. He had fought by the side of Robert Townshend, who had been killed by a cannon ball before Fort Carillon in July, 1759. He met and gained the favor of Robert's brother, Charles Townshend, a rising star in England's political world.

Townshend seems to have been deeply interested in the American. He chuckled to a minister friend over the poor portraits of the hero flooding the printshops: 'Major Rogers marches thro' the prints in a thousand various Shapes.' He apparently listened to Rogers' tales of the Lake Superior country: of the virgin copper on top of the ground, of the giant rock of copper somewheres near the 'Ontonawgon River' in the tract he had purchased from the Chippewa. Townshend and Chase Price, a friend, purchased an interest; agents would investigate and if the reports were favorable, a royal grant would be asked. Most likely Townshend's influence quickened official action on Rogers' proposals and insured him a sympathetic governmental ear.

Rogers' memorial went first to the Board of Trade, which reported on 13 September that while discovery of such a passage and even exploration of the interior had many possible advantages to the country, the matter should be referred to the military department as Robert seemingly planned an expedition as an army detachment. On 2 October the King referred the petition to the Lords Committee of Council, which the next day voted to postpone consideration. The stumbling block was the expense involved. Rogers estimated it to be a little over thirty-two thousand pounds, which was judged too high. Perhaps it might be argued that it was small in comparison to the potentialities of the discovery, but it was his misfortune to make the proposal at a time when Great Britain was low in funds and revenue. The late war had been the most expensive ever waged; many thought Canada another millstone around the neck of a government about to be dropped into a financial well. During the war the British people had been assured that the new conquests in America would pay the costs; now the gains seemed only to involve more expense. Funds simply to maintain the army necessary to guard British possessions in North America, were forcing the government to seek new sources of revenue in spite of strenuous opposition both at home and in the colonies. Economy was the slogan of all governmental agencies.

'. . . But I was told,' Rogers later testified, 'that if the Expences could be reduced within a Narrower Compass, my Proposal would be highly agreeable to his Majesty.' Before he left London he gave some reduced estimates to Charles Townshend 'and he was pleased to tell me, that he would recommend the same to His Majesty, and give me further Information about it.' There is proof that the government encouraged his belief that the project was about to be approved. His petition had proposed his appointment as 'Governor Commandant of His Majesty's Garrison at Michilimakana' as absolutely necessary for his Northwest Passage project. On 12 October Henry Conway, Secretary of State, wrote Gage that the King ordered the appointment of Major Rogers to command Fort Michilimackinac at a salary of ten shillings per diem and to 'some kind of Superintendance' over the Indians of the neighborhood, 'particularly to the Westward of that Post. . . .' Here clearly was royal approval of the first step toward the accomplishment of his proposal. As final evidence of royal favor Rogers was presented at Court on 17 October and kissed the King's hand.

The triumphant Rogers now turned toward America. He had resigned his captain's commission and lost his retirement pay, but had gained the command of Michilimackinac and a superintendency over the western Indians. Besides Conway's letter he carried two others from Viscount Barrington, Secretary at War, which seemed to assure him of financial stability. The first told Gage that Barrington was 'very desirous of rewarding' Rogers for his services. He was to be given command of some outpost as Michilimackinac (it was written before Conway's letter) and also a captain's commission in the Royal Americans. The dual pay 'would put him on a comfortable footing.' The second was a formal order that Gage reopen the question of Rogers' army accounts 'and report to me your Opinion thereon, together with the Ballance that shall appear to be due to him upon a fair Liquidation.' Conway too indicated in his letter that the King approved 'the forwarding the Settlement of Major Rogers' Accounts as far as the Nature of the Thing permits.'

Rogers seemed to have found his role in the peacetime world. Employment on the frontier meant a chance to use his particular talents: exploration of the wilderness and negotiations with the Indians. The opportunity before him was as limitless as the unexplored interior of North America.

Some months after Robert had left London there appeared a third book which has always been connected with his name:

Ponteach or the Savages of America, A Tragedy, a play in blank verse.

One particularly striking passage in Rogers' *Concise Account* had described his meeting with Pontiac while en route to Detroit in '60. Pontiac was depicted as emperor of the tribes on the Great Lakes and his negotiations with the British expeditionary force were described in terms of European diplomacy. It caught the fancy of its readers and a writer in *The Critical Review* remarked, 'The picture which Mr. Rogers has exhibited of the emperor Ponteack, is new and curious, and his character would appear to vast advantage in the hands of a great dramatic genius.' This probably led to the publication of the play by Millan. Although the title page named no author, the reviews universally ascribed it to Major Rogers. Robert himself never claimed its authorship; he never disclosed any inclination to write blank verse. It is possible, however, that Rogers played a role in its composition. The first act and the first part of the second—while they share with the remainder of the play its remarkable lack of artistic qualities—display a familiarity with frontier conditions which must have been based on first-hand information. Rogers possessed this knowledge and would have been the most likely person in London to have been consulted by an ambitious playwright. His departure for America when only the first part was finished would explain why the remainder of the play lacks even a historical interest. Scattered here and there are lines which are true of the frontier, but they seem merely isolated bits of information obviously lifted from the *Concise Account* to give a trite tale a ring of authenticity—which it as a whole sadly lacked.

The reviewers—far happier when mixing their ink with venom—minced no words about *Ponteach. The Gentleman's Magazine* gave it almost a page, but the writer was repelled by the cruelty shown by the characters. He had hoped for a contrast between the noble and perfect Ponteach and the villainous whites. His eighteenth-century sense of elegance was badly upset by the scalpings and gore; he confessed that he read it only 'with abhorrence and disgust.' *The Critical Review* writer said that while he honored Rogers as an officer and geographer, 'we can bestow no encomiums upon him as a poet. The performance before us is the most insipid and flat of any we ever reviewed. . . .' *The Monthly Review's* short, pithy comment deserves quotation:

Major Rogers, of whose Military Journal, and Description of North America, we gave some account in our Review for January last, is the reputed author of this Indian tragedy; which is one of the most absurd publications of the kind that we have ever seen. It is great pity that so brave and judicious an officer should thus run the hazard of exposing himself to ridicule, by an unsuccessful attempt to entwine the poets bays with the soldier's laurel. His journal, and account of our western acquisitions, were not foreign to his profession and opportunities; but in turning bard, and writing a tragedy, he makes just as good a figure as would a Grub-street rhymster at the head of our Author's corps of North-American Rangers.

XVI
1766

'A Pretty Sort of Deputy They Have Given You'

WHILE the London press talked of Rogers' impending departure for America, his secretary hurried ahead to New England. Soon colonial newspapers were informing their readers of Major Rogers' new appointment as 'Governor Commandant of Michilimackana and its Dependencies . . .'

On 9 January 1766 Robert Rogers arrived in New York by the regular packet and delivered Conway's and Barrington's letters to Gage. Infuriated, the general privately penned a savage attack on Rogers to Sir William Johnson:

He is wild, vain, of little understanding, and of as little Principle, but withal has a share of Cunning. No Modesty or veracity and sticks at Nothing. Be So good to Send me your Advice in what manner he may be best tied up by Instructions and prevent [sic] doing Mischief and imposing upon you.

Gage's extraordinary outburst underlines his personal animosity toward Rogers. If he had support for his charges that Rogers was unfit for the position and would do mischief, Conway's letter gave him clear authority to reject the instructions from home: 'If you know any sufficient Objections to this appointment for Major Rogers, it is left to your Judgment to make any equivalent appointment for him, till the Affair can be farther considered.' In his acknowledgments to the home authorities Gage gave no sign of his true feelings and merely temporized: 'It will be necessary to consult with Sir William Johnson, to prevent any clashing in the treating and management of the Indians.'

If there was one portion of his wide domain where Sir William tolerated no encroachment, it was his Indian department. Gage cleverly stirred up the fires of Johnson's wrath: Rogers would charge thousands of pounds to Johnson with no accountings. 'A pretty sort of Deputy they have given you.'

Sir William responded as expected. He admitted being 'Surprized . . . a good deal' at newspaper accounts of 'Gov'r Rojers [sic] and his great appointments.' Sarcasm gave way to a flood of vituperation: Rogers was an ingrate, a vain fool, stupid, ignorant, and unprincipled. ' . . . I am astonished that the Government would have thought of Such an Employment for him but since it is so, I am of Your opinion he should be tied up in such a manner as shall best prevent him from doing Mischief . . . .' He suggested that Rogers be told from whom he was to take orders regarding Indian affairs, the channels for making his reports, and that a severe limitation be placed on his power to meet and give presents to the Indians.[1]

Gage agreed and assured Johnson that if it could be clearly ascertained 'that the King's Affairs are going to Confusion, thro' Major Rogers bad management,' he would remove him from Michilimackinac. Johnson took this as a hint to set up a spy system to put Rogers under surveillance, a step which could not help but undermine Rogers' position at the post.

Rogers had his first glimmerings of Gage's opposition when he received his Michilimackinac appointment, in late February or early March. The commander in chief named him simply 'Captain Commandant' and ordered him to report as frequently as possible to the officer commanding at Detroit under whom he would serve.[2] Rogers was to obey orders according to the rules and discipline of war. 'Strictest Oeconomy' was enjoined on him 'in the small Expences . . . unavoidably . . . incurred at this Post . . . but nothing New or Chargeable must upon any Account be undertaken by you of your Own head.' There was no mention of any 'Superintendence' over the Indians: 'As in the course of your Command you must Necessarily have some Intercourse with the Savages, I have . . . put you under the Direction of Sir William Johnson' to whose instructions and future orders 'you are to pay the strictest Attention and Obedience.' To these lines Gage appended extracts from certain orders issued to post commandants relative to their treatment of Indians, concluding: 'Indians may be fed when Provision is given them by the worse Sort.'

Jarred by this revelation of Gage's attitude toward him, Robert went ahead preparing for the rehearing on his army accounts. In March he was able to go to New England where he was at long last reunited with Betsey. Yes, she would go with him to Michilimackinac. Her family frowned and fretted: no English woman except soldiers' wives had ever traveled so close to the edge of the civilized world. She was warned of hardships and dangers, but to no avail.

Besides the reunion with his wife Rogers was busy collecting documents and witnesses for the hearing and making some arrangements in connection with his Northwest Passage plans. He apparently saw James Tute, a former ranger captain, who was to be his right-hand man, and alerted him to be ready to travel to the west. While in Boston he was also approached by Jonathan Carver whom he had possibly met during the war, in which Carver had been a captain in the Massachusetts provincials. Carver, whose fifty-six years did not dim his dreams of exploring to the 'South Sea,' had taught himself surveying and map-making. Learning of Rogers' plans to discover the Northwest Passage, he had waited for Robert's arrival. Rogers seems to have felt that even if his project never materialized, it would be important to have accurate maps of the interior. Carver was told to report at Michilimackinac in the late summer.

On 8 April Rogers' rehearing opened in New York. In twelve articles he presented a claim for over twelve thousand pounds. Both Barrington and Conway had indicated that a liberal view was to be taken of the claim; obviously Amherst would have paid him had it been in perfect order. But Gage was openly convinced before the hearings began that Rogers had no justified claim and the military commission reflected his opinion.

The commissioners found as Gage expected. No standards were relaxed; diligent efforts were made to find flaws in Rogers' proof. These had existed in '61; now five years later, they had multiplied. The board's long opinion found only one minor matter in Rogers' favor—a sop to prove its fairness. Gage undoubtedly took satisfaction in sending a copy to Barrington. To Rogers he suddenly bared his iron hand. The major, given only an inkling of the finding, asked for a copy. Gage flatly refused, thereby denying Rogers an opportunity to answer the alleged defects while documents and witnesses were on hand. Indeed it seems that Rogers was not allowed even to see the report. Gage later said he had told Rogers that 'any one Lawyer of Credit and Reputation shou'd have the Perusal of the Report' but never deigned to explain why a copy was refused Rogers. The latter could send a complaint

to Barrington but could not await an answer. His witnesses
scattered and his post in the west demanded his presence.
Gage apparently never made the slightest move toward
securing Rogers a captaincy in the Royal Americans as
ordered by Barrington. Swallowing his disappointment, Rogers left for New Hampshire to pick up his wife and then to
proceed to Johnson Hall on the first leg of the long trip to
Michilimackinac. Then occurred one of the most fantastic
incidents in his life. In New York General Gage was handed
a letter which purported to reveal Robert Rogers to be a
traitor.

British army officers had not allowed the '63 peace treaty
to alter their hatred of the French. To them the recent disturbances caused by the Stamp Act and the threats of dissatisfied
manor-tenants to burn New York were French-inspired. In
late April 1766 a French sailing vessel bound for France from
San Domingo put into New York harbor. That it should arrive 'during these very Extraordinary and very Reb—ll—s
Disturbances' did not seem a coincidence; British army headquarters sniffed suspiciously at the excuse of bad weather.
    Suddenly the distrust appeared justified. A 'Gentleman'
brought several letters to General Gage.[3] They had been
delivered to him by a passenger from the French vessel who
had explained that they were from 'Mr. Hopkins.' This
obviously meant Joseph Hopkins, the former commander of
the Queen's Rangers who had gone over to the French when
the home government in England failed to extend him what
he felt to be his just deserts. Gage opened the letters carefully; rumors flew about their contents and intended recipients. Except for one, Gage never revealed their contents or
the names of their recipients. Indeed he was evasive about
the number: at one time he said 'two'; on another occasion,
'three'; and again 'four or five.' With one exception he

protected the reputation of the recipients: they were 'Gentlemen of good Character.' The exception was Robert Rogers.

The letter to Rogers was a rambling one, assuring Robert that if he preached independence to the New Englanders and ingratiated himself to the Indians, he would be rewarded by the French government. It went to curious extremes to make its secret character obvious: the anonymous signature 'Maryland' and the caution 'write me fully without signing your name.' It pointedly reminded the recipient of his intimacy with the writer and of their many mutual friends whose loyalty to the British might be dubious. Naïve and discursive, it bore little resemblance to the terse, obscure communications between traitors. Strange that the writer wrote it on such thin paper that its contents could be read by holding it up to the light. Strange, too, were the open declaration by the passenger delivering the letters that they were from Hopkins; the mention in the letter that Maryland was his home province and the request in the postscript that the answer be directed to Hopkins by name. Strange, indeed, was the delivery of the letters to a man whose first impulse was to run to General Gage. All evidence points to the conclusion that the letter was designed to damn Rogers in the eyes of others.

Gage was interested only in the opportunity to entrap the major.[4] He had a certified copy made for his records and then forwarded the resealed original to Sir William Johnson together with a request to deliver it to Rogers. He added mysteriously:

I am likewise to beg of you, for very particular Reasons, which I can't now mention, that you will give the strongest Orders to your Interpreters and Commissarys to watch Major Roger's Transactions with the Indians and that they send you Information if he holds any bad Conversation with them . . . I hope no such thing will happen, if it does, it will be chiefly at the Detroit, particularly with Pondiac, Tho' if he begins there, he will no doubt do the same at Missilimakinak. Your People should keep their Instructions secret and not divulge what you write them on this Subject.

Johnson needed no such orders: he had done this on his own initiative months previously.

In the meantime Robert and his wife had arrived at Johnson Hall and on 3 June the former received Sir William's written instructions for dealing with the Indians. Rogers was to tell the Indians that his orders originated from Sir William, who would issue all orders concerning Indian affairs. Learn to know the important men, he was told; learn their sentiments; avoid giving any umbrage to them; prevent quarrels between them and soldiers or traders; earn their confidence and esteem; discover any plots they may be hatching.

Rogers was neatly placed on the horns of a dilemma. If he fed the Indians food of 'the worse Sort' as Gage ordered, he would certainly offend them, contrary to Johnson's instructions. More than that, Indian diplomacy meant presents and presents meant expense. Robert frankly told Johnson that he wanted (to quote Sir William) 'some Latitude in the Articles of Expences, which I did not then nor since think myself Justifiable in granting him, but on the contrary during a long conversation gave him such Verbal orders as I apprehended would have been a sufficient caution to him to avoid such Expences. . . .'

Rogers and Elizabeth left Johnson Hall early in June for Michilimackinac. They went to Fort Oswego, by boat to Fort Niagara and then by portage and boat to new Fort Erie on the west bank of the Niagara River, 'a pretty little fort . . . in a small bay on a low fertile soil environed with most kinds of wood of an immense Size & height.' Here they met Pontiac en route easterly for a conference with

Johnson at Oswego. 'We smoked a pipe together & drank a
bottle of wine,' wrote Rogers to Johnson, faithfully reporting
in accordance with his instructions.[5] Betsey seems to have
been happy with her first contact with the frontier: 'she was
much taken with every place she past through on her way to
Mishilamachnac,' wrote her mother.

On 10 June Johnson received Gage's letter enclosing the
Hopkins letter. The thinness of the latter's paper was an open
invitation which Johnson did not decline. In a tizzy of excitement he dashed off a note to Gage alluding to 'a verry extra-
eordinary & alarming Discovery not to be mentioned at this
time' which made an immediate conference at Albany necessary. Gage answered, telling him that he knew what the
enclosure contained. Johnson made a copy of the letter for
himself and sent the original after Rogers. Both then bided
their time.

On 14 July Elizabeth and Robert left Fort Erie on board
the schooner *Charlotte* under Captain Lewis Gage, bowling
along 'with a fine wind.' At Detroit they probably met Carver,
who had arrived on 13 July. Soon the schooner *Gladwin*,
Captain Patrick Sinclair commanding, was carrying the two
northward toward Michilimackinac, the center of Robert's
hopes and dreams.

XVII
1766–1767

'Major Rogers . . . Is Vastly Liked and Applauded'

ON 10 August the *Gladwin* rounded the northernmost point
of the peninsula separating Lake Huron and Lake Michigan and ahead, on a barren sandy beach near the sparkling
water, was a small, weatherbeaten stockade surrounding a
few houses, fur-traders' sheds and a church: the eagerly
awaited Michilimackinac. Robert Rogers probably saw the
unimpressive post through the golden haze of his dreams.
Although immediately enveloped in a swirl of military, Indian, and trade affairs, he did not forget his Northwest Passage project. His instructions for Carver were dated only
two days after his arrival although the latter did not arrive
until the 28th. They were couched in terms of mapping the
country for the Crown. Hired at eight shillings per diem,
Carver was to proceed to the Falls of St. Anthony on the
Mississippi, at present-day Minneapolis, via the northern
shore of Lake Michigan and Green Bay. En route he was
to map the country, noting the Indian towns and their popu-
lation. After wintering at the falls, he was to send his reports
to Rogers.

Should you receive Orders from me to March farther to the Westward with any other Detachment that I may send this fall or winter
you are to do it And send back your Journals by Mr. Browe

[Bruce?] or some other safe hand but should you not receive any, you are to return by the Ilum way [Illinois] River and from thence to St. Joseph And from thence along the East side of Lake Misigan to this place. . . .

On 2 September Carver left the fort in the fur brigade of Mr. Bruce, a Montreal trader, on the first leg of his voyage of exploration. Carver may have believed that he was venturing into an untracked wilderness as he later claimed. To the singing voyageurs paddling the gaily painted canoes of the brigade their course was a well-worn water trail over which French traders had passed for decades.

Ten days later Rogers drew up definite instructions for the discovery of the Northwest Passage. The difference between the cautiously worded orders to Carver and these tend to lend credence to the claim he later made that shortly after his arrival at Michilimackinac he had received letters from Dr. John Campbell and Charles Townshend telling him to proceed in this manner: '. . . nothing could Recommend me more to his Majesty and his Ministers than those Discoveries . . . .'[1]

Captain James Tute was named leader of the party to discover the Passage 'if any such Passage there be' or in the alternative, 'the great River Ourigon that falls into the Passific Ocean about the Latitude Fifty.' Tute was to winter near the Falls of St. Anthony, pick up Carver as cartographer, and strike off in the spring to the northwest. He was to pass the second winter at 'Fort La Parrie,'[2] where a supply of goods would be sent to him.

From Fort La Parrie you will Travel West bearing to the Northwest and do your endeavor to fall in with the great River Ourgan [sic] which rises in several different branches between the Latitudes of Fifty Six and Forty Eight and runs Westward for near three hundred Leagues, when it is at no great distance from each other joyn'd by one from the South, and a little up the Stream by one from the North; about these forkes you will find an Inhabited Cuntry and Great Riches. . . .

The great river flowed into a bay of the sea which was also 'Suppos'd to have a Communication with the Hudson's Bay about the Latitude of Fifty nine near Dobsie's point. . . .' Tute was promised not only eight shillings a day salary but also a share in the reward offered by the British government for the Passage's discovery. Rogers' final words also bear out his claim that Townshend encouraged his action:

You are strictly commanded to make your Report to me at your Return, wherever I may be, Or in case of my Death to the Honorable Charles Townshend, or in case of both our Deaths to the Honorable Lords of Trade and Plantations, and for so doing this shall be your Sufficient Warrant and Instructions. . . .

For the first time in his career Rogers was not leading the expedition which carried his hopes into the unknown. He had tried to inspire Tute to face difficulties with 'Courage and Resolution.' 'Behave . . . like a man that is Devoted to his King, and Brave out every difficulty. . . .' But words were a poor substitute for his personal leadership.[3]

James Stanley Goddard, 'secretary' to Tute's expedition, commenced his duties five days after the orders were drawn up:

Wednesday morning about 6 o'clock the 17th September, 1766, set out in a Bark Canoe with Goods & proper necessaries from Michilimackinac with a light Breese from the North East up Lake Mishagan. . . .

Robert Rogers had plenty with which to busy himself. In his own words:

The Command was of a nice and Critical nature, I was not only to hold the Ballance of Justice between His Majesty's Subjects and the Savages, but likewise to preserve Harmony and Peace between the different Nations of Savages, whose perpetual broils were obstructive of Trade: Moreover I had to Govern a Garrison of His Majesty's Officers and Soldiers with a great number of the English as well as The lately Conquered French Traders, and Inhabitants, whose different Interests Diametrically clashed with each other. In this critical Situation, but resolutely undaunted in the Service of my Sovereign I was determined no thing should deter me from my Duty.

He omitted two important matters: the web of opposition spun by General Gage and Sir William Johnson, the extent of which he probably did not realize, and the clash at Michilimackinac of invisible but powerful interests battling for control of the fur trade of North America. The central figure in both was Sir William Johnson; through him they intermingled.

Sir William's power rested primarily on his position as Superintendent of the Northern Indians. This institution first arose out of the exigencies of war. In 1754 the French seemed on the verge of turning the Iroquois against the English. Until the ensuing war ended, Johnson's main role was countering French Indian diplomacy—at first simply with the Iroquois and then gradually with adjoining tribes.

Peace brought another problem. The slightest contact with the civilization of the white man robbed the Indians of their independence: they could not live without guns, axes, kettles, blankets, and even clothing. When the war's result became certain, Indians deserted the French in droves and turned to hunting furs and skins for barter. Inexorably they were drawn into the nexus of trade which bound them to the civilized world. The once proud lords of forest and mountain became exploited drudges in a cold mercantile economy.

Problems of trade began to appear. Although the army held most of the French posts, Amherst at first left all controls to Johnson. With the end of hostilities on the continent, Amherst seems to have decided to step into the picture. Early in 1761 he proclaimed an 'Open and free Trade with the Indian Nations' and instructed Johnson to promulgate certain regulations to protect the Indians. In August the latter had them ready: all traders were to be licensed, all trade to be restricted to the posts, schedules stipulated the quality and quantity of goods to be exchanged for Indian peltry.

The provisions of the Proclamation of 1763 clearly gave the home government the power to make trade regulations. Even prior to this date it had instituted inquiries through the Board of Trade designed to be the basis of a system to manage Indian trade. In 1764 Lord Hillsborough and the Board circulated a plan, one of whose provisions provided for Indian commissaries at the various posts, subordinates to the superintendent who would represent the government in all political transactions with the Indians and enforce the trade regulations under the superintendent's supervision. But the plan died a-borning: Lord Shelburne was a free trader at heart; Canadian traders and colonial governors joined forces to curtail the growing power of Sir William Johnson; the law would require a revenue-raising act and the ministry had no desire to face another Stamp Act crisis.

Sir William naturally favored the scheme. When official enactment did not immediately follow, he began to make his own regulations. Gage acquiesced and the rules seemed official. In fact Sir William mesmerized himself to the point that he began to prate of royal approval. Lord Hillsborough sharply brought him back to reality, but the unofficial character was not widely recognized in America.

Rogers seems to have been one of the few to know this fact. He dared to challenge the legality of Sir William's rules.

Undoubtedly he did not do this as a lone individual; he had thrown his fortunes in with a group bold enough to oppose Johnson: the Montreal traders.

Fur trade was of little economic importance to any of the colonies except the Hudson's Bay Company's territory, Canada, and New York. During the period under discussion the field of operations of the Hudson's Bay Company did not conflict with the other two to any great extent, but New York and Canada faced each other over a common border and fought over the same furs. The trade's importance may be illustrated by the fact that over half of the value of Canada's exports to England since 1760 was represented by furs and furs were more than a quarter of the total value of New York's exports.

One principal feature of Johnson's regulations revealed his self-interest. He sought to confine all trade to two posts, Niagara and Oswego. These were the mouths of a funnel whose neck was the Mohawk Valley and which emptied into New York City. Canada was left out entirely. Johnson's beloved Iroquois acted as middlemen—which directly or indirectly contributed to his personal advantage, and the New York merchants, his faithful supporters, were obvious beneficiaries. When Detroit and Michilimackinac came under British rule, Johnson reluctantly included the former, but it was some time before he agreed to include Michilimackinac.

Michilimackinac was unique among the posts. In most areas dominated by an adjacent fort, the Indians lived and hunted near by; it was easy for neighboring Indians to come into Niagara or Oswego. But Michilimackinac supplied far-off regions. From the beginning, French traders—principally from Montreal—had sent their agents to winter with distant Indians. British officers were inclined to follow the practice, but Johnson complained that it would allow the traders to impose on the Indians with impunity. To some extent this was true, but to enforce Johnson's rule restricting trade to the post meant not only financial disaster to the traders at Michilimackinac but also untold hardship on distant Indians who were dependent on white man's goods but unable to make the long journey to the fort.

Gage's support of Johnson's regulations impelled Montreal traders in March 1765 to petition the governor of Quebec province, James Murray, and his council, requesting the removal of the 'impediments' to the trade. If the fur trade was ruined, they warned, it would mean lower imperial revenue and less consumption of goods—particularly woolens—manufactured in Great Britain. They objected to two features of Johnson's rules: the 'Enormous Security demanded of the Traders' and 'The absolute Prohibition to Trade out of the Forts and Posts. . . .' The situation at Michilimackinac was detailed and the traders claimed that failure to supply the Indians with necessaries would disgust them, revive old quarrels, and 'kindle afresh the flames of War.'

Murray seems to have considered all fur traders a parcel of scoundrels and refused to lift a finger for them. It was true that the petty traders who followed the Indians into the wilderness were often as uncivilized as their customers. But these demi-savages were but the bitter end of a long chain by which the precious skins passed from the forest to middlemen at the forts, then to lace-bedecked merchants in Montreal and New York and into the hands of prosperous and influential London merchants. All were 'fur traders.'

Dissatisfaction with local response to their appeals caused the Canadian traders to set up a powerful lobby in London to combat Johnson and the New York merchants. Their legal representative, Fowler Walker, was hired in April 1765. While no evidence has been found connecting Rogers with Fowler and his group when the former was in London, Robert undoubtedly was sought out by them when his name was connected with Michilimackinac. The strength of this group must not be underestimated. The Montreal traders were men of affairs with substantial business relations with wealthy London merchants. The exports from Great Britain to Quebec province were important to the economy of the mother country. The imports of fur were raw, again advantageous to Great Britain. In addition Indian trade promised to increase if carried to distant tribes. In turn, more manufactured goods would be required. This brought the weight of the mercantile elements in Great Britain solidly behind the Canadian merchants. Government officials were undoubtedly subject to considerable pressure from these groups. Rogers was probably told quite plainly by the officials behind his appointment what he was expected to do.

Robert's predecessor at Michilimackinac, Captain John Howard, had brought a storm down on his head when he modified Johnson's restriction of trade to the post. Indian threats to turn to the Spanish and French traders west of the Mississippi induced Howard to allow a selected few to winter among them. The less fortunate traders complained, even to England, and there was talk that Howard had reaped a handsome profit for his favoritism. He was under this cloud when relieved by Rogers.

Rogers received no instructions from Gage about Johnson's trade regulations. Although originally in favor of them the general had begun to waver, perhaps due to a surprised realization that the home government was little inclined to make Johnson's rules official. Now he was rather impartial, asking only that when new regulations were made, that they be accompanied by a law to compel observance of them, vesting the power of enforcement in the fort commanders.

The traders gave Rogers a warm welcome to Michilimackinac, and he in turn promised to reconcile the Indians and to put the trade on a proper footing. They followed it up with a complaint of their treatment under Captain Howard. Finding that a number of the traders had gone out to winter among the Indians, Rogers—as reported to Johnson—'immediately without hesitation, gave a general permit to all Traders to go wintering, for which he is vastly liked and applauded there.'

Johnson, who had just finished complaining that 'them people at Michilimacinac taking such liberty will upset all order, & every regulation at the other Posts,' must have been infuriated. Gage agreed with him. Yet within a month the general was telling Shelburne that restricting the trade to the posts 'is found upon Tryal not to Answer . . . The Posts cannot be multiplied to the Degree Necessary to compleat it. From hence the Traders complain that they are prevented from getting the Quantitys of Furs, they could procure from Nations who live at a great Distance from the Posts, were they not restrained from going to them; which gives the French Traders an advantage. . . . It is also so contrary to the old Custom of Trade, and no People [are] more Attached to Custom, than the Indians . . . the Indians are in general way very averse to the Plan. . . .'

Johnson could make no official complaint about unofficial regulations; Gage took no official notice of Rogers' action. It was allowed to stand.

Now Rogers turned to the task of improving relations with the various Indian tribes who, the traders warned, were on the verge of discontent. Emissaries were sent to them notifying them of Rogers' appointment and of the friendship of the King. Soon the Indians were putting his ability to deal with them to the test. The Ottawa at L'Arbre Croche, a village southwest of the fort, sent him wampum belts to hasten his visit to them. On 22 September when he arrived they told him that they had been informed that a French army had landed at the mouth of the Mississippi ready to march northward in the spring to seize the western posts and then to move to Niagara where it would join an army which was to land in New York. Rogers chided them for 'such romantick foolish stories' and assured them that the Spaniards owned west of the Mississippi. 'Be strong & wise behave like men & dont fall like a foolish Child into the fire. . . .'

The Indians now flocked to the fort. A conference on 26 September with a party of Chippewa headed by seven chiefs was followed on 10 October by a meeting with almost a hundred Ottawa. Rogers gave presents liberally while reproving them for the ever-reappearing story of the French invasion. On 15 October two chiefs of the Ottawa and twenty-six of their people came in and tried a different approach with a claim that they were hungry and poor. Too often British post commanders were disgusted by such begging, failing to recognize that it was a formal, ritualistic speech well recognized in Indian diplomacy. Rogers understood and knew what was expected. The Indians were pleased.

October saw the Indians around Michilimackinac beginning to move southerly to their winter quarters. En route they stopped at the fort. Some Chippewa braves came in on 10 November from a raid on the Dakota and Rogers began to talk of halting this age-old war. His ability to let the Indians know that he was not being deceived by their tales without insulting or offending them is well illustrated by his remarks to a Missisauga chieftain who came in on 12 December supposedly bearing intelligence of great value. It turned out to be the old story of two thousand French troops at New Orleans. Rogers bluntly told him: 'You tell me the news I suppose with a design to get some rum. I give you this charge at the same time, & tell you I think it a bad way to get drink; by telling french stories for I know that what they have told you is Lies. . . .' The usual post commandant would have had the Indian kicked out of the fort. Rogers knew that diplomacy required him to give the savage the desired rum (three gallons in fact) as well as other gifts; the Indian in turn knew that Rogers was giving him these purely for diplomatic reasons and not because the tale fooled the commander of Michilimackinac.

The record of his various conferences was carefully submitted to Sir William Johnson in accordance with his instructions. It was not what Sir William wanted nor was the news from his own agent in Montreal who reported: 'The Traders that came from there [Michilimackinac] told me also that his [Rogers'] behavior towards the Indians was and is approved of by them, as well as the people of that place.'

XVIII
1767

'A Barrier . . . a Beacon . . . a Storehouse'

THE first sign of spring at Michilimackinac was the return of
the Indians from their winter retreats. Rogers was happy to
see them, hoping they were the foreshadows of the multitude
he expected in a few months. In an effort to halt the inter-
tribal wars, particularly the conflict between the Chippewa
and Dakota, which hampered the fur trade, the preceding
fall he had begun to promote a peace conference. Carver and
Tute had had instructions to urge Indian leaders met on their
journeys, to come to Michilimackinac in the late spring. The
successful meetings in the fall and the free use of gifts by
Rogers made the Indians eager to come, and by the end of
May hundreds were flocking to the small post.

Most came by canoe. It must have been like the gathering
in 1775 described the fur trader, Peter Pond. The tribes assembled at the bottom of Green Bay and embarked in a vast
canoe flotilla for their destination.

The way ther was fair and plesant we all proseaded together
across Lake Mishiagan at the end of two days we all apeard on the
lake about five miles from Macenac and aprocht in order. We had
flags on the masts of our canoes—eavery chefe his flock. My canoes
bearing the largest in that part of the cuntrey and haveing a large

Youon [Union] flage I histed it and when within a mile and a half
I took ye lead and the Indians followed close behind. The flag in
the fort was histed—ye cannon of the garrison began to play
smartly—the shores were lind with people of all sorts who seat up
such a crey and hooping that seat the tribes in the fleat a going to
that degrea that you could not hear a parson speak. At length
we reacht ye shore and the cannon seasd.

First to come in were the near-by tribes: Potawatomi,
Chippewa, Ottawa, and Missisauga. On 15 June Rogers held
a grand council with them and asked their aid in making
peace. To their pledges of help and co-operation, Rogers
returned his thanks and requested that they stay to help in
'Brightening the chain of Peace that might extend through
all the Nations & Tribes of Indians from the Rising to the
Seting Sun.'

To show his confidence in their pledge Rogers dared to send
Chippewa to escort the Dakota to Michilimackinac as the
more distant tribes came in. Beginning on 15 June the major
held a series of separate conferences with individual bands
'in which I could not help but observe a pretty general Hostile
Temper . . . There had been Injuries Provocations and Blood-
shed on both sides. . . .'

Finally on 2 July outside the fort's wooden walls was held
the 'Grand Council' with the principal men of all bands. '. . .
After many Short Speeches Replys and Rejoinders of no great
consequence,' reported Rogers, 'it appeared that there was
a general disposition to peace . . . which I had before recommended to them Separately—.' Then the red-stone pipe of
peace with its dangling white feathers was brought in, Rogers
lit it and he and the chiefs 'smoked [it] with the Formality
usual on such occasions. . . .' All exchanged 'the Strongest
assurances of Friendship and Love . . . and [promised] to use
their utmost endeavors to prevent mischief on all sides for the

future and to live in Harmony Concord and good Agreement like Brethern and Children of the same Father, begging that they might be all Treated as children in Common, have Traders sent amongst them and be Supplyed with necessary goods in their Several distant Villages and Hunting grounds which I assured them should be done. . . .' Then 'some Refreshments were distributed'—probably diluted rum—and the council was over.

The Indians looked forward to the next day when presents were distributed. Corn, cloth, tobacco, bear oil, flags, rum, and other traditional gifts of Indian diplomacy were given out by Rogers. Although his purchases for the period from 24 June to 3 July totalled about £3775, twenty-eight of the English and French traders put together goods worth about £500 for additional presents. 'We are apprehensive that the presents Allotted by His Majesty for the Indians was insufficient at so Critical a Juncture, and Therefore' they asked Rogers to give out their donation 'in His Majesty's name. . . .'

It was a successful council: over a thousand Indians came in. Familiar names are jumbled with strange in Rogers' list of the bands present: Foxes or Renards from the upper Fox River; 'St. Marys' (Chippewa from Sault St. Marie); 'Menomeneys' (Menominee from Green Bay); 'Kawmeenipte geaus' (probably Chippewa from the Kaministiquia River on Lake Superior's northwest shore); 'Wood Lake' (Chippewa from the Lake of the Woods); 'La Point' (Chippewa from La Point on the southwestern tip of Madeline Island in Lake Superior); 'Sauchs' (Sauk from the Wisconsin River); 'Puans' (Winnebago from southwest of Green Bay on the Fox River); 'Rain Lake' (Chippewa near Rainy Lake); 'Nippy gong' (Nipissing or Chippewa from Lake Nipigon); 'Winneepeek' (Cree from Lake Winnipeg); 'Minnewake' (mixed Foxes, Mascouten, and Potawatomi from near the site of modern Milwaukee); 'Souix' (Dakota from the Mississippi, near what is now southern Minnesota, northwestern Wisconsin, and neighboring areas of Iowa.)

Some Indians could not believe the word that there was an English post commander who welcomed Indians. Cree from between the Red and Saskatchewan Rivers ventured down as far as Grand Portage but no farther. They had been to Michilimackinac. Captain Howard, Rogers' predecessor, had 'kicked their Belts [of wampum] around and used them very ill.' They missed the council, certain in their belief that no successor would be different.

Rogers never saw Michilimackinac as a small, dusty post with the tainted smell of raw furs and skins. To him it was a center of colorful excitement destined to be the shining capital of a separate government. A lengthy memorandum dated 27 May 1767, set forth his views. The fur trade at Michilimackinac, he wrote, was beneficial to manufacturing and shipping of Great Britain as well as the merchants of Quebec Province. It helped to keep the Indians friendly. Traders must be allowed to go among them, he argued, repeating the familiar arguments and adding, 'Who can say what valuable Discoveries may at one time or another be made. . . ?' In at least one spot his prose revealed his dream:

It need not surely be repeated that the Case of Michilimackinac is very different, this is the Outside or Frontier British Post in America. It is, or ought to be a Barrier to all that come Westerly, South-Westerly, or North-Westerly, to the Pacific Ocean; It is or ought to be a Beacon, from which a most Extensive and as yet unknown Territory is watched and Observed. It is or ought to be a Store House fraught with all manner of Necessarys, for the constant supply of almost innumerable Bands, Tribes, and Nations of Savages . . . removed from it, Five, Six and Eight hundred, and some a Thousand Leagues, who cannot annually nor ever in their Lives visit it as a Markett, they must lose one years Hunt to make sale of another, they must leave their Familys distress'd ... [and] exposed to Enemys and perhaps perish themselves with hunger and Want, on their Way. ...

A series of rhetorical questions led to the conclusion that Michilimackinac and the territory dependent on it should be made a separate government with its own governor, lieuten-ant-governor, and council of twelve. The council, chosen from the principal merchants, would enact all necessary laws. The governor would be both commander of a 'Body of Light Troops—or Rangers, well disciplined ...' and supreme Indian agent. Rogers urged that a fixed annual sum be set for In-dian presents in keeping with the importance of a post to which, he estimated, more than a third of the Indians in North America reverted, 'besides many of the other Nations to the Westward as far as the Pacific Ocean, may be induced to visit and trade with us. ...' Rogers talked in terms of a continent at a time when the Appalachians seemed to limit all consider-ation to a narrow strip along the Atlantic.

While obviously far from a well-considered plan of govern-ment, Rogers' proposal pointed out a problem which the British government seemed to be trying to believe nonexist-ent. The Proclamation of 1763 had left a huge territory—roughly bounded on the north by the Hudson's Bay Com-pany's territory, easterly by the Alleghenies, southerly by the Floridas, and westerly by the Mississippi—without any form of civil government. There were reasons for this: it would please the Indians, discourage settlers, and keep settlements on the coast. But the plan overlooked the communities at Michilimackinac and Detroit, near modern St. Louis and Vincennes, and the traders in the region. There was no control over civilians until 1765, when a clause was inserted in the Mutiny Act authorizing any person to arrest criminals and empowering military officers to send the prisoners to the nearest colony—a poor solution, to say the least. Petitions for civil government were finding their way to London. Rogers' suggestion was timely, whatever may be argued about its wisdom.

The Michilimackinac traders backed him to a man. A letter whose signers are a roll-call of names famous in the annals of the Northwest fur trade: Alexander Henry, Isaac Todd, James Finlay, Ezekiel Solomon, Gershom Levy, Henry Bostwick, John Chinn, Forrest Oaks, James McGill, and others— recommended it and urged that the Montreal and Quebec merchants approve and send it 'properly represented' to the Board of Trade. Rogers made no attempt to hide his personal interest and drew up a memorial to the Board of Trade asking for his appointment as governor of Michilimackinac.

Alexander Baxter, Jr. carried the plan to England. He had been sent over from England—some said by the Board of Trade but more probably by Charles Townshend and others— to investigate the supposed copper mines on Lake Superior's shores. Cadotte had been into the interior with Henry Bostwick and had brought out ore samples which impressed Baxter. But the story of the British attempt to mine these copper deposits—although initiated by Rogers—is not a part of Rogers' life.

Rogers' plan never received anything but ridicule. Mails and messengers moved slowly; by the time it was under consideration, other events had overtaken it and passed it by. Rogers was then under a cloud and Johnson could blast it as 'a scheme for establishing a needy man, of bad circumstances and worse principles in the first authority, and for the next branch of the legislature of such traders as are at outposts . . . too absurd to deserve any comment. . . .' It threatened part of Sir William's authority and domain.

Rogers may not have noticed the invisible web spun around

him by Gage and Johnson. Besides his contacts among traders and Indian agents Johnson implanted suspicion of Rogers' actions in officers going to Michilimackinac. He had an ideal opportunity; Johnson Hall was a place whose famed hospitality attracted anybody bound to the frontier. On his part Gage made no effort to pay Rogers the salary as ordered— an ideal way to break a man morally—and made no motion to secure a captaincy for Rogers in the Royal Americans as suggested by the secretary at war to add to Rogers' income. He showed his feeling toward Rogers in other ways as well. As early as 24 August 1766 Rogers requested a garrison doctor because of illness being rife among the newly arrived Royal Americans. Gage answered in November that he should have made the request through his superior in Detroit. Winter delayed this answer: on 12 February 1767 Rogers was repeating his request to Gage. Receiving Gage's orders he applied to Turnbull at Detroit. The latter answered that he needed an order from Gage, but made no apparent answer to it. Desperately Rogers sent this information to Gage but the latter paid no attention.

Rogers probably had suspicions from the first that Gage and Johnson were far from happy about his appointment; he was made certain when during the Indian conference one of Johnson's Indian commissaries, Benjamin Roberts, arrived and told him that he was assigned to Michilimackinac. Astounded, Rogers wrote that Roberts told him that his appointment had been approved by General Gage. 'This step makes one think they may be some Jealousy of me by those two Gentlemen. . . .'

Although affairs at Michilimackinac were progressing smoothly under Rogers, Johnson was dissatisfied. He wanted one of his commissaries at Michilimackinac, not treating Rogers as any appointee of his. He pressed Gage: 'for several

reasons it should be well and duely inspected.' Gage avoided
any direct consent but his admission that 'Michillimackinac
seems to be the most material Post we have & certainly more
necessary for a Comissary than any other' was seized by
Johnson as tacit consent. In mid-March 1767 Benjamin
Roberts was named to the post.

Sir William could have named a no more effective trouble-
maker. Roberts had come to America with the army, but after
an unhappy time—Gage said he was 'in bad circumstances'—
he became acquainted with Johnson's oldest son and through
him solicited a position in the Indian department. Johnson
appointed him commissary at Fort Niagara; years later Sir
William said he did it more as a favor to his son than
for any other reason. Roberts—to quote a London correspondent of Sir William—'had an astonishing tincture of Vanity in
all He did. . . .' When he became Johnson's commissary, his
ego knew no bounds.

The concept of a commissary's role at a fort demanded
close co-operation between the commandant and the commissary but was certain to break down when the commissary
used the position to flaunt his power over former superior
officers. In July 1766 Roberts became involved in a violent
quarrel with Captain Jonathan Rogers at Fort Ontario at
the time of Pontiac's conference with Sir William. At Niagara
he locked horns with Captain John Brown, whose volumin-
ous file of correspondence with Gage over this point illustrates
his complete frustration by the presence of Roberts. What
Captain Brown would have finally done is anyone's guess:
at the height of the crisis his irritant was ordered back to
Johnson Hall for instructions preparatory to going to Michilimackinac. When word got around about the appointment
there were undoubtedly grins of anticipation about the next
quarrel Roberts would invoke. 'I hope the Garrison may have
more quiet in this than his last administration,' wrote one

Michilimackinac trader on hearing that Roberts was on his way.

Roberts' briefing from Johnson illustrates the latter's dramatic tactics designed to impress his audience with Rogers' alleged wickedness. The commissary later told how:

Sir William Johnson took him into his closet and Shewed him the Copy of a Letter Captain Hopkins had wrote to Major Rogers. . . . Sir William informed the Deponent, that Major Rogers had acknowledged to him the receipt of this letter, but had not communicated any part of the Contents to him or to the General; therefore, in the General's Name as well as his own, and to that effect he had since received a Letter from the General under his own hand, he desired him to look out, whether any part of the Advice conveyed in said Letter was put into execution; to enquire into the Councils that had been already, or might hereafter be held; that Major Rogers had made very great Expences, which was displeasing to the General, and that several unfavourable Reports had come from Michilimackinac; not to mention it to any one, except he saw Matters carried to extremely, and to apply to the commanding Officer of the Troop, in case of Need.

Johnson was giving Roberts a keg of gunpowder, a fuse, and a match.

What Johnson told Roberts about Rogers' expenses was not true at the time it was spoken. Rogers' accounts had started to come in. They were carefully certified and accompanied by vouchers. Johnson could do nothing but pay them, although he grumbled about the 'exorbitant prices' paid to the traders. Gage wrote Johnson in April complaining about the commissaries in general. 'Instead of Retrenching their Expences they seem to increase; and some of them so high without Authority, that they are far beyond any Expences that I am permitted to contract without Application, and Leave obtained So to do. The Expences of the Illinois, contracted by Mr. Croghan, Smallman and now Mr. Cole can not be bore. I am glad Major Rogers Acc't. are properly vouched, and hope the rest are likewise vouched, without which they should not be paid.'

When Gage learned that Johnson was sending Roberts as commissary to Michilimackinac he asked that Roberts inform Rogers that he was to incur no further expenses on Indian affairs and instructed Johnson not to pay any more drafts drawn on him by Rogers. A letter with a similar message was also sent directly to Rogers from headquarters. Rogers did not receive this news until the Indian conference was about over. His accounts were still to be drawn up and sent to Sir William.

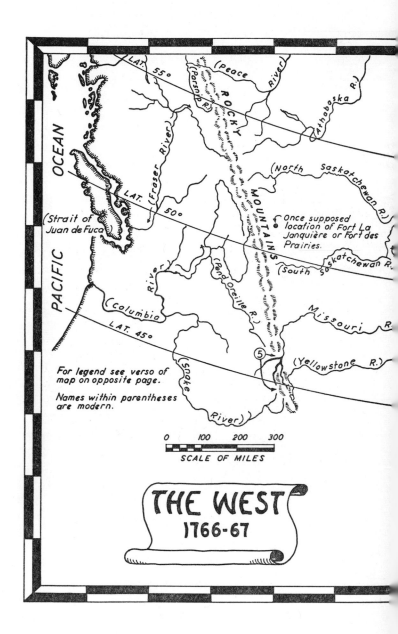

LAT. 55°

OCEAN

(Peace River)

Parsnip R.

ROCKY

Athobaska R.

(North Saskatchewan R.)

LAT. 50°

(Fraser River)

MOUNTAINS

Once supposed location of Fort La Janquière or Fort des Prairies.

(Strait of Juan de Fuca)

PACIFIC

(Pend Oreille R.)

(South Saskatchewan R.)

River

(Columbia)

Missouri R.

LAT. 45°

(5)

(Yellowstone R.)

For legend see verso of map on opposite page.

Snake

Names within parentheses are modern.

River)

| 0 | 100 | 200 | 300 |

SCALE OF MILES

THE WEST
1766-67

'Forts' northwest of Michilimackinac were merely trading posts; had no garrisons and were often mere ruins.

HUDSON

BAY

YORK or BOURBON R.

(Nelson R.)

RIVIÈRE DU PAS or PASQUIA RIVER (SASKATCHEWAN R.)

Ft. Paskoiac

Ft. Bourbon

③

Ft. de la Corne

Lac des Prairies

Ft. Bourbon or la Biche

LAKE BOURBON (L. WINNIPEG)

(LAKE WINNI-PEGOSIS)

GREAT LAKE WINNIPEG (L. WINNIPEG)

Fort des Prairies

Ft. (L. MANITOBA)

Ft. La Reine

ASSINIBOINE RIVER

L. OF THE WOODS

RAINY L.

Ft. St. Charles

Ft. St. Pierre

L. NIPIGON

Grand Portage

LAKE SUPERIOR

RED RIVER OF THE NORTH

CHIPPEWA R.

①

Cadot's Ft.

GREEN BAY

Falls of St. Anthony

④

②

BIG SIOUX R.

ST. PETERS R. (Minnesota R.)

OUISCONSIN R. (WISCONSIN R.)

FOX R.

Ft. La Baye

L'Arbre Croche

MISSOURI

RIVER

Prairie du Chien

MISSISSIPPI RIVER

Ft. St. Joseph

LAKE MICHIGAN

Fort Michilimackinac

LEGEND

(1)

APPROXIMATE location of tract purchased by Rogers from Chippewa 23 December 1760.

(2)

Both Carver and Tute followed the old trade route from Fort Michilimackinac along the northern shore of Lake Michigan, Fort La Baye, the Fox River, a portage and the Wisconsin River to Prairie du Chien. Tute's party wintered (1766–67) south of this point while Carver went up the Mississippi to the Minnesota River and wintered at (2). In May 1767 he rejoined Tute at Prairie du Chien and the expedition went northwards to the Chippewa River. Via this river, portages and other streams they made the south shore of Lake Superior and went around the west end to Grand Portage. Here the Northwest Passage project was abandoned and the hasty voyage back to Fort Michilimackinac followed the north shore of Lake Superior.

(3)

Rogers ordered Tute to winter (1767–68) at Fort des Prairies and then to 'Travel West, bearing to the North West and do your endeavour to fall in with the great River Ourigan which rises in several different branches between the Latitudes of Fifty Six and Forty Eight and runs Westward for near three hundred Leagues. . . .' After it is joined by other streams and continues another four hundred leagues, the 'Ourigan' discharges 'into an Arm or Bay of the Sea at near the Latitude of Fifty four and bends southerly and enters into the Pacific Ocean about Forty eight, nine or Fifty. . . .'

(4)

Rogers proposed in 1772 to follow Carver's route to the Minnesota River and then to proceed to the latter's source and cross via a portage of twenty miles 'into a Branch of the River Missouris, and ascend the same North-Westerly to its Source.'

(5)

At the Missouri's source Rogers claimed a portage of about thirty miles would bring the expedition to the 'great River Ourigan.' Compare to the Lewis and Clark route of 1804–05.

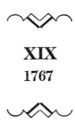

XIX
1767

'Seize . . . Major Robert Rogers as a Traitor'

THE long-awaited decision on the army claims arrived in early July from England. Not only did Barrington approve the denial of Rogers' claims but he also referred back to Gage the possibility of Rogers' being granted the King's Bounty. Rogers could only humbly write the commander in chief: 'I have only to beg you'll consider my Situation & whatever way You decide the matter in Question I shall rest satisfied; yet I pray you'll recommend my Case to his Majesty's bounty—.' He knew only too well what Gage's answer would be.

Benjamin Roberts had arrived late in June while the Indian conference was in progress: 'I never saw such hurry & confusion. . . .' For once he made no attempt to intervene between Rogers and the Indians and even reported to Gage: 'the peace he has Concluded will be an advantage to trade. . . .' Nevertheless he began to write Gage a series of complaints about Rogers. His assigned quarters were 'a wretched small room'; trading was in a disorganized state but he was restoring order; Rogers refused his request to grant the Indians free entry into the fort. There were fawning gestures to worm his way into Gage's good graces: 'I have taken the

Liberty to send Mrs. Gage an Otter Blanket . . . the greatest
Curiosity came here this Season . . . I hope hereafter to find
something more worthy. . . .' Later Mrs. Gage was sent 'a few
Brown Martins Amongst Several thousands that came from
the North West, which I was allow'd to Cull.'

About this time Rogers quarreled with his secretary,
Nathaniel Potter. The major apparently wanted Potter to take
his Michilimackinac proposals to England and Potter refused.
They parted company and Potter turned to Roberts with a
story that Rogers was planning to turn traitor. In high excitement the Indian commissary wrote Guy Johnson: 'Potter and
the Major have quarreled, he'll let me into all the Secrets he
knows. . . .' The 'secrets'—according to Roberts' version of Potter's story—were that Rogers was prepared to go over to the
French if not given independent control of Michilimackinac;
he had received 'another' letter from Captain Hopkins. He
would get part of the garrison to desert; Rogers was going out
next spring to meet Tute and his companions, who had orders
to get what they could in their hands, while Rogers on his part
was to 'take a Tour and Clean all the Coasts as he goes. . . .'
Roberts assured Guy Johnson that 'Every Appearance Talleys
so much with this information. . . .'

While in this excited state Roberts had his first clash with
Rogers over some rum seized when being taken out of the
fort without a proper pass. Rogers ordered it stored in the
'King's Provision Store' in the control of William Maxwell,
deputy commissary of the post. Roberts insisted he should
have custody; Rogers refused. This touched Roberts' megal-
omania: he told Rogers that he was not under his orders; he
wanted Maxwell's receipt; Rogers was interfering where he
had no right. Rogers curtly told him that he was being
impertinent at which Roberts blew up. He dared Rogers to
tell him this outside the fort; he was a 'gentleman' as good as

Rogers and if the latter would go fifty yards outside the fort, he would prove it.

Rogers asked the gaping spectators to note that Roberts had challenged him and ordered the Indian commissary to his room. Roberts refused, shouting he would not be ordered about by Rogers and if Rogers were not the commanding officer, he 'Dared as well be Damned as Order him to his Room.' Rogers hallooed for a file of soldiers. Roberts now called for Captain Spiesmacher, the post's second in command, who came running. Roberts appealed to him: 'they are a going to Murder me.' Spiesmacher advised him to go to his room. But Roberts refused and accused Rogers of high treason, asking Spiesmacher to arrest him: 'As the safety of the fort Depends upon you and as Commander of the Troops I order you to keep Major Rogers the Commandant in the Fort for he is a Dangerous Man and a Traitor and if you suffer him to go out of this fort you Never will see him again.'

Roberts' ravings were cut short when the soldiers carried him struggling and screaming to his room. When they set him down, he dodged by them and sprinted out onto the parade ground. There he met Spiesmacher, who told him that he was wrong and induced him to return to his room. He penned a note to Spiesmacher: 'I impeach Robert Rogers . . . for holding Secret Correspondence with the Enimies of Great Britain, & forming Conspiracies, I desire you in your Allegiance to Seize his person & papers. . . . I have now discharged my duty.' His pride bruised, he wrote a long memorial on the following day to Spiesmacher, asking for protection against the 'unheard of Violence' which had 'irreparably sullied' his military honor and civil character. He was—according to the memorial—protesting not simply on his own behalf but to uphold the dignity of his office to which Sir William Johnson had appointed him.

Roberts obviously thought Spiesmacher, like other officers,

had been told by Sir William Johnson of Rogers' evil intentions; this was not the case. When he realized his mistake, he allowed Spiesmacher to make peace, awkwardly explaining that his charges of treason arose simply because Rogers had sent him to his room and for no other reason.

Rogers wrote Gage, sounding like the other commandants who had had brushes with Roberts: 'I Beg you will be pleas'd to enform me what is the Authority Granted to Mr. Benjamin Roberts. . . in short he would if one might Believe him be Every thing and Even Commanding Officer too.' He enclosed many affidavits of witnesses to the fracas, many of which repeated Roberts' accusations of treason—a strange thing to do if he were a scoundrel secretly plotting against his country.

Roberts, too, wrote Gage. He did not breathe a word of Potter's accusations and his own suspicions. He merely said that he could not have acted otherwise 'without betraying the great trust reposed in me by you & Sir Wm. Johnson.' He was probably willing to let Potter break the news of the treason. The latter left Michilimackinac on 29 August, en route to Montreal.

On the day following Potter's departure Rogers suffered a crushing blow. Carver, Tute, and party came back, having given up the attempt to find the Northwest Passage. After wintering with the Dakota somewhere on the St. Pierre (Minnesota) River, Carver had trekked in May 1767 to Prairie du Chien on the Mississippi, where he found Tute, who had wintered further south. Tute delivered to him Rogers' orders to join Tute 'to find out the Great River Ourigan that runs into the South Sea and a Northwest Passage if Possible. . . .'

In two small canoes the party went up the Mississippi but when it came to the mouth of the Chippewa River, it proceeded up this river to the northeast rather than continuing up the Mississippi as Rogers had ordered. The men made their way to Lake Superior and followed its shores to Grand Portage without 'one Mouth full of Provisions left.' 'Captain Tute,' wrote Carver in his journal, 'Sent the interpreter with some other hands to Meet the Traders from Michilimackinac and to hurry them on as fast as possible for fear a Mutiny would break out . . . on account of our being in want of Provisions.' On 2 August four canoes came in and provisions were obtained.

On 7 August François Le Blanc came in, bound for Fort des Prairies and carrying a letter for Tute from Rogers. '. . .It is very bad to me that you did not send me in the Peltrys that you promised . . . and am astonished at your heavy Drafts on me, but that convinces me . . . you must have now Goods enough with you to compleat your Expedition. . . . I shall send some Boats up next Spring very Early, and desire, that you will push on your Journey with all Speed. . . .' Tute had no supplies; the letter hinted at Rogers' lack of finances; Le Blanc may have added fort gossip. Tute, Carver, and company could not get back to Michilimackinac fast enough. Rogers was disappointed; they in turn were enraged to find he could not pay them. Roberts gleefully reported the animosity flaring up between them. On this sad note ended the glorious dream of the golden prize of the West.

Roberts seized an opening on 17 September to renew his feud with Rogers. At the entrance to the Royal Americans' barracks he accosted Rogers with a request for quarters for the blacksmith assigned to the Indian service. Rogers offered the garrison shop until Roberts could find one, but Roberts wanted Rogers to provide it. One word led to another and another disgraceful verbal tilt followed. Finally Roberts fled to Spiesmacher, and when the latter failed to offer him protection he suffered the ignominy of being again led to his room by a guard. Now a sentry was posted there. He could not take this without a protest: he called out to a passerby to witness Rogers' refusal to allow him to continue his lawful business; he told his 'woman' in tones meant for the ears of the sentry that Rogers was instigating an Indian war to get himself out of debt and that he had broken out of jail before. The next day Roberts threatened to shoot the sentry. His bluster continued: somebody would hang for doing this to him. A memorial to Spiesmacher claimed that Rogers was acting contrary to the 'Constitution of great Britton.'

Rogers decided to send him 'down the Country' without Gage's permission. He told the latter that he could not continue to allow Roberts 'to stir up Mutiny in this place, and Make Parties and the ill and disrespectful Language he has given me. . . .' Spiesmacher asked him not to do this because of the lateness of the season but Rogers refused. Spiesmacher made no further attempt to interfere: he told Gage that before Roberts had appeared, and stirred up trouble, 'Merchants Traders and Indians seem'd well Sattisfy'd. . . .'

Roberts, afloat in a sea of self-pity with the news that he was about to be sent 'down the country,' composed a farewell worthy of a martyr bound for the stake. He was being sent in irons to Detroit 'all because I asked an Order in writing for a Forge.' He was the universal hero: 'All the Garrison Civil & Military have done every thing to prevent the usuage except Mutinying . . . all letters I fear are intercepted adieu think the only Satisfaction I have is Suffering in the Cause of my allegiance to my King & Friendship to my benefactor & friends. . . .' No letters were intercepted; in early October he left for Detroit and unfortunately for his sense of the dramatic there were no irons, no dangers. He arrived safely.

Michilimackinac became peaceful once more. John Askin, living on a farm southwest of the fort, invited Mrs. Rogers in a dignified manner: 'I Sincerely wish that the Major & you would Honour me with a visit the first good Weather.' One of the officers reported to Johnson on 28 October: 'Since Mr. Roberts left here Nothing Material has happened here.'

Elsewhere it was different. Roberts traveled eastward, spreading his falsehoods of the confusion at Michilimackinac and receiving the sympathy of his fellow commissaries. Jehu Hay at Detroit felt that Rogers' treatment of Roberts was utterly impossible 'to be shewn to one Gentleman from another.' Norman MacLeod at Niagara wailed: 'It seems we poor Commissarys are great Eye Sores to the Commandants I hope they will not have the liberty of using us in the manner Mr. Roberts had been treated with impunity.' It would have been interesting to have Captain Brown's comment on the subject.

Rogers' drafts on Johnson for the Indian conference were now being presented to Johnson, who sent his deputy, George Croghan, down to the general for a personal interview on the subject. What Croghan said may be surmised by a subsequent letter from Johnson to Gage in which Sir William said he heard that the bills exceeded £5000. He told Gage 'there must be some particular Motive' and commented on the 'more than ordinary apprehensions at present on account of the Indians.' 'I have reason to apprehend something more than common is in view, (which may not be a matter of Surprize to you). . . .' This was the signal Gage was waiting for. Croghan was sent westward with a complicated set of orders removing Rogers from his command which revealed the general's fears of Rogers' popularity with the garrison. On 21 September the general notified Sir William of his action and instructed him to dishonor Rogers' drafts.

On Sunday evening, 27 September, Daniel Claus, Johnson's local deputy and son-in-law, returned from Quebec to find Potter waiting for him with a packet of letters from Benjamin

Roberts, including on open one to Guy Johnson asking that Potter be examined under oath. The next day Claus took Potter before William Hey, Chief Justice for the Province of Quebec. The resulting affidavit was—to say the least—extraordinary. Potter swore that Rogers had confided in his secretary that if he did not get a separate government, he intended to retire 'to the French towards the Mississippi and to enter the Service of the French,' and to take all the goods he could 'by right or wrong he cared not how.' When Potter virtuously refused to join his scheme, Rogers flew into a rage and threatened Potter's life were he to reveal these plans. Potter described personal fights brought on by Rogers' violent temper. Potter concluded: 'Rogers seems to him to be cultivating an Interest with Indians, in order to retreat to them, when he shall execute his purpose of leaving the British service. . . .' This statement was a transparent mixture of half-truths, lies, insinuations, and suppositions. Guy Carleton, governor of Quebec, quickly saw its obvious weakness: 'Potter bears so bad a Character and it appears so very surprising that Major Rogers, after a confidential Avowal of no less than the Acme of high Treason, should Quarrel with the Person whom he had entrusted with so dangerous a Secret, and let him quietly slip through his Fingers, that it must stagger the Faith of even those who are most inclined to entertain Suspicions of Rogers' conduct from his General Character, and the very great Distress his Extravagancies have involved him in. . . .'

Ill, Potter pleaded his health as an excuse to avoid going southward to see Sir William Johnson or General Gage. Instead, sped onward by funds supplied by Governor Carleton, he boarded a ship for England. Mortally stricken at sea, he asked two shipmates, Henry Bostwick and Alexander Baxter—also from Michilimackinac—to take charge of his trunk and to account for his few effects to his family; he died and was buried at sea. What small effects he left were turned over

to London authorities who closely examined them but found
nothing shedding any light on the affair. But copies of the
dead man's affidavit were in the hands of Johnson, Gage, and
the home government.

Sir William was away when the affidavit reached Johnson
Hall. Guy Johnson opened it and at once hurried a letter to
Sir William. He in turn galloped back and on arrival dashed
off a note to Gage. To give his message an air of urgency he
wrote that the letters had just arrived, that Potter's affidavit
confirmed his suspicions and that the home authorities should
be informed. He turned his spleen on Rogers: '. . . a weak Vain
man; and however romantik his scheme may appear, I believe
him capable of undertaking it. . . .' To make things blacker
for Rogers, he added a falsehood: 'Potter with great difficulty
escaped from his [Rogers'] clutches and got to Montreal.'
Perhaps he sensed the obvious weakness discovered by
Carleton and wanted to cover it up.

Gage received his copy at midnight, 18 October, and—
overlooking any obvious weakness—considered it 'positive
Intelligence' of Rogers' intent to desert. He immediately
drafted orders for Spiesmacher to arrest Rogers and ordered
a warrant drawn on the 19th. The latter charged Rogers with
holding 'dangerous and traitorous Conferences with his
Majesty's Enemies, and forming designs of the most dangerous nature, with intent to raise commotions and disturbances
in the Upper Countries, and to kindle a war betwixt the Savages and His Majesty's Subjects. . . .' He was to be divested of
all command, his person seized 'as a traitor to his King and
Country' and held in custody until he could be sent either
to Montreal or Detroit.

The accusations concerning the disturbances were obviously
based on Potter's affidavit. What evidence he had about

treasonous conferences and an Indian war has never been unearthed. It is sufficient to point out that Rogers was never tried for a single crime charged in the warrant which damned his reputation forever.

All dispatches were on their way west the day they were written.

Sir William Johnson with obvious satisfaction now assumed general command of the campaign to demolish Rogers' reputation. First he supplied a ramrod to stiffen Gage's back. The latter having reconsidered Potter's deposition, in a moment of objectivity confessed some doubt about its veracity. Johnson braced him: 'I do not doubt but that Potter will make the most of his discovery from his Character, at the same time I believe his acco't is within Compass & that probably he could say more if he Choose it.' When Gage received the dispatches containing the affidavits concerning the encounters between Rogers and Roberts, he was frank in admitting he did not know which one was most at fault. Johnson—with Roberts at his side—wrote: 'Mr. Roberts might have been more cool; when we consider the man he had to deal with and the discoveries he had just made of his designs, it will in great measure account for his conduct. . . .'

XX
1767–1768

'A Low Cunning Cheating Back Biting Villain'

GAGE'S first orders had already left Detroit when the second set arrived. Ensign Robert Johnston of the Michilimackinac garrison, then in Detroit for treatment of a gun wound, volunteered to deliver the latter and by forced marches despite bad weather overtook the first couriers and arrived in Michilimackinac on 6 December.

Spiesmacher dared only to confide in Lieutenant Christie who ordered the fort gates closed and the men under arms. Spiesmacher then engaged Rogers in conversation on the parade until Christie marched up with a file of armed men and surrounded them. Then Spiesmacher arrested the dumbfounded Rogers for high treason.

Rogers retained his composure, surrendering 'very calmly' as one officer admitted. He simply said that as it was Gage's order he would submit and offer no resistance, as he was confident of his ability to prove his innocence and loyalty to the King. He was then led off to Spiesmacher's rooms. The garrison officers found this attitude sinister. To Lieutenant Christie it proved Rogers was 'As subtil & deep as Hell itself.' Ensign Johnston was sure that while Rogers 'seemed to bear up with a good deal of Resolution . . . even at this time he was forming the most horrid Plot. . . .'

Rogers' quarters were immediately seized and his wife was

dispossessed. Windows were nailed up, doors locked, sentries paced up and down. A court of inquiry under Lieutenant Christie examined all of Rogers' papers. To its disappointment, they were merely 'his plan of Lake Huron, St. Clear, Supperior and part of the River of Missisipi, the Journals of the Detachment he sent from this to find out the North West passage with their orders etc a few Indian speeches.'

On the day following his arrest Spiesmacher informed Rogers he was determined to send him immediately to Detroit. Other officers persuaded the captain that this was impossible and he decided to hold Rogers until the schooner came in the spring. Rogers and Elizabeth were placed in another house under guard and went at least three days without proper food in bleak December. It was a week before they were permitted back in their own quarters.

Now all wrote Gage to deny connections with Rogers: Carver, Tute, and the others. Spiesmacher lamely tried to explain why he had approved Rogers' Indian expenditures: '. . . I thought it not of Consequence whether I signed it or not.' Rogers too wrote Gage. He blamed his removal on a plot to wrest control of Indian affairs from him. He recognized the role played by Hopkins' letter, denied answering it, and told how Hopkins had made a similar proposition in London which he had rejected and named Colonel William Amherst as a witness. He claimed credit for keeping the Indian tribes on the Mississippi from going over to the Spaniards.

Two Indians visiting the fort on 10 December brushed by sentries to shake hands with Rogers. They asked Spiesmacher why he was imprisoned and—to quote the captain—said they 'look'd upon him as a good father to them and that the [y] thought the English troubling him for being So, but they were determined to Stay some time to See whether he was Sent off, and if he is Sent off . . . Some English men Should

Suffer for it as all the Indians at any rate was to ware with the English in the Spring.' The incident was told to both Gage and Johnson as an illustration of Rogers' 'badness.'

Shunned by the officers, Rogers and his wife turned to the non-commissioned officers and men for company at the holiday season. The men liked Rogers and this made the officers 'Suspect his dissigns Evel.' Spiesmacher finally ordered no visitors for Rogers without written permission.

Cut off from all outside companionship Robert and Elizabeth faced a long, dreary winter. While the winds howled and snow swirled they could only daydream of a dramatic rescue from Robert's predicament. Suppose the Indians suddenly descended on the fort and set them free? Rogers would brave the storms of winter, travel to New York, appear before Gage, and demand the right to clear his name. Rogers' orderly, David Fullerton, a simple but devoted soldier, overheard these musings. Thinking them serious he went to Joseph Ainsse, a young Frenchman well-known for his intimacy with the Indians. Ainsse visited Rogers, but apparently saw that there was nothing to the supposed plan. He turned around, went to Spiesmacher, and, perhaps led by questions from the officers, turned the rescue into a story that Rogers wanted the Indians to get him to New Orleans where Captain Hopkins was waiting with four battalions of soldiers. He even produced a note purporting to have been signed by Rogers promising Ainsse a hundred pounds annually for five years for taking him to Hopkins.

Spiesmacher immediately put Rogers in solitary confinement. Despite the season his cell had only an open barred window. Elizabeth alone dared to speak to him through the window but ceased after a sergeant took her by the shoulders and threatened to boot her away. (It became garrison gossip that he had 'kicked her Arse away from the window.') Irons were prepared by the Indian commissary's blacksmith which were between six and seven pounds in weight and in the form of horse fetters. The band around one of Rogers' legs was too tight and a soldier later recalled how on one occasion Rogers tried to hobble across the room to speak to Mrs. Rogers at the open window. '. . . He had almost fainted with pain in crossing the Room, the Deponent was obliged to assist in getting his legs upon the Bed, and imagine it was owing to the Irons being too small.' Elizabeth, too, protested to Gage about her husband's 'Strict Confinement (which was so severe, that no Person was permitted even to speak to him, & your Memorialist insulted . . .)' and about the 'great Hardships & Cruel Usage which was unprecedented for one only under suspicion. . . .'

The garrison officers sent 'down the country' letter after letter describing the plot. Ensign Johnston's version was typical:

Major Rogers, that experienced chief to all manner of wickedness and treachery, had formed a deep and horrid plot to kill me, send Captain Spiesmacher, and Lieut. Christie, prisoners to the Indian country, plunder the garrison, and put all the soldiers to death, who were not in the plot. . . . He then with the Indians and what part of the troops that would follow him, was immediately to set off to surprize the garrison of Detroit and give it up to plunder . . . and then proceed to Old France, (via New Orleans). . . . The Particulars of the dark Plot are many, the Proofs positive.

They tried to outdo each other in damning Rogers. To Lieutenant Christie he was 'a low Cunning Cheating back biting villain.' Johnston's appelations have already been quoted. To Spiesmacher he was 'more and more as subtile and [as?] Hell its Selfe.'

The story and characterizations of Rogers spread eastward, growing more exaggerated as they moved. When Johnson Hall heard the news, Guy Johnson added his bit with a breathless account of the 'Traiterous plot . . . fortunately discovered Just at the point of execution. . . .' The letters went on to army headquarters in New York. Eventually they were released to the newspapers.

The press had turned on its hero either by accident or design: a series of articles before the announcement of his trouble depicted Rogers as unable to get along with the Indians. He was reported killed by them—for his 'abuses of them in trade,' said one paper. A supposed inhabitant of Michilimackinac then appeared in New York who told how the Indians captured the hated major and were on the verge of torturing him when he was rescued by a detachment from the fort. It is curious why the newspapers consistently showed Rogers as unpopular with the Indians when the opposite was true.

Early in May the story of Rogers' 'treasonable machinations' broke, and by June the 'horrid villany' was spread through all the colonies as portions of the letters from Michilimackinac were released to the papers. Rogers' name was forever stigmatized.

London was not neglected.

While Gage delayed in reporting his actions, Johnson took the initiative, hurriedly sending home copies of Potter's affidavit and Hopkins' letter with a covering letter and comment which successfully turned the government against Rogers. (To read Johnson's statements makes it difficult to realize that when the court-martial of Rogers was held, he was unable to give one iota of assistance to the prosecution.) Shelburne wrote Gage that the charge 'deserves the strictest Enquiry, and, if proved, a very exemplary Punishment.' The Earl of Hillsborough gave like assurance to Johnson.

By coincidence Rogers lost his patron at a time when he

needed official support: Charles Townshend died suddenly on
4 September 1767. A letter announcing his death to Johnson
reported that while 'they talk oddly of Major Rogers' in New
York 'yet he was looked upon in London As . . . very intel-
ligent.' But the English public eventually learned the worst.
The Gentleman's Magazine of July 1768, speaking of letters
from Fort Pitt, reported 'one very extraordinary article in
these letters, which positively asserts, that the famous major
Rogers was turned traitor to his country, and is now in irons
for a conspiracy in order to surprize several fortresses, to kill
the commandants, plunder the garrisons, and desert to the
enemy.' It was a backhanded tribute to Rogers: when vil-
lainies were attributed to him, they were of the superhuman
variety.

On 21 May the schooner *Gladwin* dropped its anchor off
the shore opposite Michilimackinac. Excitement reigned at
the fort. A few days before the *Gladwin* came into sight, Indians had begun to collect about the stockade. First came
Ottawa from Grand River and L'Arbre Croche, but they were
unarmed and professed friendship. Then came the Chippewa
with three war chiefs at their head, sinister in war paint and
with guns and tomahawks arrogantly displayed. They gathered on the shore: English gorgets and medals were angrily
wrenched from necks and disdainfully hurled into the water.
Spiesmacher, hearing that they were inviting the Ottawa to
join with them in rescuing Major Rogers, held a council and
bought peace with lavish presents.

Under heavy guard Rogers and Fullerton, who was also
under arrest, were brought to the water's edge, Rogers still in
irons. Two boats, with armed men interspersed among the
rowers, carried them to the *Gladwin*. Rogers was put into the
hold, to lay in ill-fitting fetters on the ballast stones for ten
days, until the schooner made Detroit late on 5 June. 'From

the pain I suffered, together with the cold, the bone of my
right leg was split, and the marrow forced its way out of the
skin,' Rogers later reported. Elizabeth was aboard, probably
half-frantic with indignation, shame, and concern for her
husband.

In Detroit Captain Turnbull removed Rogers' irons only
to allow him to walk to a cell in the barracks; they were
replaced and were on when he sailed on the *Charlotte* on 19
June bound for Fort Erie. From there he was taken to Fort
Niagara where he arrived on 29 June.

Here he came under the jurisdiction of Captain Brown,
who seems to have felt some sympathy for Rogers—possibly
because of his own brushes with Benjamin Roberts. Although
he kept careful guard over Rogers, he removed the irons in
the daytime and later entirely upon advice of the fort doctor.
Although Rogers had no money, Brown ordered credit supplied to him in order that he might have proper provisions.
Others had left Rogers in the dismal darkness of the cells;
Brown supplied candles, an unusual touch of kindness.

Here Elizabeth was allowed to join Rogers. With her his
courage seemed to return and he began to prepare for his trial.
There was a stream of requests to Gage: please appoint judges
acquainted with the service in the interior, please have a trial
soon; arrest Roberts, Spiesmacher, and Christie for inhuman
treatment; enclosed are the defense's witnesses. When he
left Niagara, Elizabeth went on to Boston to seek evidence
to discredit Potter. Affectionately she wrote her husband
from Oswego and Albany; she was carrying his unborn child.

Gage decided to hold the trial in Montreal: perhaps he was
afraid of sympathy for Rogers in New York. Hector The-
ophilus Cramahé—a noted attorney destined for a brilliant
career on the Canadian bench and in its government—was
to prosecute Rogers as Deputy Judge-Advocate. Gage was

confident of a conviction, fearing only that the prisoner might escape. Afraid that a civil trial, which alone had jurisdiction over treason, would rule out most of the evidence as hearsay, he drew up new articles of accusation for a court-martial and sent them to Cramahé with an outline of the case.

Gage made every effort to discover evidence against Rogers, but depended particularly on Spiesmacher and Roberts. The latter was warned:

It behoves you in a very peculiar manner to support the Accusation you have made by Evidence or corroborating circumstances that may Amount to a proof; As great Censure must fall upon you if after the decisive manner in which you have expressed Your Sentiments upon this Subject, the Accusation against Major Rogers should fall to the ground.

Rumors flew as Rogers was brought eastward: one had him rescued by Indians. He arrived in Montreal Sunday evening, 17 July, ill[1] and under heavy guard. Here he finally was permitted to consult an attorney but denied the privilege of talking to him in private or to interview witnesses. The attorney was a Mr. Williams, 'a Gentleman of the Law of good character' (according to Governor Carleton), whom Rogers saw for the first time on 25 August.

He recorded this event in an affectionate letter to his wife which attests to the deep ties between them at this time: 'I could most heartily wish it was in my powar to be with you to attend you in your present condition but my Dearest that cannot be at least for some months—but I don doubt you will have a good time, and I hop a Son—that he may Inherit your Fortun—and be a comfort to you in after times.' He was confident about the outcome of his trial and told her he expected to go to England as soon as he was cleared 'but shall go to portsmouth. . . .' He interrupted his writing for the interview with Mr. Williams and then told her that the attorney 'is clever and I shall be Honourably Acquited and that I shall have the Happiness of Seeing you this winter. . . .'

Elizabeth's letters have been lost but there is a tiny clue attesting to her loyalty to her husband. Her arrival in Boston on 17 August was noted in the press. Immediately after this item came the first defense of Robert since the news of his 'treason' broke: 'It is said by some that the Major is innocent of the crimes he is charged with.'

Evidence now, not name-calling, was needed to convict Rogers. Gage suddenly found a strange change in the attitude of his informants. Lieutenant Christie who had declared he wanted to be the hangman of the villainous Rogers, wrote: 'I have no Knowledge of any of his designs but what was inform'd me by others. . . .' James Stanley Goddard was supposed to know of Rogers' evil designs; at Gage's request Carleton questioned him and found he knew nothing of value which might be used against Rogers. But most jolting of all was Johnson's answer to Gage's request to send the evidence he possessed to Cramahé: 'I have sent the necessary papers to Canada, tho' I apprehend they will not be of such Importance, as I gave Rogers but few Instructions, and no Conversation with, or opportunity of Seeing him since his departure for his post. I find it presupposed that he cannot be hurt. . . .' This was the man who had told the general that he had 'particulars' to prove Rogers' villainy, whose letters damned Rogers' reputation on both sides of the Atlantic.

After Cramahé had listened to the witnesses and read the papers sent to him, he knew the truth: the case against Rogers was built on sound and fury. But he had dutifully prepared the strongest possible case against the prisoner when the trial opened on Thursday, 20 October before a panel of British officers presided over by Lieutenant-Colonel Valentine Jones.

XXI
OCTOBER 1768

'I Doubt not to Be Able to Convince the World'

GAGE'S new charges opened the trial. Rogers had 'contrary to his Duty and Allegiance to his King and Country, formed Designs of a Traiterous and Dangerous nature of Deserting to the French . . . and Stirring of the Indians against His Majesty and His Government.' He had held 'a Correspondence with His Majesty's Enemies' and had disobeyed 'his Orders and Instructions . . . in having undertaken expensive Schemes and projects, and lavished away money amongst the Savages, contrary to his Instructions, but Conformable to the Council given in a letter . . . by an Officer in the French Service. . . .'

First witness for the prosecution was Benjamin Roberts. He recited his tale under Cramahé's questioning. Johnson had shown him a copy of Hopkins' letter; Potter had told how 'Rogers wanted him to engage in some bad affairs. . . .' Roberts could not cite a single act or word by Rogers in his presence to support the charges.

Potter's affidavit was introduced but it failed to agree with what Roberts testified that Potter had told him. Roberts specifically stated that Potter had told him of seeing a second letter from Hopkins acknowledging an answer from Rogers; this all-important information was noticeably absent from the affidavit. Roberts mentioned some details supplied by Potter on how Rogers planned to make a 'Sweep' of everything he could; the only preparation described in the affidavit was not among them. Potter mentioned a public row with Rogers and named Roberts as a witness; Roberts failed to corroborate the affidavit in this particular. But both agreed that Rogers 'had Villainous designs in his head. . . .'

Next to appear before the judges was Captain-Lieutenant Frederick Christopher Spiesmacher. No, from the date of his arrival in August 1766 to July 1767 Rogers did nothing to attract his attention until the arrival of Roberts. Then Rogers had said he was dissatisfied, would write England and would not stay if something better was not done for him. Spiesmacher obviously had been impressed by Benjamin Roberts' statement to him that Potter had spoken 'of the Major's engaging some of the Soldiers to assist him in going off to Captain Hopkins by the Missisipi.' Yet neither Potter's affidavit nor Roberts' testimony made a single reference to this point. Spiesmacher explained that he had meant to write Gage concerning his suspicions of Rogers but the warrant had arrived too soon.

He went on to describe the Ainsse incident, a peculiar circumstance in that at no time was Rogers a participant before his eyes. He told of listening to one of Fullerton's conversations with Ainsse in which the major's orderly said that Rogers intended to join Captain Hopkins then believed to be at New Orleans. (Neither Ainsse nor Fullerton, who testified for the prosecution, mentioned such a statement in their testimony.) Asked if Rogers had ever held private councils with the Indians, he could remember only one and admitted that Rogers had told him about it. Asked about rewards to Ainsse he minimized them and lied about the date when he appointed the Frenchman garrison-interpreter. On cross-examination by both Rogers and the court it appeared that he had deliberately neglected to forward Gage's orders that the witnesses requested by Rogers should be sent down from Michilimack-inac. Asked for a list of the papers seized from Rogers, he avoided a direct answer, saying he had a written list among his papers but never produced it or testified to what it showed.

Next came Benjamin Frobisher, who had joined Spies-macher to listen to Fullerton's conversations with Ainsse. Frobisher denied any knowledge of Rogers' conduct except what he had overheard but even here admitted that, 'He cannot exactly relate everything. . . .' Lieutenant John Christie's testimony followed. Aside from the Fullerton incident he actually helped Rogers' case. 'He had no personal knowledge of Major Rogers' Conduct relative to the Articles now exhibited against him. . . .' He recalled that Rogers had told him that he had forwarded Hopkins' letter to Gage 'but the Boat was cast away up the Lake.' Fullerton, turning King's witness to save his skin, testified that Rogers had sent to Ainsse to request the Indians be kept around the fort in order to rescue him and Mrs. Rogers. Fullerton added: 'All he heard the Major say, was, that he wished to get out of the hands of those among whom he was, in order to go and deliver himself to general Gage at New York.' There was no mention of any proposed meeting with Hopkins; Fullerton said he had never heard of more than one letter.

Joseph Louis Ainsse then detailed the curious plot in which he was supposedly involved. He testified that he had visited Rogers after the latter's arrest but the major had said nothing until asked by the witness 'to let him know all his affairs. . . .' He did not attempt to give Rogers' answer in the latter's words but said that the prisoner 'gave him to under-stand he intended to go to New Orleans, where he supposed Captain Hopkins was, and begged he would get the Indians to assist in freeing him. . . .' Three days later Ainsse went to Spiesmacher, plans were made to entrap Fullerton within ear-range of the hidden Spiesmacher and Frobisher. He told of two different conversations with Fullerton under these circumstances; Spiesmacher and Frobisher mentioned only one. While describing the conferences with Fullerton, Ainsse did not mention any reference to Hopkins; both of the listeners claimed there was. Ainsse told of getting a note from Rogers as a reward for his proposed escape, but totally destroyed the value of his testimony when he refused to identify the paper produced at the court-martial as being it.

Several soldiers testified. Corporal Alexander Johnson said he heard Rogers admit intending to escape but without intent to harm anyone. Another said he had intended 'only to go into the Woods to screen himself from his Creditors.' Ensign Robert Johnston, who had once written that Rogers was forming 'the most horrid Plot,' now could only state that he heard Rogers say he had received the Hopkins letter which was forwarded to Gage but the boat carrying it had been lost in Lake Huron. The prosecution then introduced a copy of the Hopkins letter.

Cramahé put into evidence six more documents: Rogers' commissions to Carver, Goddard, and Tute and three letters to Tute. These were obviously to prove the charge that the major had undertaken expensive schemes. Spiesmacher was reintroduced to testify as to the Indian expenses but could only state that he did not exactly remember them. The prosecution then rested after seven days of testimony.

Under contemporary practice Rogers was given the privilege of using counsel in the preparation of his case but not in the actual trial. Here his future depended on the agility of his own mind and tongue. He opened his defense with a slashing statement carrying the attack to his prosecutors. Gage 'was pleased to denominate me a Traitor to my King and Country.'

Under this heavy accusation my Name and Reputation have been blasted, and I have been branded with Infamy without the Ceremony of an Examination—Under this Infamous Accusation I have been imprisoned and Loaded with Irons, and suffered the utmost Tortures both in Body and mind. . . .

Rogers swiftly touched upon the variance between the warrant and the charges at the trial and pointed out that the evidence produced against him seemed to be as much concerned with what he did after his arrest as with proving that his arrest was justified. He promised an accounting as Michilimackinac's commandant but pointed out that Spiesmacher had deprived him of important documents.

He then discussed the prosecution's proof. The charge of planning to desert to the French depended on Potter's affidavit, a piece of evidence which deserved little notice because he did not have an opportunity to question the maker. The complaint that he sought to arouse the Indians depended solely on one conference which he had disclosed to Spiesmacher, which was held with open doors and which was reported to both Gage and Johnson. He showed how ridiculous the Hopkins letter was:

Indeed I never thought the Letter of any Material Consequence. I was to be a great Man whenever Mr. Maryland became Prime Minister of France, provided I should seduce the People of New England, and the Indians of Michilimackinac to the French Interest.

Little evidence, Rogers commented, had been offered to prove the charge of lavishing money on the savages. He would offer his accounts which had been examined, approved, and signed by the officers of the garrison.

He then turned to the Northwest Passage expedition. He told how he had proposed in London to find the passage and how, after arriving at his post, his London agent, Dr. Campbell, sent him word to proceed as did Townshend and others. 'These Letters were amongst my Papers at Michilimackinac when I was Confined, and taken from me by Captain Spiesmacher.'

As for his alleged attempt to escape:

However unwearied my Enemies have been upon this Subject, I doubt not to be able to Convince the World, that the utmost extent of my Offence in this Particular has been no more, than either my mentioning the Apprehension I was under of being Carried down to New York and Confined in Prison for my Debts, or some Romantic Conversation between Mrs. Rogers and me, merely to pass Time during my Confinement, and never intended to be put in Execution, which might accidently have been overheard by a Servant, and by him thought in Earnest. . .

This seemed weak until Rogers in rapid succession showed that no actual escape was planned or possible. The plot was supposedly hatched between 8 December and 1 February, yet no mention was made either to soldiers or traders; the Indian chiefs whom Ainsse claimed Rogers wanted, were at winter camps over three hundred miles from the fort. Not one plan was 'within the compass even of a Possibility.' A winter trip to the Mississippi or New Orleans with or without Mrs. Rogers was beyond imagination. Then Rogers struck hard at the testimony of Ainsse about Hopkins' supposed presence at these places:

Nor was it ever imagined, by any Person I ever Conversed with, that Mr. Hopkins was either at the Mississippi or New Orleans, and not withstanding Mr. Ainsse says, I gave him a Note for Five Hundred Pounds to undertake this Journey, I utterly deny that Note, and do declare upon my Honor, I never saw it, untill it was produced in Court by the Judge Advocate, nor will any Person who knows my hand-Writing, judge I wrote that Note.

After a few more effective thrusts, Robert concluded:

Nevertheless, when the Court shall have heard the Evidence now to be produced on my Part I have not the least Doubt, but I shall be Honourably Acquitted.

Rogers opened fire on Potter's reputation with affidavits which were not copied in the record and with the testimony of Henry Bostwick in whose house at Michilimackinac Potter boarded. There were no fights between Rogers and Potter as the latter claimed; Rogers had been kind to Potter when the latter was ill. Bostwick also testified to Ainsse's poor reputation because of his part in the Indian massacre at Michilimackinac in '63.

Ensign Johnston was recalled by the defense to testify to Potter's bad reputation in Michilimackinac and to Rogers' ill-treatment. In answer to a question from the court he admitted that there had been room in the *Gladwin's* cabin for Rogers and a guard 'but he had Captain Spiesmacher's Orders to put him in the Hold, which Orders he produced to the Court.'

Rogers' Indian interpreters testified that 'Major Rogers never held any bad Discourses with the Indians, but in General exhorted them to live in Peace and Quiet. . . .' They and a trader thought Rogers gave less presents to the Indians than the former French commandants. Soldier after soldier took the stand to swear that they had never heard of any attempt by Rogers to 'seduce' the non-commissioned officers and men of the garrison to escape until the supposed plot was 'discovered.' They also gave details of Rogers' ill-treatment and the insults to Mrs. Rogers.

The defendant then confidently introduced what should have been part of the prosecution's case: 'An Account of the Distribution of Goods made by Major Rogers to the Several Indian Nations in the District of Michilimackinac during the

Time of his Command there, Commencing 10th August 1766 and Ending the 8th December 1767.' The total was £5792 ... 2s. Vouchers for all bills except one were produced bearing certificates by the post officers that the distributions had been actually made and were absolutely necessary. Among the signers were Benjamin Roberts and Captain Spiesmacher. Rogers introduced his accounts for flour, meat, and firewood supplied the garrison. Such vouchers as he had were presented and a trader was called on to verify one whose voucher was missing. The court could now pass judgment on all his expenses.

Rogers closed his case with a bold attack on his enemies. Briefly alluding to his services in the late war and to his appointment at Michilimackinac as a reward for them, he described his work until Roberts appeared and induced Gage 'with untrue Affidavits' to treat him as an enemy to his country. The orders to arrest him came to officers who 'were easily induced to Treat me with Inhumanity, and to brand my Name with Infamy in all the Public News Papers upon the Continent. . . .' His irons, his being thrown into the hold of the *Gladwin* were described.

He then turned to the evidence. The failure of very few of the prosecution's witnesses to testify to anything that they had seen or heard was pointed out; the unreliability of hearsay evidence was noted. He commented on the weaknesses in the proof of all articles. Gage's instructions regarding economy related to garrison affairs; in Indian affairs he had discretion. 'The Court will determine from the Evidence I have given whether I exceeded my Authority, or lavished away the Publick Money.'

Cramahé in rebuttal called Christie, Spiesmacher, and Frobisher to contradict Rogers' contentions that he had been deprived of various papers. Yet after they testified it was clear that papers of Rogers had been confiscated and the prosecution failed to have Spiesmacher deny seeing the specific letters mentioned by Rogers such as those from Campbell and Townshend. The captain had said he had a list but he made no effort to produce it—a fact which undoubtedly was not lost upon the court. Cramahé made no effort to contradict Rogers' bold denial of the supposed note to Ainsse; in view of the major's unquestionably destinctive handwriting it can only be presumed that the note was a clumsy forgery.

At 11 a.m. of what was to be the final day of the hearings, 31 October, the court reconvened and allowed Rogers to show by a trader, Gershom Levy, that a boat carrying letters from Rogers to Gage and others had been lost en route from Michilimackinac in the fall of 1766. This explained the loss of the original Hopkins letter. The judges then took the case under consideration. Their verdict was not guilty.

XXII
1768–1775

'A Affair of Party and Faction'

MONTREAL was stirred by the drama of the court-martial. Spiesmacher told Gage 'the populace . . . are all in Rogers' favour.' Roberts wrote: 't'is Surprising the Number of Friends he has got here. . . .' Johnson wrote Gage that the public was being induced 'to deem the whole as a Malicious attack upon a man of worth.'

The witnesses for the prosecution were worried by the reaction in New York to the verdict. All tried to anticipate the accusation that they had failed to support their charges. Roberts said the trial proved 'there was reason for Suspicion. . . .' Spiesmacher blamed the verdict on the fact that the witnesses 'were only allowed to Say what they persinaly know. . . .' This was a strange remark in view of the liberal admission of hearsay and supposition testimony against Rogers. They then picked a scapegoat: Ensign Johnston. Even Sir William Johnson joined in the chorus against the man. Johnston learned of Johnson's part in the attack on him and quickly wrote Gage a letter revealing how Sir William poisoned the minds of officers going to Michilimackinac. After Johnson had taken Johnston into the 'private room' of Johnson Hall and enjoined him to secrecy, the officer could not avoid thinking any act of Rogers was proof that the latter was the 'disaffected and bad Man' full of the 'bad Intentions' described by Sir William.

Gage received the news when he returned to headquarters from Boston on or about 24 November. He did not acknowledge its receipt until 5 December and then said he had not had time to read the record. It was not until the 19th that he wrote Carleton to release Rogers from close confinement and to allow him the freedom of Montreal, 'tho' he is still to consider himself as under Arrest. . . .' Gage's deliberate delay and the slowness of the mails kept Rogers in jail until February, although he had been acquitted in October. Gage sent the record home and waited to hear what the government would say.

Although even Johnson wavered about payment of Rogers' accounts in view of their certification, Gage refused to permit payment. The decision of the court-martial—in effect denying the charge that Rogers had disobeyed Gage's orders regarding expense—did not change the general's mind. He sharply wrote Colonel Jones indicating his disagreement with the verdict on this point and complained that the trial had become 'a Affair of Party and Faction.' Rogers might well have used the same words to characterize his arrest.

Rogers languished in his Montreal cell. The day before Christmas he wrote his wife in a far-off Portsmouth, acknowledging the receipt of a letter of 25 October: 'It Really gives plesure to know you are in perfect helth. . . .' Elizabeth had apparently regretted not accompanying him to Montreal; Rogers told her that 'you have done Every thing for me and much mor than you could had you a come to this place.' He hoped the mail from New York, expected the next week, would bring orders for his release; 'I Shall Imediently Set out for portsmouth.' His future plans would wait 'till I can tell you by word.'

The expected release did not come and early in February Elizabeth gave birth to a son without the comforting presence of a husband. The baby was christened 'Arthur' by his grandfather in Queen's Chapel on 12 February 1769. The name honored both the minister and Elizabeth's younger brother then in the army and stationed in Gibraltar. No letter from Rogers to Elizabeth of this period is known, but there is one to his brother-in-law, Samuel Livermore, on 16 February noting 'I have wrote to Mrs. Rogers and pray God I may heare She is in perfect Helth.'

When finally allowed to walk the Montreal streets, Rogers received a cordial welcome from the regular officers stationed there. Roberts wrote to Gage that 'the Garrison of Montreal seem much in his favor, he drinks and games as usual.' On 9 May they met face-to-face; unfortunately we have only the confused details set down in Roberts' hysterical letter. Roberts apparently told Rogers he was a rascal and should keep on the other side of the street. Rogers answered the streets were free, called Roberts a 'puppy,' pulled his nose, and forced him down on his knees. Moaned Roberts to Johnson: 'Notwithstanding all . . . everybody seems prepossessed in his favor.'

Finally on 1 March 1769 Charles Gould, Deputy Judge-Advocate of England, wrote Gage concerning the verdict of the court-martial. After a formal recital of the charge he stated:

His Majesty is pleased to approve the Opinion of the Court of Acquitting said Major Robert Rogers of each of the said Articles of Charge and to Order that he be released from the Confinement; at the same time it appears to His Majesty, that there was great reason to suspect the said Major Rogers entertaining an improper and dangerous correspondence, which Suspicion the Account afterwards given of his meditating an Escape tended to confirm.

This weak excuse of Gage's action left Rogers still under a cloud and enabled Gage to complete his plans to strip Rogers of any office in spite of the court-martial verdict. In the General Orders of 1 May 1769, Gage repeated the above finding, thus negating the effect of the verdict in the eyes of army personnel. Then he wrote England refusing to reinstate Rogers to the command of Michilimackinac.

Released on 3 June, Rogers went directly to New York and was given permission by Gage to go to London. The latter also certified that he had given Rogers no pay as commandant of Michilimackinac. Robert then went to Portsmouth to spend a few precious days with his wife and son Arthur. But creditors were on his heels: he could only hope for redress from the home government. On 18 July he sailed again for England.

Early in September he again set foot in London. Now alone, with a besmirched reputation, he faced an up-hill battle. Even as he was approaching England's shores, Gage and Johnson were trying to insure his failure. 'It is needless to trouble you by giving you any Caution about his assertions,' wrote the general to Barrington, while Sir William adopted a more lofty tone: '. . . it is highly improbable that persons of consequence could be so far imposed upon. . . .'

At the outset Rogers first claimed his pay as commandant of Michilimackinac, a limited objective which could not engender much opposition. However, he was arrested on complaint of an impatient creditor and thrown into debtors' prison. His stay was short; he was rescued by 'An Unexpected Friend' and all London was repeating how 'he fought his Way thro the jaylers & turnkeys. would pay no fees.'

The setback only seemed to spur his drive. His pay was given to him; the government was considering an application to pay a commissary's salary for the time he was at Michili-mackinac and a memorial for lands in New York. There seemed no end to his applications: for continuation of his pay as commandant at Michilimackinac and for payment of his Indian accounts.

Writing Elizabeth was a welcome diversion. With no mention of any reversals or of prison he told her of his 'heart of Gratitude an [d] Sincear Love to you and our Dear Son . . .'; of his longing for letters from her; of his hopes of concluding his affairs in the near future and of leaving for America.

A rash of rumors concerning awards to him flooded London and made its way to America dismaying his enemies. '. . . With his cursed impudence he hums all the great people and I firmly believe, he will succeed beyond what every one in America who knows him, could Expect,' wrote one London correspondent to Johnson.

The rumors were wrong: things were not progressing too well for Rogers. He decided to concentrate on the payment of the Indian accounts and substituted a new, well-presented brief and petition on the subject. In telling fashion he pointed out that the accounts had been properly certified, that he had orders to appease the Indians, that he had been found not guilty of the charge of squandering funds.

Considerable support gathered behind him from not merely people in general but also influential officials. General Conroy wrote: '. . . Being acquitted he seems to have a right to the same justice & consideration of his accounts which others have.' John Pownall added: 'I cannot refuse the request of Major Rogers that I should say to you what I really think that the Case of his accounts now before the Treasury is attended with circumstances of great hardship inviting their Lordships compassion.' Charles Jenkinson agreed with these sentiments. Benjamin Roberts later sourly observed: '. . . Mr. Fitzherbert & several Lords of Trade espoused Rogers' Cause Mr. Touchet was his first friend; General Williamson to whom he is related by Marriage, was very Strenous in his behalf & engaged General Conroy & most of the Officers of Artillery on his Side. . . .'

The Lords of the Treasury decided to submit the question of Rogers' authority to General Gage. Rogers protested: his creditors would not wait. He desperately asked that the court-martial verdict be considered a report on the accounts or that he receive the money simply as a reward for his services.

His letters to his wife changed: there was no longer any mention of a date for coming back to America. Yet he did not reveal his worries; the dread specter of debtors' prison hanging over his head was given no attention. Instead he talked of his son: he was sorry to hear that he was ill; 'My love to my Young major . . . I shall take care to Send you Some perty things for Atty. . . .' His desperation forced the Treasury lords to relax their firm stand. They were willing to advance a sum to relieve his 'present distress' but the matter would still be referred to Gage. Rogers was asked to prepare a schedule 'of such part of those debts . . . to Sundry People in London . . . for which he is Liable every day to be arrested.' Rogers asked for £3894; he was allowed on 15 May £3000.

This was only a stopgap, but for Elizabeth's sake he exuded optimism: '. . . three days ago I had his majestyes warrant for three thousand pounds Sterling and am in a fair way to Recover my ould accounts but that will take time. . . .' He thought he would follow his letter in about twenty days.

Elizabeth had seen such promises before; his long absence did not make her appreciate that Robert was actually a prisoner of his creditors who would have thrown him into jail had he made one step toward America. Her letters apparently took on a sharp tone. Robert tried to make her see how he had to wait for the money in order to discharge his debts and to help 'in Seeing you in a house of your own which you so much desiar.' But he became indignant when she accused him of living extravagantly. He told her that he hoped his letter would 'Show you how Villenious those persons are that has Set you on your High Hors about my Extravagant Living in London . . . It is impossible for any man on Earth to be more Industerious than I have been since I arrived in London.'

He had indeed been busy. Memorials, petitions, briefs supporting his position, requests had to be prepared and revised; there was the perpetual round of government officers to see busy secretaries in order to keep the memorials and petitions from being buried and lost under a mass of other papers, the facing of impatient creditors, the humiliation of begging for extensions of time to pay, the trying visits to friends and influential people to seek their favor and loans. He tried everything; he circulated the fur trade report hoping to enlist supporters Benjamin Franklin, for example—to urge the separate province of Michilimackinac.

Gage finally answered the Treasury's inquiry. He admitted that the vouchers appeared authentic and regular but denied that there was sufficient reason for the expenditures. 'The Pretences given for incurring the Expence are in general such as may continually be given at every Fort in the Indian Country, and if allowed as Valid at one Post, would have served as an Example to the rest and soon Entail an annual Expence of between Thirty and Forty Thousand Pounds for Indian presents.'

The watchdogs of His Majesty's Treasury were properly impressed. They wrote Gage that they approved of his conduct and hoped he would continue to take precautions to prevent similar expenses. Rogers' petition was denied.

Early spring 1771 found Robert back in debtors' prison. Now—among other requests—he pressed a memorial to the Privy Council asking for compensation for services, sufferings, and losses while in the service. It was referred to the Treasury, which passed it on to Barrington. The Secretary at War, with no signs of undue haste, reported it was the same matter which had been referred by him to Gage when Rogers had applied for the King's Bounty in 1767. He was still awaiting an answer from the general. The Treasury conveyed this message to the Privy Council. At every turn Rogers was blocked by General Gage.

In the meantime he was released from jail. His stay was again brief, but he emerged to find that all his belongings had been sold—he later claimed—'without attention to value, and the produce, with a shameless disregard to justice, converted to private use, without success.' He kept his despair to himself; outward confidence fooled many watching him. There was even a brief moment of glamour reminiscent of better days. *The London Evening Post* of 1 October reported:

Tuesday last, about two o'clock, after Major Rogers had passed through Dartford, the post-chaise man who drove him told him a highwayman hovered around the chaise. As soon as the fellow came to the Major, he seized him by the hand and pulled him into the chaise. The highwayman answers the description in an advertisement of Sir John Fielding's. The Major carried him to the Mayor of Gravesend, and after an explanation there, sent him to the Rotation-house in Bow-street.

In November he petitioned for a pension and a renewal of his commission as major. In vain. Early in 1772 he prepared a memorial to the Lords of the Treasury containing a full statement of his demands for his services and prayed that they direct his application to be presented to the House of Commons. Again he was turned down.

Tireless, he tried a new tack. Seven days after the adverse action by the Treasury he petitioned the Privy Council for support of an expedition to discover the Northwest Passage. He reduced the size and cost from that proposed in 1765 and detailed a three-years journey. The route, too, was changed; now he proposed to follow the Minnesota River to its source, then make a short portage to the Missouri, and follow this second river to its source. Another portage of about thirty miles would bring the expedition to the 'Great River Ourigan' which leads 'through a vast and most popular Tract of Indian Country' to the Straits of Annian and the Pacific. This would take two years: here the second winter would be spent. The following spring every inlet, nook, and bay northwards would be explored for the passage. If discovered, the expedition would follow it to Hudson Bay. If not, the party was to proceed to the extreme westerly projection of North America, cross to Siberia, and return to Great Britain via Russia.

Rogers sought the aid of all: the Royal Society of London and Benjamin Franklin were only two. Jonathan Carver, who had come to England to ask compensation from the government and had had his faith in Rogers restored when he found that Rogers had acted in 1766 with some encouragement from persons of authority, asked to be allowed to join the expedition. Rumor magnified the progress of the application: the press reported that the Lords of Trade had approved the measure and that 'it now lies at the Treasury Board, that a proper estimate may be made of the expence.'

As usual rumor outsped truth. The proposal had been referred to the Lords of the Committee of Council for Plantation Affairs, who passed it on to the Lords Commissioners of Trade and Plantations. They reported, detailing advantages similar to those set forth in 1765, and stated that while no success was assured, 'we must, in justice to ye Services & Experiences of the Proponent, observe that he seems in a particular manner qualified for conducting this laborious & different adventure. . . .' But they felt that the proposal should be referred to 'that Department of Governm't, to which ye consideration of such cases seems more properly to belong.' The Lords Commissioners did not suggest which department. There the application was permitted to rest, gathering the dust of centuries until picked up by curious historical researchers.

Desperation forced Robert to write humbly to Gage asking for a decision so that the government could take some action on his request for the King's Bounty. The general cleverly treated Rogers' letter as a request for a reversal of his former decision on his accounts: he said 'no' to Rogers. However, he never sent any decision to Barrington and thus successfully blocked a review of Rogers' petition. The major was totally defeated; no retreat was possible.

The next scene was inevitable: on 16 October 1772 Robert Rogers was committed to Fleet Prison at the suit of Matthew Pearson and eight other creditors. On oath the latter claimed a total of almost fourteen hundred pounds—not a great sum but it might just as well have been a million. Rogers had no funds.

When the 'jigger' (door-keeper) closed the gates on the unhappy Robert and the 'collegians' of this new 'College' surrounded him with cries of 'Garnish! Strip or Pay!', it symbolized the end of the dynamic Robert Rogers whose career has been followed to this point. No penniless man passed two years in that 'Prince of Prisons' standing 'Close by the Borders of a Slimy Flood which now in secret rumbles thro' the Mud,' without irreparibly damaging his character. Perhaps it was here that the heavy drinking, mention of which crops up in his later life, began.

There are only a few reminders of the days the major spent

in the Fleet. On 17 November 1772 his petition to the House of Commons was redrawn but never used. The following spring a newspaper printed a rumor that he might be appointed lieutenant-governor to St. Vincent but there seems to have been nothing behind the story. On 14 June 1773 he petitioned the king for a tract of land sixty miles square 'on the Banks of some great and convenient River or Lake' in America so 'that he might compromise with his creditors. . . .' This petition mentioned his distress for want of every necessity and the injury to his health caused by imprisonment. Warm personal recommendations of Rogers from Lord Loudoun, Earl of Eglington, General Monckton, Colonel Amherst, Colonel Harvey, Colonel West, Colonel Grant, Colonel Abercrombie, and Captain D'Arcy accompanied the memorial but they had no effect.

Few letters to Elizabeth during this period have been preserved but those in existence seem to show that Rogers felt there was at least one person on earth who was still interested in his fight for freedom. One dated 18 March 1774 is a warm note reflecting his love and complaining only of the dearth of letters from her. 'Good news' promised in it was revealed in his letter of 7 April 1774: a suit against General Gage if the latter did not give a favorable answer to a memorial sent to him, while the general was temporarily in London.

Gage, as might be expected, did not give the desired answer, with the result that on 8 April as the general was about to sail for America, a sheriff served him with a writ demanding twenty thousand pounds damages for injuries sustained by Rogers. Allegations charged him with trespass, assault, false imprisonment, and unlawful conversion of goods. Gage was being sued as if the officers at Michilimackinac were his agents: he 'beat bruised wounded and ill treated' Rogers; he 'Imprisoned him and without any reasonable or probable Cause against the Laws of this Realm . . . and . . . put . . . Divers Iron

Chains Iron Manacles and Iron Fetters on the hand, and legs of the s'd Robert . . . and . . . the Said Robert . . . underwent and suffered great Pain Torture and Anguish of Body and Mind. . . .' Rogers was assaulted 'with force and arms to wit with Swords Bayonets Sticks Staves Clubs & Fists. . . .' The list of goods and chattels were the usual grossly exaggerated numbers found in legal writs: '. . . 5000 printed Mapps 500 other Mapps 5000 Printed Books 100 Books of Accompt 500 other Books 5000 Deeds 5000 . . . Receipts 100 Bills of Exchange 100 Promissory Notes 20 Indian Slaves 500,000 Beaver Skins 10,000 other skins 1000 Gallons of Rum . . .' and so on.

Rogers later claimed the suit was brought at the insistence of his creditors. Undoubtedly he was willing to lend his name to it if it promised relief. It may have been designed to compel the government to give some attention to his memorials in order to spare Gage a civil trial. The latter stoutly professed his innocence to the Treasury lawyer charged with his defense, but his confidence did not keep him from inquiring if Rogers' action was barred by the statute of limitations.

In the meantime a new bankruptcy law was passed. Rogers immediately sought his release by complying with its requirements. He published proper notice of his intent to petition for a discharge, then appeared at Quarter Sessions and filed a schedule vesting in the Clerk all his real and personal estate except what the law allowed him to keep: wearing apparel, bedding, working tools, and not over forty shillings. He was discharged on 4 August 1774 after almost twenty-two months in the Fleet.

Rogers immediately petitioned for a return to his retired-captaincy status and pension which was granted—probably in return for a withdrawal of his action against Gage. He was compelled to mortgage his retirement pay in order to live and began another barrage of petitions asking for full pay and royal consideration for his losses. There was some talk of attaching him to the East India Company, but no additional officers were being sent there. Interest in the Northwest Passage proposal revived and Richard Whitworth, a member of Parliament from Stafford, lent his assistance. According to Jonathan Carver only the trouble in America put a stop to the expedition. Finally in the spring of 1775 following a petition to Lord Dartmouth, Rogers was given the retirement pay of a major and sufficient funds to enable him to return to America.

After six years of disappointment and failure Robert Rogers sailed back to his native land, a broken man of forty-three bearing the marks of debtors' prison, who could only aspire to a quiet future with his wife and son.

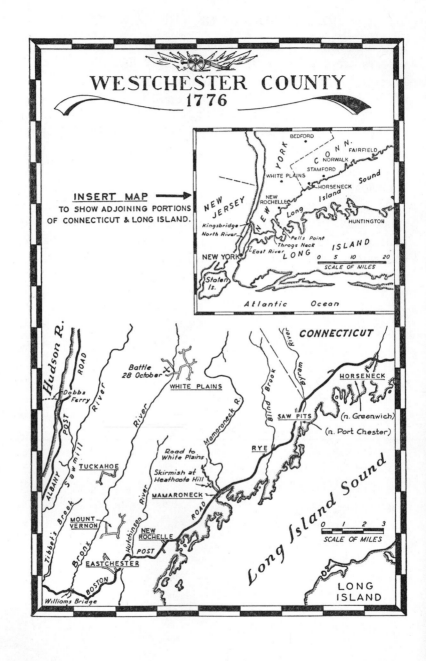

WESTCHESTER COUNTY
1776

INSERT MAP
TO SHOW ADJOINING PORTIONS
OF CONNECTICUT & LONG ISLAND.

BEDFORD

NEW YORK

C O N N.
FAIRFIELD
NORWALK
STAMFORD

WHITE PLAINS

NEW JERSEY

NEW ROCHELLE

HORSENECK

Long Island Sound

HUNTINGTON

Kingsbridge
North River

Pells Point
Throgs Neck
East River

NEW YORK

LONG ISLAND

Staten Is.

0   5   10   20
SCALE OF MILES

Atlantic   Ocean

Hudson R.

CONNECTICUT

ALBANY POST ROAD

Sawmill River

Dobbs Ferry

River

Byram River

Blind Brook

Battle
28 October

WHITE PLAINS

HORSENECK

Mamaroneck R.

SAW PITS

(n. Greenwich)

(n. Port Chester)

TUCKAHOE

Tibbet's Brook

Bronx River

Hutchinson River

Road to
White Plains

Skirmish at
Heathcote Hill

RYE

MOUNT
VERNON

MAMARONECK

BOSTON ROAD

Long Island Sound

NEW
ROCHELLE

POST

EASTCHESTER

0   1   2   3
SCALE OF MILES

BOSTON

Williams Bridge

LONG
ISLAND

XXIII
1775–1776

'Major Rogers . . . Is Empowered To Raise a Battalion of Rangers'

ON 4 June 1775 Robert Rogers sailed from Gravesend, England, on the snow *Baltimore* bound for Maryland. Early in August he landed on an alien shore. He knew nothing of 'Liberty and Property'; the revolt around Boston meant little. To the people he was merely a ghost from the forgotten past. There was a brief reference to his former glory—not for his benefit but merely to add lustre to another rising star: 'The late Duke of Newcastle scrupled not to acknowledge Col. Washington and Maj. Rogers "two of the bravest and most experienced officers in the King's service." ' The press eagerly printed news he brought from abroad but omitted his name.

Robert turned northward. He first wanted to see his brother James, now a leading citizen in a small Green Mountain settlement under New York jurisdiction, to arrange some financial matters. Then Portsmouth was next with Elizabeth and his son, now six years old.

Arriving in Philadelphia on 22 September he was arrested by order of the local Committee of Safety on suspicion, being a retired major in the British army on half pay. However the Continental Congress indicated that if his half-pay status was the only basis of the charge, he should be released on giving his word not to take up arms against the Americans. He gave this parole and was released.

Arriving in New York he wrote General Gage an apology for suing him, trying to excuse himself by blaming 'the great Importunity of my creditors. . . .' It obviously rankled him to take this role; he told Gage that John Pownall, Secretary to the Board of Trade, had 'strongly recommended' this move because the government would give him no employment while he remained in disfavor with Gage. Expecting the general to accept this tactless attempt to obliterate the past, he sent a copy of this letter to Pownall and requested some employment from the government 'on an Annual Stipend. . . .' He also sent a memorial to Lord Dartmouth asking for some position in government service.

Rogers left for Albany on 10 October, but 'fever and ague' —a return of his malaria—made this a ten-days journey. A fortnight was spent in Albany and Stone Arabia looking over possible land grants and then he went on to Kent where he passed five or six days with his brother James.

Preoccupied with his financial worries, Rogers was blind to the serious situation in America. He had been absent on the frontier and in England during the period of ferment in the colonies; like most professional soldiers he had been indifferent to the political world. The men among whom he was now moving were deeply involved in a revolution in which not only their fortunes but their lives were at stake; to them a person must be friend or foe. Rogers had turned down suggestions that he join the colonists; he was a retired British army major on half pay wandering through the countryside.

On 13 November he called on Dr. Eleazar Wheelock in Dartmouth College, hoping to interest him in land grants. Wheelock, filled with patriotic ardor, found even the plainness of Rogers' garb suspicious. 'He treated me with great respect; said . . . [he] had been offered and urged to take a commission in favor of the colonies but, as he was now on half pay from the crown he thought proper not to accept it.' A wild tale hid his imprisonment for debt: 'he had fought two battles in Algiers for the Dey. . . .' Wheelock was noncommittal to Rogers' offer of his services to obtain a land grant for the college and the major left, promising to let the doctor know where to contact him. Wheelock then penned a description of the interview to General Washington with an addition showing how the major was still a legendary figure:

But yesterday two soldiers . . . on their return from Montreal, informed me that our officers were assured by a Frenchman, a Captain of the artillery, whom they had taken captive, that Major Rogers was second in command under General Carleton; and that he had lately been in Indian habit through our encampment at St. John's, and had given a plan of them to the General; and suppose he made his escape with the Indians, which were at St. John's,

Ignorant of the gathering storm clouds Rogers went to Portsmouth where he was reunited with his wife and son. No evidence of what happened has been found but his next letter to her was in his former affectionate style, indicating that he at least felt that it had been a happy reunion. He could not stay long; he wanted to complete the acquisition of some land grants in New York province and soon was on the road southward.

The journey brought him near the battle lines around Boston, and he went to Medford to present his credentials to Washington. He asked for the latter's permission 'to go unmolested where my private business may call me, as it will take some months from this time to settle with all my creditors.

I have leave to retire on my half-pay, and never expect to be called into the service again. I love North-America, and I intend to spend the evening of my days in it.' The answer apprised him of the suspicions aroused by Wheelock. He wrote 'Dearest Betsy' that 'it was luckey I went to Medford . . . as many persons have given a verrey unfavorable representation concerning my coming to America. . . .'

At Washington's request, General Sullivan 'Strictly examined' Rogers. He reported that Rogers' passes seemed genuine; that he had admitted all in Wheelock's letters except the story of being in Canada. Sullivan tried to find something suspicious, although he was 'far from thinking that he had been in Canada. . . .' He guessed that Rogers might have a commission as governor at Michilimackinac to stir up the Indians against the colonists 'and only wants for an opportunity to get there. . . .' There was nothing to susbstantiate this opinion and Washington let Rogers go on but refused to give him any pass.

As the major was heading for Albany, Washington asked General Schuyler to look into the stories about him. On 5 January 1776 the general reported to Washington that 'I believe there is no truth in the intelligence sent by Mr. Wheelock. . . .' Washington, in answer, agreed but added that Rogers should be watched as he was 'much suspected of unfriendly views to this country. . . .'

Rogers left Albany for New York to obtain his land grants from Governor Tryon. Fear of mob action had forced the latter to transfer his home and office to the packet *Duchess of Gordon,* anchored in the harbor under warship protection. The rebel Provincial Congress—which controlled the affairs of the colony—allowed visitors to pass back and forth between the town and the ship; even the provincial Council was rowed out at times to meet with the governor. Rogers, too, obtained permission to pursue his land grants on board the *Duchess of Gordon.*

During these negotiations General Henry Clinton appeared in New York. He had left Boston with an expedition to attack Charleston but his ship, the *H. M. S. Mercury,* had turned aside to sail into the harbor on Sunday, 4 February. Clinton held a series of interviews with various persons, including one with Rogers on the 8th. He scrawled a record of the conversation in his illegible handwriting in a private notebook:

[Told]Major Rogers that if he chose to join me, I did believe that his services would be such as would induce me to recommend him to gov't & the commander in chief [He] said if he could get rid of the oath he would I told him he was the best judge how it was tender'd to him & if he was reconciled to coming I should be glad to receive him but no positive conditions.

This evidence clears Rogers of the long-standing accusation that contrary to his parole he was seeking a position with the British army in America. Desperately in need of funds from any source, he here turned down a tempting offer. General Sullivan had obviously disbelieved Rogers' protests in Medford that 'it cannot be supposed that Major Rogers could derogate one tittle from his Parole of honour given at Philadelphia' and his suspicions have come down through the years. Here is proof that Rogers was telling the truth.

War now drew closer to the town of New York. Provincial troops daily increased; trenches appeared, trees were cut down, redoubts erected, cannon moved, barricades were thrown up in the streets. Despite the protests of the New York Provincial Congress, General Lee cut off all communication with the British ships. The cleavage between patriot and tory became clearer; men were forced to make their choice. Yet blinded by his own personal affairs Rogers on 22

March asked permission to send to the *Duchess of Gordon* the surveys of the tracts granted to him and that William Cockburn and Joseph Blanchard, deputy surveyors, be permitted to go on board to make required returns. He had a rude awakening: William Alexander, the Earl of Stirling but an American general, ordered him out of town at once. Rogers complied and went to Philadelphia. He had at last made up his mind: he would seek a commission with the patriots but if he was not successful, he would go to Florida and sail back to London, still in pursuit of government employment.

Although he tried to keep his application to the American Congress secret less it prejudice his chances in London should he be forced to go there, the British learned that he was 'at the Congress, together with the warriors and Chiefs of the different tribes of Indians. . . .' A British officer wrote home that 'Major Rogers commands a powerful force of Indians. . . . The Indians consider him as their God, and the Congress are constantly loading him with honours it is a pity he was so neglected by Government, to whom he might have proved a material acquisition.'

Rogers had no such good fortune. Congress was suspicious of employing a retired British officer on half pay although there was a precedent in General Charles Lee. Rogers returned to New Hampshire to collect recommendations to support his application.

He naturally sought his wife but something happened. Elizabeth Rogers made this claim when she later sought a divorce:

The last time your Petitioner saw him, which was about two years since, he was in a situation which, as her peace and safety forced her *then* to shun & fly from him so Decency *now* forbids her to say more upon so indelicate a subject.

There is no further light on what occured. One thing only is certain: Robert Rogers never again saw Elizabeth Rogers or Arthur.

Rogers obtained the desired recommendations and again set out to the south.

In New York patriot persecution of loyalists quickened; the latter struck back with minor plots. When some of these were brought to light, the imagination of the patriots ran riot: Washington was to be assassinated; tories were under arms ready to seize the town; New York was to be set on fire. Washington believed the tories capable of any crime.

Rumor traced the 'plot' to Governor Tryon and Rogers' name came into the story because of his visits to the *Duchess of Gordon*. That he had always had the permission of the patriot authorities for these visits, that he had been out of the province when the 'plot' was supposedly formed, that his name was not conspicuous in the many affidavits given by frightened people hoping thereby to escape imprisonment, counted little in Rogers' favor. Word of 'a plot as deep as hell' —a reminiscent phrase—was quickly transmitted to New Hampshire where the House of Representatives voted on 25 June to choose a committee to confer on the expediency of seizing Rogers 'in consequence of sundry information against him as inimical to the rights and liberties of this country. . . .' On 2 July it voted to arrest him, but its quarry had left weeks previously for Philadelphia.

Washington ordered Rogers' arrest: he was taken in South Amboy. The general examined him and Rogers laid all his cards on the table. Washington reported:

The business which he informs me he had with Congress, is a secret offer of his services, to the end that, in case it should be rejected, he might have his way open to an employment in the

East-Indies, to which he is assigned; and in that case he flatters himself he will obtain leave of Congress to go to Great Britain.

Washington, obviously believing Rogers an enemy agent, sent him in custody on to Philadelphia. While the general forwarded 'letters found on him which from their tenour, seem calculated to recommend him to Congress,' Washington made his position clear by asking Congress to consider 'whether it would not be dangerous to accept the offer of his services. . . .' He and his officers met in council, agreed that Rogers 'is not to be sufficiently relied on,' and forwarded the minutes to Congress. There was no room for Rogers in the American army.

While innocent of being involved in any plot against Washington or the patriots and sincere in the offer of his services, Rogers had himself to blame for much of his predicament. He had continued to communicate with the royal governor of New York beyond the time when such negotiations seemed innocent. Seeking to insure some position he failed to make a clean break with Great Britain. He still failed to understand that Great Britain—not merely its army in America—had become the 'enemy,' that any employment by its government was aid to the enemy. His disclosure shows that he did not even consider that anyone would think he would serve in the British army in America, yet it was the most probable thought which would occur to the Americans. His naïve plan brought on his head redoubled suspicion.

Rogers had to remain in jail while 'a momentous matter'— the Declaration of Independence—was under consideration. Finally on 6 July Congress gave him a moment: it voted to return him to New Hampshire 'to be disposed of as the Government of that State shall judge best.' When he realized that his services were not wanted, Rogers asked permission to go to England by way of the West Indies but this was denied.

Rogers had two choices: meek submission to imprisonment or a desperate attempt to escape. The latter would throw him into the British service. If it was merely his parole which had kept him from accepting Clinton's offer, the arrest by the Americans relieved him of any obligation. But this was probably a small matter for he had been honorable about the offer of his services to the patriots. More probably he was hurt and bitter about his rejection by the government of his choice. Had his background cultivated a willingness to be a martyr to shining patriotism, Rogers would have bowed his head to the commands of Congress. But he was a son of the frontier where a fierce individualism grew wild, ready to revolt against man or government if supposed rights were infringed. He knew that he faced little chance of a fair hearing: his choice was inevitable.

It happened as Rogers' legend would picture: during the night of 8-9 July he vanished from prison. Ten days later he was climbing aboard the British flagship in the fleet off New York. Closeted with the British command from the moment of his arrival, Rogers was soon assured of a welcome he had not found on the other side of the lines. On 6 August General Howe reported to Lord Germain:

Major Rogers, having escaped to us from Philadelphia, is empowered to raise a battalion of Rangers, which, I hope, may be useful in the course of the campaign.

XXIV
1776–1795

'The Most Miserable State of Wretchedness'

LOYALISTS were flocking to the British, hoping to help end the uprising in a hurry. Recruiting progressed rapidly. Some of the new soldiers were men of principle, who had refused to abandon their loyalty to the home government and were now anticipating the joy of avenging the losses, insults, and beatings endured at the hands of the Sons of Liberty. Others were adventurers, looking forward to gain when the obviously stronger side would prevail, or scoundrels interested merely in the loot of war. The loyalist regiments were weird combinations with one common denominator: few had any experience as soldiers.

When Robert Rogers surveyed these recruits of '76 for the 'Queen's American Rangers'—farmers and townspeople who scarcely knew one end of a gun from the other—he must have despairingly recalled the experienced and sturdy New Hampshire men of '56 in his first ranger unit. These men now facing him in ragged line, were not 'rangers,' yet inevitably they acquired the once proud title of 'Rogers' Rangers.'

British officers looked askance at the outfit. During the previous war the regulars had been forced to accept the aid of the rangers in the mountains and forests of northern New York province. But here in the southern portion of the province the wilderness had disappeared. Conditions were not unlike European battlefields. Here townspeople and farmers had no special qualities or training to stand in line with British regulars. Something else had developed in the British mind: a tendency to 'look down' on all Americans. Shortly before he left London in 1775, Franklin told of the reflections cast 'on American courage, religion, understanding, etc. in which we were treated with the utmost contempt, as the lowest of mankind, and almost of a different species from the English of Britain. . . .' An English writer in 1776 was repeating a widespread belief when he described American troops as being 'effeminate, new raised soldiers, commanded by officers without knowledge or experience.'

Rogers was under a cloud: his court-martial and his suit against General Gage. Undoubtedly many British army officers felt that their side had been a second choice by Rogers who had picked it when given no alternative. They resented any attention given this rough, old man undoubtedly bearing the marks of debtors' prison. What particularly rankled the regular officers was the fact that Rogers did not award commissions to 'gentlemen.' In British regiments these were bought and sold within a rather restricted group of recognized 'gentlemen.' Rogers carried on the colonial system of awarding commissions to any man who could enlist a certain number of men. This had its obvious faults which soon became noticeable in loyalist and patriot units alike.

A later report on Rogers' unit presented the British officers' point of view:

. . .Many of those officers were Men of mean extraction without any degree of education sufficient to qualify them to bear His Majesty's Commission . . . many . . . had been bred Mechanecks others had kept Publick Houses, and One or Two had even kept Bawdy Houses in the City of New York . . . Mr. Brandon . . . kept a Tavern and eating house in New York . . . Captain Griffiths kept a dram Shop in the flea Market New York . . . Captain Eagle was still more illeterate and low bred than Fraser . . . Walsh was the last [least?] exceptionable . . . a petty constable in the City of New York. . .

There were some factors which might have induced Rogers to recommend these men as officers. Daniel Frazer had served twenty-three years in the regular army, had been wounded at Ticonderoga in '58, and had been recommended to Rogers by a British general for a lieutenancy. John Brandon had served in the French and Indian War and in the Loyal Irish Volunteers in Boston under Gage. Patrick Welsh had served fifteen years in the 35th Foot, four years as lieutenant and adjutant in a Connecticut provincial unit, and four years in the same rank in a New York outfit. John Eagles and John Griffiths had no military experience yet had demonstrated their loyalty and leadership by raising loyalist units in hostile territory. A few officers as Gymes and Armstrong went un-challenged, being acceptable to the officer class as former members of Lord Dunmore's Virginia unit of the same name.

The contempt and coolness of the British officers, who made no effort to conceal their feelings, came as a shock to the loyalists, who expected a warmer welcome. Ill-bred or not, tory officers risked their lives to raise men for the unit. For example, William Lounsbury was killed in late August when surprised with his recruits in Westchester County.

This incident seems to have been the first news of Rogers' unit received by the patriots. The local Committee of Safety reported to Washington 'That in his [Lounsbury's] Pocket book was found a Commission signed by Genl How to Major Rogers empowering him to raise a Battalion of Rangers with the rank of Lieut Col Commandant. That annexed to this was a Warrant to this Lounsberry signed by Rogers appointing him Captain of one of these Companies & a Muster Roll of the Men already enlisted.

Washington issued warnings about Rogers' unit in order to kindle partriot fires. On 30 September he wrote Governor Trumbull of Connecticut that unless the enemy measures were counteracted, the enemy would raise an army 'of our own people.' On 4 October the President of the Continental Congress was told of the necessity of raising men and of offering a suit of clothes as well as pay and bounty. The general added: '. . . I question whether that will do, as the enemy, from the information of one John Nash, who with six others were taken by our guards, are giving ten pounds bounty for recruiting and have got a battalion under Major Rogers nearly completed, upon Long Island.'

Connecticut, meanwhile, worried about Rogers' position, just across the narrow ribbon of Long Island Sound. Governor Trumbull told Washington (13 October) that many inhabitants had joined Rogers, giving him full intelligence of 'every inlet and avenue into the towns of Greenwich, Stamford and Norwalk. . . . The design of Rogers, as far as we can learn, is from Huntington to make a sudden descent in the night more especially on the town of Norwalk, not only to take the stores there, but to burn, and destroy all before them.' Letters from former inhabitants now in Rogers' unit were enclosed to underline his fears.

Rogers' reputation undoubtedly increased patriot apprehensions. Every reference repeated that he was 'a famous partisan or ranger in the late war.' His name conjured up visions of silent, grim giants suddenly appearing out of the darkness and swooping down, Indian-fashion, on a town with tomahawk and torch. Patriots tried to exorcise Rogers with insults: he was now 'the infamous Major,' but it failed to quell the fears of citizens along Connecticut's southwestern shore.

At first Rogers established headquarters at Flushing, on the north shore of Long Island. A sloop was used to pick up recruits hiding on the New York and Connecticut shores. During this period (22 September) an incident occurred about which there has been much speculation. Actually nothing more substantial is known about it than is told in the brief entry in the diary of Captain William Bamford of the 40th Foot:

Nathan Hale, a Cap't in ye Rebel Army, & a spy was taken by Maj'r Rogers & this m'g hang'd. . . .

There is one school of thought which believes that Hale was captured when he hailed a British warship from the New York shore and was recognized, and that Rogers' connection with the incident is merely that he was halted while en route to Howe's headquarters in his sloop and asked to bring Hale in. His appearance with Hale induced officers in New York City to believe he had made the capture.

There are no records of the strength or uniform of the Queen's Rangers when General Howe finally moved (12 October) in pursuit of Washington. There seem to have been ten companies or a strength of about five hundred men. Provincial units were to be clothed in green coats lined with white baize, white waistcoats and breeches, and dark brown leggings. The facings were to be white, green, or blue. The last color was apparently that of the rangers. Uniforms and material for the provincials were sent to Howe from Great Britain during 1776 but whether they were received and distributed before his move into Westchester County cannot be determined.

On 18 October the British army finally began to move inland after landing on Pelham Point. On the next day it took a position facing East Chester, with the right wing stretching toward New Rochelle. Rogers' unit was here, less at least seventy-two men detached for service with the artillery. On the evening of the 20th he was ordered to seize the village of Mamaroneck. At break of day he swung into action; the American militia fled—to quote a contemporary patriot—'with the utmost precipitation,—As usual.' There is some question about the amount of stores Rogers found: the patriot already quoted claimed that all were moved 'except some Onions. . . .'

The Queen's Rangers then camped on Heathcote Hill near the village. Rogers used a near-by schoolhouse as headquarters; one of the scholars, dismissed for an unexpected holiday, recalled the Colonel many years later as 'a very rough looking red eyed man.' As night came on, strong outposts were set to the north and east, but only a weak one to the west where the British army was located. Meanwhile the Americans were watching the British movements. Informed of Rogers' position, Lord Stirling decided to execute a coup to revive lagging American morale. Seven hundred and fifty men, of whom six hundred were from Delaware and Maryland, and the remainder from Virginia, were placed under the command of Colonel Haslet of Delaware. They, the cream of the Americans under one of the ablest field commanders, were to attack Rogers under cover of darkness.

Local guides led the Americans around so that they approached the tory unit cross-country from the southwest. A single outpost—a young Indian from Long Island—was easily dispatched with a sword and the Americans pushed on to complete the coup.

Rogers had become dissatisfied and had ordered Captain Eagle's company of about sixty men to be stationed to the southwest. This move was not known to the Americans and when their vanguard of Virginians under Major Green attacked the post, they thought they were hitting the main body of the enemy. Surprise and overwhelming strength gave the Americans an initial advantage. Some tories quickly surrendered; others took advantage of the confusion in the dark and by shouting imprecations against Rogers and his crew, managed to escape to the main camp.

Rogers had been aroused at his headquarters by the melee and had hurried to join his men on Heathcote Hill. Exhilarated by their easy victory and expecting only scattered resistance, the Americans came on, only to be met by heavy gunfire. Over the din was heard Rogers' rough voice: 'Steady, boys, steady! Fire! Fire!' In the confusion the American guides disappeared; the raw loyalists stood firm. Colonel Haslet decided to withdraw, content with the trophies of his initial surprise: thirty-six prisoners, and a variety of spoil.

The Americans were jubilant over a 'victory'—which in sober fact had but the proportions of an outpost overrun and a repulse by a numerically inferior unit. Colonel Haslet spread the canard thicker about 'the late worthless Major; on the first Fire he skulked off in the dark.' This refrain was eagerly repeated: 'Major Rogers . . . it is said, was the first that run off. . . .' Patriot newspapers gladly spread it throughout the colonies. Americans gleefully reassured one another: 'This blow will ruin the Major's Rangers.' Lord Stirling publicly on parade thanked the officers and men of the detachment.

How he observed the day is described in a soldier's diary:

Tuesday 22 [October] . . . there was a gallos ordered by Genl Starling to hang three of the prisoners at 12 o'clock.

The only frank statement made by the Americans is contained in the report by Colonel Robert H. Harrison, Washington's secretary, to the President of the Continental Congress: 'By some accident or other the expedition did not succeed so well as I could have wished.'

General Howe reported the engagement to Lord Germain on 30 November. The initial loss was blamed on the fact that 'the carelessness of his centries exposed him [Rogers] to a surprise from a large body of ye enemy by w'h he lost a few men killed or taken; nevertheless by a spirited exertion he obliged them to retreat, leaving behind them some prisoners & several killed or wounded.'

Americans behind the British lines under a flag of truce noted the open coolness between Rogers and the regular officers. They thought it a result of the fight at Mamaroneck, little realizing the basic reason. Reports circulated that Rogers had been dismissed in disgrace. Actually he continued in command of his unit. One penetration into the enemy lines shortly after the skirmish at Mamaroneck to release British prisoners was noted by an officer in his diary. Loyalists continued to risk their lives to recruit for him; when caught, there was the inevitable 'melancholy spectacle' on the gallows.

American leaders knew Rogers was still in command and tried to destroy him. In mid-November, while retreating across New Jersey, Washington desperately needed the troops he had left with General Charles Lee on the east bank of the Hudson. Lee did not immediately send them, explaining that he had a chance to hit Rogers' corps. Washington assented, believing a smashing defeat of Rogers' unit to be essential.

Lee failed; he blamed 'the timidity or caution of the enemy, who contracted themselves into a compact body very suddenly.'

Noncombatants in Westchester County, regardless of sympathies, began to suffer from pillaging. Troops on both sides as well as the criminal element among civilans were responsible. Undoubtedly men from Rogers' unit participated. However, all marauders soon saw how civilians dropped all signs of resistance at the dread words 'Rogers' Rangers!' Soon every robber band loudly proclaimed its membership in that unit to its victims; all suspicion was directed to a unit which the Americans and even some British were happy to condemn.

Westchester inhabitants constantly appealed for protection. In December 1776 they petitioned the New York Provincial Congress, complaining of their 'continual danger of being made prisoners, and . . . plundered by Robert Rogers' party . . . who daily make Excursions in divers parts of said County, and taking with them by Force of arms many of its good inhabitants, also their stock, grain, and every thing . . . laying waste and destroying all they cannot take with them.' The petitions were also bitter about patriot troops who 'did plunder and distress them more than the very enemy. . . .' In May 1777 the Committee of Safety in Bedford told General George Clinton that their town had become a frontier, 'there being a Sartain Company of Robers, otherwise Called Rogers Rangers, that keep Consealed in Parts of North Castle & Corlandt Manor. Hardly a Night Passes but there is Some Roberies Comitted or Some of our good men Captivated and Draged in a most Barberous maner to the Enemy.'

By this date Robert Rogers no longer commanded the Queen's American Rangers. In January 1777 Alexander Innes was appointed Inspector-General of the Provincial Forces in the British Army with orders to reorganize these units. He shared the feeling that most provincial officers were not proper persons to hold commissions and objected to 'Negroes, Indians, Mulattos, Sailors and Rebel prisoners' in the ranks.

Innes later described what happened to the Queen's American Rangers:

... Mr. Rogers had introduced into this Corps a number of persons very improper to hold any Commission and their conduct in a thousand instances was so flagrant that I could not hesitate to tell the General, that untill a thorough reformation took place, he could expect no service from that Battalion which in the course of the winter had been reduced to one fifth of its original strength principally by desertion.

On this representation the General [Howe] determined that Lieut Col'o Rogers should retire on his pay and give the Command of the Corps to Lieut Col'o French then Major of the 22nd Regiment. . . .

Rogers quietly stepped aside. A removal from command in this fashion was unusual and when some of his captains were later displaced in similar style, they complained bitterly. There is no explanation why Rogers made no protest. Can it be that he had little heart for combat with his countrymen? He continued to recruit, it appears, but there was an increasingly greater absence of reports about him. Defeated, tired, despondent, he left the limelight for the shadows.

Elizabeth Rogers claimed the center of the stage for a brief moment in 1778. On 26 January she signed a petition for divorce which was presented on 11 February to the New Hampshire legislature which alone had power to dissolve marriages in the province. Elizabeth painted a dismal picture of an unhappy marriage from the moment in June 1761 she married Robert 'at that time of some Character and distinction,' not for love but out of 'obedience to the Will of her parents, friends &c.' Rogers' absences to South Carolina,

Detroit, and England seemed in her petition willful abandonment of her. At Michilimackinac 'she underwent every hardship, and endured every species of ill treatment which infidelity uncleaness and drunken barbarity could inflict on one bound by the tenderest & most sacred ties to succor. . . .' She ended with the veiled reference to Rogers' condition when she last saw him which forced her 'to shun & fly from him. . . .'[1]

While much of what she alleged is demonstrably false, Elizabeth's case does not lack a sympathetic side. She had a small child; her father who had supported her, was dead; there was not even the slightest possibility that Rogers would ever return to her side,—a fact singularly mentioned in her petition. He had been in debt when he married her; he was in debt when he last saw her. She had never had for any period of time financial security supplied by her husband. She had to think of her future and that of her eight-year-old son.

The divorce was granted.

The New Hampshire legislature—like the other states—wanted no tories ever to return. In November of the same year it passed an act naming certain persons—including 'Major Robert Rogers'—who were not to return to its soil. If any did, he was to be seized and transported to British territory. A second return meant death. There was no need for including Rogers' name in a second act confiscating loyalist property. He had none.

There are only fragments to Rogers' story at this point. In the fall of 1778 he was in Quebec on recruiting service. He then went to England: there is the inevitable petition for a land grant—now for lands on the east bank of the Penobscot River. In April 1779 he was back in New York. On half pay, he was in desperate straits.

Sir Henry Clinton, now commander in chief, seems to have had faith in Rogers' ability to attract men to the British side. On 1 May Robert was ordered 'to raise for His Majesty's Service Two Battalions of the able bodied Rangers' to be known as the 'King's Rangers.' With his brother James as second in command, Robert apparently hoped to attract many old friends from northern New England over the Canadian border. Expecting a swarm of volunteers, Robert sent James ahead in July 1779 with an advance party and asked General Haldimand who commanded in Canada to help them. The latter obviously resented any recruiting in his sector for Clinton's forces and made no move to help James until dire distress from lack of funds dampened their ardor.

Robert followed in the British frigate *Blonde*. This ship put into Penobscot Bay with other vessels in time to force the Americans to abandon on 13 August their efforts to take Fort Migibiguaduce (or Fort George). Rogers went ashore and made his way to Fort Howe at the mouth of the St. John River where he reported considerable success in recruiting. However, the difficulties engulfing his officers in Quebec required his presence and in mid-December he undertook the difficult trek to that city. He seems to have only made matters worse. Apparently he was drinking to excess and Haldimand complained that 'he at once disgraces the Service, & renders himself incapable of being Depended upon. . . .' James apologized for him: 'I am sorry his good talents should so unguarded fall a prey to Intemperance.'

Robert left Quebec in March; in June he was reported imprisoned for debt in Halifax. Released, he made his way to Penobscot Bay and boarded a schooner bound for New York. En route a Pennsylvanian privateer, the brigantine *Patty* under Captain Read, captured the vessel and on 10 January 1781 the *Pennsylvania Gazette* reported that 'the famous Major Rogers, of the British army . . . is now safely lodged in the new gaol.'

There was little excitement: the ghost of Major Rogers of the Rangers had finally been laid. New heroes or villains had claimed the public's attention. There was simply an old-appearing man in the jail whose health deteriorated so rapidly that he was obviously no 'formidable Enemy.' Rogers tried to arrange for his exchange but he seems to have remained a prisoner at least for the greater part of 1781. There is no certain evidence of his being back with the British until 10 May 1782. He probably left these shores with the defeated army when New York was evacuated and returned to London a lonely, broken exile.

Inevitably there were the newspaper notices that 'the celebrated Major R- - - -s, the American partisan, so distinguished for extraordinary vicissitudes of fortune during the two last wars . . .' was back in debtors' prison. He was in debt during at least part of the remainder of his life. The bare records of his withdrawals of half pay show assignments to creditors in 1784, 1788, 1793, and 1794.

His last days were passed in Southwark where his drinking continued. Sometimes in his drunken frenzies he would relive old days, calling out names and places to the bewilderment of his landlord, John Walker. Inevitably his health broke down: there is a record of a wasting cough and bloody phlegm. A fall which affected his mind heralded the end which finally came on 18 May 1795. The London press noted his passing; typical was the item in *The Morning Press*:

Lieutenant Col. Rogers, who died on Thursday last in the Borough, served in America during the late war, in which he performed prodigious feats of valour. He was a man of uncommon strength, but a long confinement in the Rules of King's Bench, had reduced him to the most miserable state of wretchedness.

His landlord hurried to claim Rogers' half pay to the date of his death and to take out administration on his estate. It was only one hundred pounds; if there were any other creditors, they did not bother to appear.

Two days after his death Rogers was buried in the churchyard still by the old inn, Elephant and Castle. There is an account of a hastily read funeral service in the rain, of fidgeting gravediggers anxious to finish their task, and of two unnamed mourners who hurried off at the end of the committal service.

The tragedy was over.

The total failure and miserable ending of Rogers' career did not entirely blot out the memory of him and his rangers in the 'Old French War.' New England remembered it. It fired the imagination of young Francis Parkman when during his student days he began to prepare the foundation of his famous studies of colonial America. Nothing epitomizes the drive of Parkman's early life as the line he wrote after a famous description of the rangers in the woods, summer and winter: 'There were those among them for whom this stern life had a fascination that made all other existence tame.' Through his books on the French and Indian War and Pontiac's conspiracy, Rogers became immortal.

The grip of Rogers and his rangers on Parkman's imagination even induced him to depict a ranger's personal feelings in the only poem he is known to have written.[2] It is far from great poetry yet there are a few lines which might have come to Robert Rogers in that fleeting second before death claimed him. Perhaps as his pain faded, Rogers' tortured mind fled the squalid surroundings and recalled a scene as the rangers' whaleboats were drawing up under the cannons of Fort William Henry at the head of Lake George after a scout:

The rich green hill, the waters still,
  The pure and amber skies;
Our toil and woe are well nigh done;
  Strain, comrades, at the oar!
There lie the walls that shelter us,
  On yonder guarded shore.
I see the frowning rampart,
  The rigid palisade,
And slowly rolled in swelling fold,
  Old England's flag displayed.
Hark to the rolling of the drum,
  And the gay trumpet-note,
That, softened on the greedy ear,
  O'er the calm waters float!
And see! and see! on yonder plain,
  The long and glittering line;
The red coats glow in the evening rays,
  The bustling bayonets shine;
How, 'twixt those shadowy western hills,
  Upon the bright array
The sinking sun pours duskily
  His last departing ray!

APPENDIX

Portraits of Robert Rogers

THE best known 'portrait' of Robert Rogers is a mezzotint entitled *MAJOR ROBERT ROGERS, Commander in Chief of the Indians in the Back Settlements of AMERICA,* published by Thomas Hart in London on 1 October 1776. What seems to be the original edition bears the legend under the drawing 'Ioh Martin Will excudit Aug. Vind.'

This shows a three-quarters' length view of the supposed Rogers standing, facing the viewer and looking toward the latter's left. He is in uniform but has two Indian-decorated belts slung over his left shoulder and is wearing the high, so-called 'Indian stockings.' His gloved right hand is on his hip, the left holds a musket. Three Indians appear in the background to Rogers' left.

This was one of the series of 'rebel officers' sold by Thomas Hart. (Before news arrived of his escape to the British, rumor said Rogers was the American commander of the Indians.) All these portraits have been pronounced fictitious. Charles Henry Hart, 'Frauds in Historical Portraiture, or Spurious Portraits of Historic Personages,' *Annual Report of the American Historical Association for the Year 1913,* I (Washington, 1915), 87-9. Careful examination of the supposed portraits bears out this conclusion. All have the same narrow shoulders and small but definite paunch. Despite superficial changes the postures are similar, as are the uniforms. The faces seem to vary yet all possess cupid-like lips, large, protruding eyes, and prominent noses. Comparison of some of the drawings with authentic paintings of the subject reveals such dissimilarity as to throw doubt on the entire series. Thomas Hart was interested in making some money from the current interest in the American rebellion; the veracity of the portraits mattered little.

There are various copies of this print. The drawings are cruder, with Rogers' nose becoming more and more ugly.

A French mezzotint showing a half-length figure of Rogers in an oval bears the title: *MAJOR ROBERT ROGERS Comandeur en Chef des Indians dans les Habitations derrieres d'Amerique*. It bears a legend 'peint par Thomlinson a Nouvelle Yorck,' but reveals its origin with the note following the title: 'Se vend a Londres chez Thom. Hart.' It is similar to the Hart portrait but the musket and Indians in the background are gone. There are some changes in the face by the French artist who was copying the English print.

There is a third print entitled *Robert Rogers, Commandeur der Americaner*. The original of this seems to have been in a German history entitled *Geschichte der Krieg in und ausser Europa, Elfster Theil* (Nürnberg, 1777). I have a copy as a separate print. It is a poor copy of the Hart portrait and merits attention only as a curiosity.

William Loring Andrews in his *Essay on the Portraiture of the American Revolutionary War* (New York, 1896), at pp. 36-7, lists a portrait of Major Rogers in the famous set issued by Du Simitiére, all of which were supposedly 'drawn from the life.' No library possessing supposedly complete sets reports any Rogers' portrait therein. Andrews may have believed the French print already described to be a part of the set or may have had in mind a portrait unknown at the present time. Perhaps he was thinking of the rare print entitled *Le Major Robert Roger* [sic] *Commandant en Chef les Troupes Indiennes au service des Américains,* which seems an obvious copy of the Hart portrait except that Rogers is looking to the viewer's right. Some of the trimmings around the oval enclosing Rogers' figure—shield, ribbons, palms, flags, cannon-balls, cannon, and so on—resemble the decorations on the Du Simitiére prints.

Failure to be certain of what print Andrews had in mind probably matters little. He admits that the Du Simitiére prints 'are adjudged poor portraits, even if they were "taken from the life." '

There are a few prints of a clearly spurious portrait showing a tall soldier grasping the hand of a crouching Indian and entitled *Major General Rogers*. For a copy of this see *The Bulletin of the Fort Ticonderoga Museum*, VI (July, 1940), 20. Its true character can be perceived by putting it beside Benjamin West's painting entitled *The Death of General Wolfe at Quebec*. The Indian in the print is West's Indian down to the tattooing and feathers. 'Rogers' is the chief figure in West's left-hand group; the head and arms have been reversed. The musket slung over the 'general's' back is obviously the gun hanging from the soldier on the extreme right side of West's painting.

No contemporary description of Rogers has been found. Apparently all contemporaries thought him too well known. 'The famous Major' was mentioned many times by all, but except for the suggestion given by Stark family tradition, his exact appearance is unknown.

SOURCES
And Textual Notes

ASIDE from 'The Life of Robert Rogers' by Allan Nevins printed in the Caxton Club edition of *Ponteach* (1914) there has been little effort made to explore Rogers' life. This fact combined with the prejudice and legends surrounding his controversial career made necessary prolonged critical work in original sources. Documentation of this study could not be compressed into available space. Interested scholars will find detailed notes on deposit in the New-York Historical Society and The Clements Library. The following indicates merely the principal sources of the chapters. Rogers' own books, *A Concise Account of North America* (1765) and *Journals* (1765), were of course consulted on all points.

Chapter One

The Methuen town clerk's office has the vital statistics and town meeting records; the assessor's office has the assessment rolls. Baptism and church records are in the town's First Congregational Church. Slight genealogical clues are in Susan Burnham Greely (grandchild of James, Robert's brother), 'Sketches of the Past,' *Loyalist Narratives from Upper Canada,* ed. James J. Tallman (1946).

Rogers' early life in New Hampshire is based principally on the land, probate, and court records (New Hampshire Historical Society). *Township Grants . . . in New Hampshire . . .* Vol. XXVII (1896) and *Provincial Papers . . .* Vol VI, ed. Nathaniel Bouton (1872) are printed records of value. Muster rolls may be found in C. E. Potter, 'Military History of New Hampshire . . . ,' *Report of the Adjutant General of . . . New Hampshire for . . . 1866* (1866). For Stark family tradition see Caleb Stark, *Memoir and Official Correspondence of Gen. John Stark* (1860).

Chapter Two

For the beginnings of the '55 campaign see 'Journal of Colonel John Winslow . . . ,' *Collections of the Nova Scotia Historical Society,* IV (1855); *N. H. Prov. Papers VI* and *New Hampshire Provincial Papers. Vol. XIV,* ed. Isaac W. Hammond (1890). The diaries both manuscript and printed which were consulted in connection with the various campaigns are too numerous to list but none describes the contemporary Champlain valley as well as *Peter Kalm's Travels,* ed. Adolph B. Benson, 2 vol. (1937).

Used in connection with every chapter from this point were *The Papers of Sir William Johnson,* ed. James Sullivan et al., 12 vol. (1921-57); *Documents Relative to the Colonial History of . . . New-York,* ed. E. B. O'Callaghan et al., 15 vol. (1853-87); *The Documentary History of . . . New-York,* ed. E. B. O'Callaghan, 4 vol. (1850-51).

1. I find no contemporary evidence that Wentworth planned a fort in 1755 at either the Upper or Lower Coös or that Robert Rogers built Fort Wentworth either at Groveton, N.H., (as claimed by Potter, *Mil. Hist. N. H.*) or at the junction of the Ammonoosuc with the Connecticut (as claimed by Kenneth Roberts, *Northwest Passage Appendix,* 1937). There was a fort at Groveton during the Revolution but it was not in existence during the French and Indian War. A typescript entitled *Mysterious Fort Wentworth* by the author is on deposit with the New Hampshire Historical Society in which this point is discussed with full citation of authorities.

2. Roger's original report fails to identify which side of the lake on which he landed. In his *Journals* he states that it was the west side and that the fort he watched being constructed was Fort Carillon. It is my opinion that the latter post had not been commenced at this time, that he landed on the east side and saw the square entrenchment built at the foot of the portage and later described by a French deserter. A typescript entitled *The Location of the First French Fort of 1755 at Ticonderoga,* by the author and on deposit in the Fort Ticonderoga Museum Library, contains a more complete exposition of my theory. I imagine it will always be a disputed point.

Chapter Three

Manuscript sources include photostats of Rogers' reports in the Mary Cochrane Rogers collection at Fort Ticonderoga and material from the Public Record Office, London, C. O. 5 and W. O. 34. Printed sources include *Correspondence of William Shirley,* ed. Charles Henry Lincoln, 2 vol. (1912). A secondary reference of value used in connection with this and following chapters is Stanley McCrary Pargellis, *Lord Loudoun . . . in America* (1933).

1. An untitled map in the Crown Collection endorsed '1757. Mr. Abercrombie. A Sketch of Ticonderoga' has a dotted line from Lake George to Wood Creek and a notation reading: 'here Cap't Rogers carried his boats across to Wood Creek.' Rogers apparently landed near present-day Huletts Landing and followed the valley between Spruce and Hogback Mountains to the brook flowing down to Wood Creek, passing north of Dresden Center to the inlet north of Chubbs Dock. Consult *New York-Vermont, Whitehall Quadrangle, Geological Survey, U.S. Department of the Interior (July 1902 ed., reprinted 1942).* Harrison K. Bird Jr., who has lived in the locality since childhood, believes Rogers landed at modern Glenburnie and followed the trail to Wood Creek, an easier route. I have found evidence that this route was known to British in 1756.

Chapter Four and Five

The Earl of Loudoun Papers (Huntington Library) are the principal source of these chapters. Also consulted for this and following chapters were *Military Affairs in North America 1748–1765 . . . Cumberland Papers,* ed. Stanley Pargellis (1936) and *Correspondence of William Pitt,* 2 vol. (1906). 'A plain Narrativ of the Uncommon Sufferings . . . of Thomas Brown' is from *The Magazine of History,* Extra No. 4 (1908). Of value was John Knox, *An Historical Journal of the Campaigns in North America,* 3 vol. (1914). I suspect the authenticity of 'Joshua Goodenough's Old Letter,' ed. Frederic Remington, *Harper's New Monthly Magazine,* XCV (1897) yet many details ring true. P.R.O. C.O.5 supplied some material as did John Macomb's Letter Copy Book (MS) in the New York State Library.

Chapter Six

In general the sources are the same as for Chapters Four and Five.

1. There is no proof that a prisoner or deserter betrayed Rogers' party to the enemy. Yet according to one French source an old Indian 'sorcerer' had predicted that the English would be seen 'before long' just before the report by Indian scouts of the tracks of Rogers' expedition. It was common for Indians to have conjurers 'foretell' what was already known. The Indians had captured the sutler: he may well have been the source of the sorcerer's prediction.

2. This battle started the famous legend of 'Rogers' Rock.' The story has different forms. During the retreat, according to one version, Rogers slid down the precipice. Others, dubious that anyone could slide down the high, almost perpendicular slope, claim Rogers reversed his snow-shoes at the brink and threw his knapsack over the edge to make the Indians think he slid down. No contemporary evidence on the point was discovered but the story is old. The spot is called 'Rodgers' Leap' in a land petition of 1 September 1766.

3. Early praise ('No men in this world ever behaved better. . .' Macomb to Hutchinson, 21 Mar. 1757) was followed by criticism when French claims that they suffered few casualties came to British ears. See Hauck-Saunders to Loudoun, 29 May 1758, Loudoun Papers. But a letter from a British regular officer captured after the battle described a 'very unequal combat' and claimed that 'it was impossible for a party so weak as ours to hope for even a retreat.' Pringle to Haviland, 28 Mar. 1758, Rogers, *Journals*, 90–102. This halted criticism.

Chapter Seven

Among the manuscript sources are the James Abercromby Papers (Huntington Library), Captain Alexander Monypenny's Orderly Book from March 26, 1758 to May 5, 1759 (Fort Ticonderoga), and the Thomas Gage Papers, American Series (Clements Library). The printed sources include the *Pitt Corr.* and the *Cumberland Papers*. Of particular note is John W. Shy's *James Abercromby and the Campaign of 1758* (typescript), a thesis submitted to the Graduate College of the University of Vermont, June 1957.

1. I do not believe the death of Howe had the instantaneously demoralizing effect commonly attributed to it. Many contemporary comments fail to mention it. See Samuel Morris' Journal (Clements Library) and Eyre to Napier, 10 July 1758, *Cumberland Papers*. Later when it was realized how the death of Howe left the army in the hands of incompetent field commanders as Abercromby and Gage, the importance of the incident increased and writers have related the loss to the poor discipline shown by the army.

2. I find no contemporary evidence to support the tradition that Captain John Stark of the rangers tried to give Lieutenant Clark, the engineer, advice how to attack the French position. It is as dubious as the legend that Stark was responsible for the successful defense of Fort William Henry in March 1757.

Chapter Eight

Among the manuscripts in the Gage Papers of great importance is the general's letter copybook entitled *Letters Winter Quarters 1759* (Clements Library). At P.R.O. the bulk of the Amherst Papers is in W.O. 34; C.O. 5 was also useful. An unusually good diary is the one by Robert Webster (Fort Ticonderoga). Pertinent portions of Monypenny's orderly book for the '59 expedition are printed in *The Bulletin of the Fort Ticonderoga Museum*, VI (1942). Other printed sources include *The Journal of Jeffery Amherst*, ed. J. Clarence Webster (1931) and the *Journal of William Amherst in America* (n.d.).

Chapter Nine

W.O. 34 and the Gage Papers are among the principal manuscript sources. Rogers' report of 1 Nov. 1759 (erroneously dated the 5th in printing) and his remarks set forth in his *Journals* are the principal source of value concerning the raid on St. Francis; stray details were taken from many places, e.g. the manuscript affidavit of Frederick Curtiss dated 4 Oct. 1760 (Connecticut State Library). Valuable is the 'Courtmartial of Lieutenant Samuel Stephens,' printed in Roberts, *Northwest Passage Appendix* (the man in question spelled his name 'Stevens').

Rogers sent a map of his route to Amherst but it cannot now be found. Rogers to Amherst, 20 Mar. 1760, W.O. 34/51. His landing place in Missisquoi Bay is known because engineers found the charred remains of his boats while making a survey of Lake Champlain after the war. *A Survey of Lake Champlain . . . by William Brazier Draughtsman, 1762* (Clements Library). Rogers apparently swung almost easterly and hit the marshes west of modern Frelighsburg. Then proceeding to the northeast he again hit bogs around Lake Selby and south of Brome Lake. As he turned more directly to the north he was again in the swamps between Roxton Falls and Actonville. This would bring him to the St. Francis near Joachim de Courval where tradition places his crossing.

The village of St. Francis (more properly 'St. François') was composed of two sections: one spread between the mainland and the islands in the river's mouth, containing about 47 families and the Indian village about 4 miles further up the river on the northeast bank. See Map No. 5 in the atlas prepared under the direction of General James Murray entitled *Plan of the Part of the River St. Lawrence . . .* and commonly called the 'Montressor Maps' (Clements Library). Odanak now lies on the site of the Indian village.

On his return I believe Rogers went down the Passumpsic valley to the Connecticut. His request that supplies be sent to the Wells River and his time schedule support this rather than the tradition that he swung for some unknown reason southeasterly to the Upper Coös.

Contemporary newspapers, especially the *New-Hampshire Gazette*, were full of reports of the raid but must be used with caution.

Chapter Ten

W.O. 34 and T. 64/21 contain many manuscripts of value (P.R.O.); the Gage Papers (Clements Library) and the Robert Rogers Collection in the New York Public Library were also of value. Printed sources have already been cited. Maps of Fort Isle aux Noix as it existed in 1760 are practically unknown: the one on Map No. 15 of the 'Montressor Maps' (Clements Library) is a rarity. The Mary Cochrane Rogers Collection (Fort Ticonderoga) has many photostats of value relating to ranger accounts.

Chapter Eleven

Scattered items relating to Rogers are in the Rogers papers in the New York Public Library, the Ayer Collection in the Newberry Library, C.O. 5/59 and 5/154 (P.R.O.), the Cadwallader Collection in the Historical Society of Pennsylvania (Croghan's letters and accounts), and the Burton Collection in the Detroit Public Library. Many hitherto unknown details may be found in 'Petition of the Representative of Robert Rodgers [sic] Praying the Confirmation of his Title to a Tract of Land,' *Records of the U.S. Senate, 27th Congress, 2nd Session* (National Archives), which is principally a mass of affidavits; the Indian deed to Rogers, formerly a part of this file, is now in the Detroit Public Library.

The basis of the text on the Detroit expedition to 4 Nov. is Rogers' *Journals.* From the latter date the basis is the 'Journal of Robert Rogers. . . ,' ed. Victor Hugo Paltsits, *Bulletin of the New York Public Library,* XXXVIII (1933). 'George Croghan's Journal 1759–1763,' ed: Nicholas B. Wainwright, *The Pennsylvania Magazine of History and Biography,* LXXI, Part One (1947)—the better of the two versions of Croghan's journal—is followed for events from 4 to 12 Nov. I suspect that Rogers' field notes were lost in the storm of 12 Nov. and that he attempted to reconstruct the events to this date from memory. From this point I have followed Rogers because Croghan's attempts to minimize Indian opposition color his reporting.

The trip was followed on maps of the U.S. Geological Survey. Helpful as a contemporary account was the *Journal of Chaussegros de Léry,* ed. Sylvester K. Stevens et al. (1940).

1. That Croghan's statements cannot be taken uncritically is revealed at this point. In his journal he states that the presents were given to the Indians because he informed Rogers 'it was necessary & would be for the good of his Majestys interest.' When complaints were made about the costs he blamed 'ye premrtory orders of ye officer Comm'd'g to do my Duty in ye Indian Department Cost what it wold.' Croghan to Monckton, 19 Apr. 1761, Cadwallader Coll.

2. This is the meeting with the Ottawa described by Rogers as having taken place on the 'Choagage River.' Historians have assumed this to be the meeting with Pontiac described by Rogers in his *Concise Account* (240f.) and Parkman was one of the first to identify the river as the Cuyahoga. Croghan's journal clearly shows that these assumptions are not true. This fact is taken as a reflection on Rogers. I do not know why: Rogers does not mention Pontiac in his journal of the trip; he does not identify the spot where he met Pontiac in his *Concise Account*. Actually he is being blamed for the unsupported assumptions of many generations of historians.

3. The events in the journals and the description in Rogers' *Concise Account* indicate that it was at this point Rogers met Pontiac. Undoubtedly he exaggerated Pontiac's prominence. It should hardly be used to cast reflections on Rogers; it is still accepted practice for travelers to far-off places to add glamor to their experiences.

Chapter Twelve

The manuscript sources include W.O. 34/48, 34/88, and T. 60/21 (P.R.O.), provincial land and court records (New Hampshire Historical Society), and the Rogers papers in the New York Public Library. Printed sources include 'The Reminiscences of James Gordon,' *New York History*, XVII (1936) and the excerpts from the New York Land Papers in *Journals of Major Robert Rogers*, ed. Franklin B. Hough (1883).

Chapter Thirteen

Of great importance is the collection of Rogers' letters to his wife in the Clements Library. That she preserved these in spite of her divorce complaint seems to throw doubt on the sincerity of her allegations. An important letter from Arthur Browne to Robert and Elizabeth Rogers of 12 May 1763 is in the Gratz Collection in the Historical Society of Pennsylvania. Other sources include W.O. 34 and the Chatham Papers 30/8/96 (P.R.O.) and the provincial land records in the New Hampshire Historical Society. For letters of a creditor of Rogers see the *Letterbook of John Watts* (Collections of The New-York Historical Society for the Year 1928).

Chapter Fourteen

A journal of Pontiac's attack is wrongfully attributed to Rogers in *Diary of the Siege of Detroit,* ed. Franklin B. Hough (1860). Jehu Hay was the writer. Manuscript sources include W.O. 34 (P.R.O.), the Gage Papers (Clements Library), the Rogers papers in the New York Public Library, the Letterbook of James Sterling (Clements Library), and the various documents collected on the siege by William L. Jenks and on deposit in the Clements Library. A printed source of value is 'Expedition to Detroit' [John Montressor's diary], ed. J. C. Webster, *Transactions of the Royal Society of Canada,* Series III, XXII (1928). A photostat of the important complaint against Hopkins by Rogers et al. dated 12 Nov. 1763 is in the Clements Library.

1. A notation of a letter now destroyed and later accusations of Sir William Johnson have been interpreted by some writers to indicate that Rogers was engaged in illegal and discreditable transactions at Niagara at this time. McCracken to Johnson, 24 Jan. 1764, *Calendar of the Sir William Johnson Manuscripts,* compil. Richard E. Day (1909), 202; Johnson to Gage, 23 Jan. 1766, Gage Papers, A.S. Examination of both sources reveals no mention of Niagara; Rogers was here only eight days. Correspondence from the post during the period contains no complaint about Rogers; indeed Captain Browning clearly indicates that he would have welcomed Rogers' presence during the winter. Browning to Gage, 5 Dec. 1763, Gage Papers, A.S.

Chapter Fifteen

Of great importance to the text is the file in P.R.O. listed as T.S. 11/1069, No. 4957. This is Rogers' suit of 1774 against Gage and contains Gage's explanation of the events from 1766, letters and petitions he considered important, and the record of Rogers' court-martial. Clements Library has in addition to the Gage Papers the letterbook of Charles Townshend, 1763–1766, containing stray but important references to Rogers. The conveyance of 10 Oct. 1765 by Rogers to Townshend et al. is written on the reverse side of the Indian deed of 23 Dec. 1760. Other pertinent papers in P.R.O. may be found in C.O. 5, P.C. 1/10/51, C.O.

323/18, F.O. 83/9, C.O. 5/70. Carver's original manuscript journal in the British Museum (Add. MS 8949) has several important references to Rogers. For the jail-break in New York see *New-York Gazette,* 19 Jan. 1764; *The Boston Post-Boy and Advertiser,* 23 Jan., 6 Feb. and 13 Feb. 1764; *New-York Mercury,* 23 Jan. 1764.

Chapter Sixteen

In addition to the items cited for the preceding chapter there is the important letter from Gage to Johnson of 13 Jan. 1766, owned by James S. Schoff of New York, petitions of Carver mentioning Rogers in P.R.O. (P.C. 1/54 and Ti 45), and items in the Gratz Collection (Historical Society of Pennsylvania).

1. Johnson was righteously indignant that Rogers would probably use his position to aid himself and his friends in the fur trade. Both Johnson and his commissarys used their positions in the same way. The state of public morality may be seen in the fact that General Gage, who passed on Johnson's Indian accounts, was soliciting the latter's assistance to add to his personal fortune through land speculation.

2. Gage couched his appointment in military terms to restrict Rogers' power (although Rogers actually was not in the army), but later claimed that it was a civil appointment to excuse his non-payment of the salary he had been ordered to pay Rogers. Certificate of Gen. Thomas Gage, 26 June 1769, Gage Papers, A.S.; Rogers' Memorial, 1769, C.O. 5/70; Barrington to Gage, 1 Nov. 1767, Gage Papers, E.S.

3. I surmise that the man who brought the Hopkins letter to Gage was Redmond Magra, formerly of the 22nd Regiment. See the comment in Brown to Gage, 4 Jan. 1768, Gage Papers, A.S.

4. Gage never explained why the French would want trouble at Michilimackinac when they no longer owned Louisiana. This point has troubled some historians, but instead of questioning the charges against Rogers they have blandly stated that Rogers was accused of plotting to betray his country to the Spaniards; one even went so far as to compare him to Aaron Burr. Spain is not mentioned in any accusation against Rogers.

5. Rogers to Johnson, 28 June 1766, Gratz Coll. This is important because it proves that Rogers was not at the conference between Johnson and Pontiac at Oswego in July 1766. On that occasion Captain Jonathan Rogers, commandant of Fort Ontario, quarreled with Johnson's commissary, Benjamin Roberts. It has been accepted 'fact' that Robert Rogers was the 'Captain Rogers' involved in the fight. Many historians have interpreted the encounter to show his determination not to be bound by Johnson's orders, his jealousy of Johnson, and in general to reflect on Rogers' character. Actually it showed Roberts' propensity to flaunt his authority as commissary in the face of former superior officers and to quarrel with them.

Chapter Seventeen

Besides manuscript sources already cited there is James Goddard's *Journal of a Voyage under the Command of James Tute* in the Redpath Library, McGill University and the collection of photostats known as the Robert Rogers Papers in the Minnesota Historical Society. An all-important printed document is the *Journal of Major Robert Rogers*, ed. William L. Clements (1918). Too seldom considered is the Canadian view of the fur trade in the United States. See Marjorie Gordon Jackson, 'The Beginnings of British Trade at Michilimackinac,' *Minnesota History*, XI (1930); Margaret G. Reid, 'The Quebec Fur Traders and Western Policy, 1763–1774,' *The Canadian Historical Review*, N. S., VI (1925); and W.S. Wallace, 'The Pedlars from Quebec,' *Canadian Historical Review*, N.S., XIII (1932).

1. The failure of the prosecution at Rogers' court-martial to challenge this statement with definite proof of what papers were taken from Rogers at the time of his arrest prevents casual dismissal of this claim. There were several parties arriving at the fort shortly after Rogers who might have brought the letters. On 24 Aug. a portion of two companies of the Royal Americans under Captain Spiesmacher came to relieve the company of the 17th Foot which had been the garrison. Four days later a flotilla of canoes came in. Carver was a passenger in one of them.

2. There seems to be no question that the French post known as the Fort des Prairies was on the Saskatchewan quite near to Fort Pasquia.

See the map presented by Peter Pond to Lord Hamilton in April 1785 and printed as 'Map No. Two' in Henry R. Wagner, *Peter Pond, Fur Trader & Explorer* (1955). Just east of the forks of the Saskatchewan is a point marked 'This is the highest Post the French Traders possess'd.' Carver wrote in his manuscript journal that he and Tute were ordered to winter 'at a Place Call'd by the French Fort la Prarie Not far from Lake Winepeck it being the Furthest Trading Post the French Ever had to the Sea and Northwest Passage. . . .' There is some dispute as to its exact site. See W. M. Stewart, 'David Thompson's Surveys in the Northwest,' *The Canadian Historical Review*, N.S., XVII (1936).

3. Note that Rogers planned in 1766 a penetration of the West in a northwesterly direction, thus anticipating the path of the Montreal 'pedlars' who in turn prepared the way for Alexander Mackenzie.

Chapter Eighteen

Rogers' Indian accounts are attached to his petition dated 10 Jan. 1770 in P.R.O., Ti/456; his *Estimate of the Furr and Peltry Trade in the District of Michilimackinac* is in C.O. 5/85. The Minnesota Historical Society has photostats of many documents of value to this chapter.

Chapter Nineteen

The principal manuscript sources have already been cited. A printed document of interest is *George Croghan's Journal of his Trip to Detroit in 1767*, ed. Howard H. Peckham (1939).

Chapter Twenty

The basic source is the Gage Papers. Contemporary newspapers of value include *Boston Chronicle*, 22 Feb., 2 May, 13 June, and 29 Aug. 1768; *Virginia Gazette*, 7 Apr., 30 June, 18 Aug., 1768.

1. Claus to Johnson, 26 Sept. 1768, Rogers, *Journals*, (ed. F. B. Hough) 252. The editor concludes from the remark that the prisoners were beginning a salivation that Rogers was suffering from syphilis. Actually mercury was used in connection with many diseases including malaria from which Rogers suffered. I doubt that Rogers had syphilis because no one else took the opportunity to cast aspersions on him. In view of the fact that there was no official report of any illness of Rogers, I should not be surprised to find that Claus was repeating a bit of idle gossip.

Chapter Twenty-one

The court-martial proceedings have already been cited.

Chapter Twenty-two

Besides sources already cited the manuscripts include the following in P.R.O.: C.O. 5/154, C.O. 323/27, C.O. 324/21, C.O. 5/1075, C.O. 5/70, T. 24/41, T. 29/40, T. 29/41, Ti/456, Ti/478, Ti/484, Ti/518; Guildhall (London) Library (on Fleet imprisonment); the Earl of Dartmouth Papers, Patshull House, Wolverhampton. There is an interesting letter from Rogers to Livermore of 18 Feb. 1769 in the New Hampshire Historical Society proving that he had not become friendly with Ensign Johnston. Notices of Rogers in contemporary newspapers are too numerous to cite.

Chapter Twenty-three

The principal new manuscript source is the Henry Clinton Papers in Clements Library, particularly the entry in the *Journal of an Expedition to the Southern Colonies under the Command of Maj'r Gen'l Clinton,* a separate notebook. Printed records of value include the *American Archives,* ed. Peter Force (1843–51), *Letters and Papers of Major-General John Sullivan . . . Vol. I,* ed. Otis G. Hammond (1936), *Letters on the American Revolution 1774–1776,* ed. Margaret Wheeler Willard (1925), and *Calendar of Historical Manuscripts relating to the War of the Revolution in the Office of the Secretary of State, Albany, N. Y.,* 2 vol. (1868).

Chapter Twenty-four

New manuscript sources include John M. McDonald, *Interview Volumes,* Hufeland Memorial Library, New Rochelle; *Papers of the Continental Congress,* National Archives; the Haldimand Papers, British Museum, Add. MSS 21,800, 21,810, and 21,820; Guy Carleton Papers, Colonial Williamsburg; and the Paymaster-General's Books in P.R.O., 4/36, 4/41, 4/51, 4/54, and A.O.V. 5/111. Rogers' paroles while in American hands are in the Historical Society of Pennsylvania. Printed sources include 'Bamford's Diary,' *Maryland Historical Magazine,* XXVIII (1938); *Letters Written by Ebenezer Huntington During the American Revolution* (1915?); *The Writings of George Washington,* ed. John Fitzpatrick, Vol. VII (1932) and Vol. XXII (1937). Some details and full documentation for a portion of the period of this chapter may be found in the author's 'The Early Days of the Queen's Rangers August 1776–February 1777,' *Military Affairs,* XXII (Summer 1958).

Rogers' death was noted in the British press and he was not buried under the name of Richard Rogers in the churchyard of St. Mary-Newington which was torn down in the following century and whose site was paved over for a street. Neither is he buried in a Bennington, N.H., cemetery: the Robert Rogers lying there was a contemporary of the Major, who passed at least a portion of his life in Londonderry, N.H., with his wife Sarah.

1. The strangest result of a search to find any evidence to support Elizabeth Rogers' statement in her divorce petition concerning her experiences at Michilimackinac was the discovery of, not transgressions by Rogers but mention of the 'uncommon freedom' of Ensign Robert Johnston with Elizabeth: 'common fame says to the extent of carnal conversation with her.' Daniel Morison, *Narrative of an Outrageous Action of Burglarly and Felony. . . ,* MS (Detroit Public Library). There was something to the story: Rogers was reported to be jealous of Johnston. Turnbull to Gage, 25 Sept. 1767, Gage Papers, A.S. Events proved—at least to my mind—that Elizabeth and Robert were close. Had she cause to leave him, Rogers' arrest would have provided her an ideal opportunity. Instead she remained by his side.

Elizabeth married John Roche, a sea captain said to have been famous for his unholy expletives and excessive potations. Joseph B. Walker, *Life and Exploits of Robert Rogers the Ranger* (1885). Tradition claims that Roche started for London from Quebec 'by dead reckoning' and landed in Portsmouth, N.H.

2. 'The New Hampshire Ranger' by 'Capt. Jonathan Carver Jr.,' originally printed in *The Knickerbocker Magazine*, XXVI (1845) and reprinted in Charles Haight Farnham, *A Life of Francis Parkman* (1900). For clear evidence of Parkman's great interest in Rogers see *The Journals of Francis Parkman*, ed. Mason Wade, 2 vol. (1947). One entry with Parkman's italics reads: 'General Hoyt has journals, letters, etc., of great interest, and a *complete unpublished life of Rogers*.'

INDEX